"The notes assembled here begin," Mr. Cantril writes, "with the phase of his thinking after he turned to the psychology of visual perception with all the ramifications that he saw this subject had relevant to the nature and range of human experience."

Approaching his subject from the base of optics and the psychology of vision, Adelbert Ames went on to examine the nature of reality as it presents itself to the experiencing human being. A closer scrutiny of this book will reveal a noble, almost heroic, effort to reach the very frontier of man's possible comprehension of himself and his self-created world.

The inclusion of a series of letters from John Dewey to Adelbert Ames, Jr., almost all of them hitherto unpublished, lends special interest to this volume.

Adelbert Ames, Jr., was born in 1880 and died in 1955. After graduating from Harvard he studied for and practised the law, and later studied art and painted for a period of four years. His interest in painting led to investigation in physiological optics, and he held a research fellowship at Clark University from 1914 until the United States entered World War I. After serving as an aerial observer with the Army throughout the war, Ames went to Dartmouth College where he remained as a research professor, first in the Department of Physiological Optics, and from 1945 until his death, in the Dartmouth Eye Institute. Mr. Cantril's close association with Mr. Ames began in 1947.

Hadley Cantril is Senior Research Counsellor at the Institute for International Social Research at Princeton, N. J., and a Research Associate in the Department of Psychology at Princeton University, where he was professor and chairman of the department until 1955.

# The Morning Notes
## of
## Adelbert Ames, Jr.

# The Morning Notes
## of
## Adelbert Ames, Jr.

INCLUDING A CORRESPONDENCE WITH
### JOHN DEWEY

EDITED AND WITH A PREFACE BY
### HADLEY CANTRIL

RUTGERS UNIVERSITY PRESS

NEW BRUNSWICK       NEW JERSEY

# Preface

The purpose of this volume is to enable more people to have an opportunity to become acquainted with a very remarkable man whose mind was of a rare and original quality. In a conversation with one of Ames's friends, Whitehead once remarked "So you know Adelbert Ames. There's an authentic genius!" In the last letter Ames received from John Dewey and included in this volume is the comment: "I think your work is by far the most important work done in the psychological-philosophical field during this century."

I have a deep conviction that Ames was ahead of his times and that as the years go by the impact of his thinking will become more and more apparent and should, therefore, be available for those who may want to study it carefully and trace its development. Furthermore, my own conscience would forever remain unsettled if others were not able to share, at least in a remote way, some of the stimulation these notes have provided me personally and from which I have—with Ames's enthusiastic blessing—so freely borrowed in my own thinking and writing.

In writing these notes, Ames was merely thinking out loud. He had no intention whatever that any of the notes would ever be published and consequently never reviewed them to resolve apparent inconsistencies, to delete repetitions, or to improve his initial expression. The fact that Del Ames was an amateur in psychology, philosophy, and biology gives his notes a refreshing boldness and originality, just as it also intersperses them with occasional statements which professionals in the field may feel are somewhat naïve. In preparing these notes for publication, I have deliberately not "edited out" any passages which reflect an ignorance of the historical development of currents of thought akin to some of his own, nor have I attempted to polish the original rough-hewn record of his thoughts.

In the dedicatory address given on the occasion of the opening of the Perception Demonstration Center at Princeton University, the distinguished American philosopher Horace Kallen included this thumbnail sketch of the career of his Harvard classmate.

After a pleasantly conventional sojourn at Harvard College Ames became a successful, but not a satisfied, lawyer. Then he turned away from the career

*v*

of law to a career of painting. . . . He passed from the practice of the art to an analysis of its fundamentals—particularly of seen color and form. He constructed very delicately graded color scales, but soon felt that he must give up the analysis of the seen to probe into the activity of seeing. The psychophysics of vision led to the physiology of the organs of vision, their role in the organism, and the psychology of visual stimulus and response. Ames took expert guidance in the study of each. . . . The rest of the record is better known; the settling in Hanover; the study of optics; the devising of camera lenses patterned like the lenses of the human eye; the discovery of the perceptual defect called "aniseikonia" and of aniseikonic glasses which correct it; the establishment of the Dartmouth Eye Clinic; the unyielding struggle to say in words what he had come to understand regarding the interplay of vision and action in the human being's self-altering upkeep of his being human. At some turn in these passages of his personal history, Ames realized that words could not be enough. The invention, testing, and perfection of the perception demonstrations followed this realization. In so doing, Adelbert Ames kept insisting, he was but a member of a diverse team in whose achieved consensus no one's role can be segregated from any one else's. . . . To me, there is something integrally American in this record, with the frontiersman of the mind taking over and transvaluing the faith and works of the frontiersman of the woods. There is likewise something suggestive of Leonardo.

For the sake of the record, it is appropriate to indicate how and why the complete set of demonstrations devised by Ames were set up by us at Princeton and how our collaboration began.

Briefly told, the story is somewhat as follows. In the summer of 1946, John Dickey, President of Dartmouth College, told me about the demonstrations Mr. Ames had created and asked if, as a friend and psychologist, I would come and see them and give him my impression. He thought they might interest me. Mr. Dickey had heard conflicting reports. Many people had seen the demonstrations since they first began to appear in 1938. Some thought them rather interesting, but said they were nothing more than ingenious optical illusions. A few others who had seen them apparently believed that they were of vast potential significance and importance, but had not quite explained why they felt as they did. At that time the name of Adelbert Ames, Jr., was to me only a great name in the field of physiological optics. I had previously heard nothing of the demonstrations.

So one day I drove to Hanover, was shown the demonstrations by Mr. Ames, and immediately felt that they were most significant. It seemed to me that here, at long last, there were concrete illustrations of phenomena that we had been clumsily trying to spell out and investigate in the area labeled "social psychology." Here, for example, one was presented with demonstrations, rather than arguments, showing the interdependencies between our perceptions, our actions, and our purposes. The phenomena I experienced in the demonstrations, as then set up in the basement of the Choate House in Hanover, N.H., provided me one of the most exciting days of my life, confirming as they seemed to in simple and direct fashion the fact that our perceptions, our attitudes, our prejudices are learned significances for purposive behavior, significances which we ourselves have created in order to act effectively and which we are unlikely to alter unless and until our action is frustrated or our purposes change.

But even more exciting on that summer day was the sense of disturbance I had because of my own incomplete understanding of my own naïve experience as I went through the demonstrations with Mr. Ames. The "illusions" became paradoxes to be explained. And I spent many days thereafter, having trekked from Princeton to Hanover on weekends, alone in the basement and then in communion with Mr. Ames, trying to intellectualize for myself what I at first only vaguely sensed was valid and important. It was necessary to bridge the gap between naïve experience and conceptual abstractions and to become aware of the level of abstraction on which we were operating. For there is always the danger that anyone, especially the scientist, may tend to mistake the conceptual abstraction for what it refers to, embrace it eagerly because of the feeling of security it affords, forget that it obscures uniqueness and differences, that it is a function of some human purpose and is at best partial and tentative.

Most of the attempts to put our thoughts on paper were in the form of informal interoffice memoranda. The articles first published met considerable resistance from many psychologists, while others systematically ignored the phenomena described and the explanations that appear most intrinsically reasonably to account for them. In view of this reaction, I was therefore particularly struck by a remark made by Einstein when I was showing him the "revolving trapezoid window" in his home one evening. I mentioned in the conversation how "stimulus bound" psychologists opposed the point of view we were trying to develop. He smiled broadly and said, "I learned many years ago never to waste time trying to convince my colleagues."

"Morning Notes" is the phrase Ames used to describe his informal working memoranda. The notes contained here are those I have selected from six bound volumes which contain the complete set beginning with 1941. Some of the notes consist only of a short paragraph; others are several pages long. One copy of these notes is housed in the Baker Library at Dartmouth College, another copy is in the Firestone Library at Princeton.

A word should be said about the way in which Ames wrote these notes.

He had the habit of putting a problem to himself in the evening just before he went to bed. Then he "forgot" it. The problem never seemed to disturb his sleep. But he often "found" the next morning on awakening that he had made progress on the problem. And as soon as he got to his office he would pick up his pencil and pad of paper and begin to write. He always said he didn't know just "what would come out," and dozens of times he would call me at Princeton in the middle of the morning, ask, courteously, if I had a few minutes, and say, "Hadley, listen to this. I'm surprised at the way it's turning out and I think it will interest you." It was almost as though he himself were a spectator.

We had hundreds of hours of communion alone together. Occasionally an interested colleague sat in. But Ames was best when he was talking with only one other person. Larger groups cramped him. He never wanted to "argue"; he just wanted, as he put it, to "sail" where the wind blew. In a separate volume also housed with the sets of Del's notes in the libraries I have put some of my own notes made between 1946 and 1953, since they occasionally capture the spirit of our communion as well as some of its results. Perhaps my own chief role in the process was to help set and formulate problems which we tried to think through. We had planned to continue our discussions of "reality" during the summer of 1955, the time of Ames's death.

Soon after I met Ames, we managed to get foundation and other funds to finance our work and time together. The Institute for Associated Research was established as a nonprofit mechanism to receive money. It followed the principle of an "informal organization," thanks in large part to the skill and understanding of John Pearson, who had been with Ames as his right-hand administrative expert and friend. Except for the sympathetic and courageous backing of the late Dr. Alan Gregg of the Rockefeller Foundation, Ames's work both in vision and in visual perception and our later work together might never have got off the ground.

Because of Ames's method of thinking and working and the complex vocabulary he developed to represent his ideas accurately, it was difficult for him to prepare any lengthy manuscript for publication. He was much more concerned to get his ideas down in his informal memoranda and let his demonstrations of perceptual phenomena serve as his vehicle of communication. The bibliography of his publication relative to the field of psychology included at the end of this volume is therefore a very short one.

The Notes are arranged chronologically. Occasionally I have quite deliberately included some of the repetition of ideas found in the original notes. For, like a pole vaulter, Ames generally had to take a running start to see if at the end he could jump a little higher. I have omitted all of the more technical discussions of problems of vision and the construction of demonstrations. Ames's great contributions to the field of physiological optics have been recorded elsewhere by competent experts, and a complete set of his writings in this field has also been housed in the Baker Library at Hanover. The Notes assembled here begin, then, with the phase of his thinking after he turned to the psychology of visual perception with all the ramifications that he saw this subject had relevant to the nature and range of human experience.

The correspondence between Ames and John Dewey is included with very little omission because I felt sure that many professional philosophers would be interested in this exchange. I am most grateful to Mrs. Dewey for allowing me to include her late husband's correspondence here.

In addition to the Rockefeller Foundation, others generously contributed to the work that a small group of us did in the years between 1947 and 1955: the Office of Naval Research, Mr. and Mrs. J. P. Stevens, and Mr. E. K. Hall, Jr. Our informal group consisted of the late Charles H. Bumstead, Albert H. Hastorf, W. H. Ittelson, Horace Kallen, Earl Kelley, F. P. Kilpatrick, Merle Lawrence, Ross Mooney, Seymour Robins, Charles Slack, Hans Toch, Warren Wittreich, and a number of others who were with us for shorter periods. Mrs. Alice Weymouth served as Ames's devoted secretary, and her assistance in assembling these notes is most gratefully acknowledged. Mr. Kimball Whipple was indispensable in the design and creation of the demonstrations in perception. Miss Beatrice Miers and Mrs. Pauline Smith have aided in the task of preparing this volume for publication. Professor Sidney Ratner kindly read the manuscript and gave valued advice and encouragement. Finally, I am especially grateful to Mrs. Ames for her permission to prepare this volume from the complete notes and to Dr. Adelbert Ames, III, for his editorial counsel.

This book is published under the aegis of the Institute for International Social Research, established with an endowment from the Rockefeller Brothers Fund, because Ames's thinking and its implications are so integral a part of the Institute's approach to research.

HADLEY CANTRIL

*Princeton, New Jersey*
*May, 1960*

# Contents

# The Morning Notes
## of
## Adelbert Ames, Jr.

# The Morning Notes

August 4, 1941

We localize the visual impression, not the object. The object is only one of the factors in the situation that gives rise to the visual impression. The visual impression is a sensation and is derived from past experience, i.e., it is the significance of past experience. From one aspect, past experience is more truly the source of the visual impression than the object. It would be nearer the truth to consider the significance of past experience as the source of impressions and the immediate situation as a catalytic agent which is responsible for the particular significances sensually experienced. That is, the organism brings to an immediate situation a potentiality for sensually experiencing the significances of all past experience. The stimuli from the immediate occasion bring into being, in terms of sense response, those particular significances which may be present in the immediate situation.

Late April, 1942

### RE: WHITEHEAD AND PRAGMATISM

Whitehead believes we live in a world of *functional* activity in a continual state of *becomingness*, i.e.—"that every actual thing is something by reason of its activity whereby its nature consists of its relevance to other things and its individuality consists in its synthesis of other things so far as they are relevant to it."

The activity of other things in the past is recorded in the physiology of the organism which determines pragmatically the relevance of those "other things," and this relevance is disclosed only pragmatically; that is, through experience, past, present, and future.

Our hypothesis, built on Whitehead's concepts, gives a simple and perhaps a better account of the nature and origin of sensations than his "presentational immediacy" (external object or events) directly recognized in sensations which by "symbolic reference" acquire "causal efficacy."

*3*

We conceive that we cannot directly know external events; that our senses and sensations and ideas give us, at most, a prognosis of their significance. What is known can never exactly correspond to the immediate occasion. At best their relationship can only be a similarity or analogy. The degree of this similarity may vary, but we can never know the inherent nature of objects and their relationships as such.

The fact that *we can never know* what we commonly consider as facts and truth is rather appalling. It is as if nature had set about to create a super hoax with humans, like donkeys chasing the "feed bag." But we are in that situation as long as we insist on believing that knowledge of the constitution of things as such, and their relationships, is the final goal.

We have believed that our knowledge discloses the innate constitution of things apart from their relationship to us. We fail to realize that we can know nothing about things beyond their significance to us.

Philosopher James inveighed against this error. He considered as immaterial and irrelevant the matter of correspondence between our knowledge and external events. James was only interested in the degree to which our knowledge worked as disclosed by pragmatic experience. James kept insisting that the only test of knowledge is "does it work." Implicitly the word "work" means to be successful for a purpose.

It is only when we recognize that so-called facts and truths in themselves are not the ultimate goal, but have value in so far as they show us the ever becoming reality and contribute to our purposes, that we shall cease to be hoaxed.

In adopting "significance disclosed through purposeful action" our hypothesis follows James. We differ from James's pragmatism, however, in that our point of view provides an understanding which he did not have of the nature and origin of sensations. It also makes physiology a much more indispensable part of the whole. It accentuates purpose, direction and "becomingness" more than James did. . . .

Finally, this new point of view elucidates Whitehead's great contribution: namely, that there is no conflict between the concepts of permanence and becomingness or between determinism and free will. Since the essence of nature is purposeful direction, both (determinism and free will) are necessary. Direction must be from somewhere, from something.

The permanent determined aspect of nature, up to the present, is the anchor without which becomingness and free will could not move on and be. . . .

November 17, 1942

As long as the physicists in their investigations in determining the relationships between the external phenomena and the dioptric image were limited to measured determinations of the characteristics of the dioptric system of the eye, they were on sound grounds, but when they included subjective judgments they stepped out of their field. It was natural that they should have included subjective judgments because, under normal conditions, the subjective judgments correlated so exactly with their scientifically determined factors, i.e., laws of geometrical optics. This confirmed their belief that in all important respects there was an important correlation between the dioptric image and what came to consciousness and caused them to think they were capable of saying the final word on all the problems of vision.

January 2, 1943

Due to the fact that science deals only with determined, repeatable aspects of nature, it only works in these aspects. It does give us a great deal that we cannot get from sensations. Why? Because all we can get through sensations is limited by our physiology, and the contribution of science is that its instrumentation has increased the range of our value differentiation. It has not added any more values but has increased the range of already developed values in the repeatable aspects of nature.

February 4, 1943

Learning consists in acquiring more knowledge about the relationships of determined aspects of reality. You cannot learn a becoming aspect; becoming aspects are made known through disclosure, not through learning.

February 15, 1943

Our sense responses disclose the probability of future events for the same reason that "dope sheets" disclose the probability as to which race horse will win or not win a race: namely, because our sense responses are recordings of observations of the result of action in connection with past events of a similar nature. The race horse dopester keeps a record of the performance of all race horses. When any particular horses are going to race, the averages of their past performances disclose a reliable probability as to their relative future performance.

So the human being keeps a record of the result of all action following the experiencing of particular visual sensations and records them against the characteristics of the visual stimulus that gave rise to his visual sensations. When, in later use of his eyes, a similar visual stimulus is given rise to, the results of past actions come to mind in the form of sensations of "whereness" and "whatness" which disclose to him the probable effectiveness of particular types of action.

In ordinary, commonplace environments, i.e., those that have been experienced many, many times before, the probability that action based on sensations will accomplish the desired results is sufficiently high for practical purposes.

It is only in carefully controlled laboratory environments that a really high repeatability of action following stimulation can be demonstrated, but, even under these conditions, the correctness of action remains a probability. It can never be a sure bet.

May, 1943

### SUPERSTITION

Scientists are the super-superstitionists. By their identifying *value* in inanimate objects, they become the magician (soothsayer) of the modern age.

Superstition is irrational thought proceeding from ignorance.

May 20, 1943

It is only through relative motion between the organism and the other events that their spatial relationship to the organism could be disclosed. Movement, relative change, and therefore time necessary for it are conditions for the disclosure of relative spatial relationships. They cannot originate, therefore, in the *immediate* event. They must have their origin in the past as the result of change, therefore action, and the action must be purposeful to provide a basis for meaning and significance.

That purposeful change, action, is a condition for the existence of space is very interesting.

Similarly it must follow that becomingness is a condition for the existence of change.

Further, it must follow that purpose is a condition for the existence of becomingness.

It follows from the above that the mathematical and geometrical concepts of space have a humanistic origin in which both sensation (significance) and the physiology of the organism play a role.

August 3, 1943

### PROGNOSTIC NATURE OF SENSATIONS

Consider what is meant by the term "prognosis" as applied to sensations. A prognosis has to do with future events that have not yet occurred. It, therefore, cannot be those events themselves. At best it can only be something in our minds, a sense or concept.

That is, the organism is continually comparing the prognosis of the continually changing new external events with his determined frame of significances.

If they conform, i.e., "work," he is no longer interested; but in so far as they do not, he has to take stock of the situation.

There are three possibilities—either his frame of significances may be wrong, or his immediate sense response may be wrong, or both. In any case, he has a problem to solve.

August 20, 1943

Each of us knows two worlds. One, uniquely personal, is the significance to us of other things. This world is disclosed by our sensations. The particular "thatness" * at a particular "thereness" of our visual sensations of a person we look at is an example of an element that constitutes this personal world. The other, an impersonal world which we share with all other humans, is the significance of other things to each other irre-

---

* Editor's Note: Throughout the Morning Notes the reader may find Ames using words which will at first seem strange, annoying, and unnecessarily esoteric. However, in an attempt to express precisely what he meant, Ames made constant use of the unabridged dictionary, searching for a word which meant what he meant. "Thatness" is an example, defined by Webster as "'The quality of anything which makes it 'that'; quality of forming a self-existent entity."

spective of their relevance to us. This world is disclosed to us by our concepts. The concept of the spatial relationships of the various buildings and streets in our home town, irrespective of our immediate personal position, is an example of an element that constitutes the impersonal common world.

It is commonly thought that the first personal world is a subjective world, a humanistic creation of man's own making, and the second unpersonal world is an objective world existing in its own right quite apart from man or his doings. But as has been pointed out, especially by Whitehead, this objective world has no existence in its own right; it is only the meaning or relevance of the other things in the world to an organism of man's particular nature and purposes. The same external world would have an entirely different meaning, and therefore objective aspect, to organisms of different nature—consider protozoan, or a tree, or a fish. This meaning (relevance) of other events has been disclosed through pragmatic action in the past. This concept does not imply that nature only exists subjectively, for instance, that if a person wasn't present to look at an object there wouldn't be anything there. There is a "functional activities" there. But all that we, as one of the functional activities that make up the world, can know of the other functional activities is their relevance to us, how they may affect us; that is, our knowledge of those activities as they exist objectively.

Both the subjective and the objective worlds are essentially humanistic in their essence. The difference between these two worlds is not that one is subjective and humanistic and that the other is objective and nonhumanistic, but that one is uniquely personal to the individual experiencing it, disclosing those aspects of nature that can be experienced by him and by him alone; while the other discloses the humanistic aspects of nature that can be the common experience of all men. These aspects must be impersonal, that is, exclusive of individualistic significances (cf. modern science).

Sensations are uniquely personal. You ask me "where" an object is. If I can see it, its "thereness" is perfectly definite to me, and I say "there it is," but that doesn't mean anything to you. You cannot share or participate in my sensation of "thereness." To disclose the "whereness" of the object to you, I must translate my unique personal world of sensation into objective terms common to us both. I do this by relating the object of my thereness to some other objective aspect. For instance, I can say, "*It* is right in *front* of *you*." You will then know "where" I see it. But that knowledge does not enable you to share my personal sense of "thereness." Or I may say, "*It* is right in *front* of *me*." In so doing I am simply calling your attention to the position of my body for you as one of the objective events of this common objective world.

The impersonal objective world potentially includes all relationships between other activities that have a determined significance to man; i.e., is essentially determined. The personal sensorial world potentially includes significances that are also determined.

However, we are related to the immediate becoming aspects of nature only through the personal sensorial world. The "becoming" aspects of nature are made apparent to man not directly, but only in so far as through action in carrying out his purpose man is frustrated. It is only in the solving of his frustrations that the characteristics of the becoming aspects make themselves evident.

August 23, 1943

For example, if I look at an object, I have a sensation of its particular localization. Its particular localization can have two types of significance to me. I can sense it as having a particular "thereness" which enables me to act effectively relative to it as moving towards it, touching it, or kicking it. That is its importance to me personally with my particular unique background involving its significance for my particular potential purposeful action. This significance exists irrespective of the relation of this object to other objects in the field of view or its relevance or significance to other persons.

Or, its localization can be significant to me in terms of its "whereness" to other objects irrespective of its "thereness" to me. Normally our sensations include both of these types of significances. The first type is uniquely personal and is how other things enter into the unity of my own experience. This unity of my own experience is how I exist "formally" (Whitehead). These "formal" significances, so to speak, cannot be shared or communicated with anyone else.

The second type of significances are irrespective of the localization of the object relative to me but have only to do with its spatial relation relative to other objects in the field. This significance does not involve the spatial localization of my body, or a synthesis with my individuality, or my potential purpose. It involves only the relevance of one thing to another. It is the significance of things as they exist objectively, that is to say, "existing abstractly, exemplifying only those elements of their formal contents that have a common human significance." From this type of common significances we have evolved and formulated conceptual frames of significances or references. There are innumerable types of these common frames of reference.

May 23, 1945

## OBJECTIFICATION

Objectification is the attributing to otherness (other functional activities) of specific significances.

That "objectification" attributes aspects to otherness that do not inherently exist does not mean that it, in itself, is useless or apart from reality. It is an inherent part of reality.

But for it we could not communicate with each other.

But for it we would not have the means for carrying out our purposes or those of the human race.

However, objectification, due to its very nature, can in no way disclose the direction and probability of the becoming aspects of Reality or the direction and probability of individual or collective human purpose.

The direction and probability of human purpose can only be disclosed by the integration of the personal potential purposes evolved and tested by past experience, with those of other functional activities.

This integration can take place only in the now of continuing experiences when and where the organism is related to otherness through their mutual impingement and interaction.

The danger of objectification arises only when we make the superstitious mistake of substituting it for the whole of reality. And that danger can be very great.

The ultimate and only actual significance there can be for an organism can exist only in regard to its purposes as affected by the impingement and interaction of otherness in the now of its continuing experience.

In so far as we consider any objectified significance as causal, we will be led into error.

So in the problem of re-education, an adequate understanding for the successful handling of a specific case is only possible to the extent that the purposes of the subject in the *now* of its continuing experience are known.

May 30, 1945

### IMPORTANT

We are now defining sensations as prognostic directives for action. This definition is incomplete because whenever we have sensation, the situation is always one in which there is an *alternative* choice to do one thing or another, or at least to *do* or *not* to do something about the sensation.

The only situation in which we do not have a choice is that of *reflexes*, and in that situation there is no *sensation in consciousness*. The concept sensations implies something in consciousness.

Our definition of sensations therefore should be—"Prognostic Directives for Alternate Action."

July 9, 1945

### CORRESPONDENCE; ILLUSIONS

The concept of correspondence implies similarity or identity between sensations, percepts or concepts of objects, qualities, etc., that exist in consciousness, and those same objects, qualities, etc., that exist externally.

When a lack of such correspondence exists, that which is in consciousness is conceived of as illusions or autisms, on the assumption that the external objects and qualities are real. This, in turn, leads to the confusing conclusion that illusions and autisms are outside of reality.

It would be equally logical to assume that the illusions and autisms are real and that the external objects and qualities are illusions. But that assumption is apparently denied by the fact that we can demonstrate that the external objects and qualities *actually* exist.

But actually this *cannot* be demonstrated. Objects and qualities are specific and determined. We know no such things exist in their own right in nature. There is also the evidence of modern physics, that nature in its essence is a becoming flux.

So we find ourselves in confusion and double talk.

James recognized this dilemma when he absolutely refused to have anything to do with the concept of correspondence. This whole dilemma is primarily due to our insistence upon indulging in the superstition of objectification. This, in turn, is due to the insistence of conceiving sensations and percepts as referring to objects and qualities existing in their own right.

This dilemma and confusion can only be avoided by realizing that what exists in consciousness is not there to bring to our attention objects and qualities existing as such, but as prognostic directives for potential alternative achievements to enable us to further our purposes in integration with the furtherance of the purposes of the other functional activities, organic and inorganic, which, with us, constitute nature.

August 11, 1945

## VALUE CONCOMITANT WITH CONCEPTS OF USEFULNESS OF EXPERIENCED OBJECTS

Bear in mind and think more about the fact that when we have a concrete experience of an object, such as a chair, we fore-sense the experience we would have if we sat in it. This fore-sense, accompanied by motor impulses to our bodies and limbs, is a value, not a conceptual factor.

We cannot relate abstracted concepts to such fore-sensing.

It is these combined integrated fore-value responses that constitute the valueful nature of the concretely experienced reality. Abstracted concepts of specific usefulness cannot be integrated or weighed as "fore-value responses" can, and therefore can never be a substitute for them.

August 31, 1945

## EXPERIENCE
(Most Important)

Experiences can be divided into two types:

I. Those that alter our perceptual process.
II. Those that do not.

I. For experiences to *alter* our perceptual processes they must have a bearing on our purpose, i.e., either further it or interfere with the carrying out of one or more or our innumerable specific purposes.

The degree to which we are altered by such experiences is related
a. to the intensity of our purpose;
b. to the probability with which the external phenomenon is related to accomplishment of the purpose.

II. We have innumerable purposes:

a. We have *temporary* purposes brought into play by transient circumstances such as answering a letter.

b. We have *periodic* * purposes, for instance, satisfying physiological needs varying with night and day.

c. We have innumerable *more permanent* purposes, nonperiodical, the existence of which in our "now" varying with the "field of external events" existing at the time as purposes related to the war and peace.

d. We have *ultimate* purposes that always exist in our "now" irrespective of the nature of the field of external events existing at the time, as self-loyalty, family loyalty, race loyalty.

We have the capacity of being conscious of purposes that do not exist in our "now." Such purposes are "*abstracted* purposes."

We have also the capacity of having in our consciousness the significance of the now external events as related to such *abstracted purposes*. (It should be borne in mind that such events, not being related to the specific "now" purposes of our biological continuum are also semi-abstracted.)

These capacities of sensing the *potential* significance of (1) concrete external events as related to totally or semi-abstracted purposes, or of (2) totally or semi-abstracted external events as related to concrete purposes, or of (3) totally or semi-abstracted external events as related to totally or semi-abstracted purpose, constitute our conceptual world as differentiated from our experiential world.

Our actions can be effective in carrying out our purposes only to the extent we make use of these abstracting capacities.

Without them the field of effectivity of our action would be limited to that field from which our physiology received impingements. In vision this would be limited to that field from which light rays enter the eyes.

These abstracting capacities enable us to extend our "visual field," i.e., for the purposes of action, around the world and into the future.

But besides extending our field of effective action, these abstracting capacities have a direct effect on the nature of our purposes.

This is due to the fact that the very existence of a purpose is predicated upon our being able to do something effective in carrying it out.

The intensity of our purposes, our faith in them, is directly proportional to our capacity to carry them out.

Action consummating purpose is a function of purpose. Purpose is meaningless without the possibility of fulfillment.

* Editor's Note: In the Notes Ames uses "periodic" sometimes in the sense of an occurrence repeating itself at regular intervals and at other times as an event that takes place during a certain extent of time.

*However,* the inherent character (nature) of a purpose does not have its origin in the knowledge of how to carry it out.

The nature of purposes has its origin in another level. Purposes have to do with the directional becomingness of the particular organism which senses the purpose.

This is disclosed to the organism through his experiences in "becomingness."

This is disclosed through prior prognostic experience that has disclosed what does or does not further its becomingness.

The nature of an organism's becomingness is to be found in the accumulated alterations of the organism's perceptual processes, purposes, and values. That is, the "now" of a specific organism's perceptual world is the high-water mark of the synthesis of the becomingness of purpose (value) of that organism as related to the becomingness of all other functional activities constituting reality.

That it is our perceptual world and not our abstracted world that is most basic and is directly related to our purposes is disclosed by the fact that in a concrete situation it is our perceptual response (sensations) and not our abstracted concepts that determine our actions (distorted room).

September 17, 1945

### VALUE—SENSATION

A sensation is an experienced value which has been created by purpose, i.e., our perceptual world is a valueful humanistic creation.

A sensation is also a prognostic directive for action toward creating new value.

A sentiment is a value abstracted from its concreteness.

September 18, 1945

### MISFORTUNE—ERROR—SIN—FRUSTRATION
### (Preliminary Notes)

I. Misfortune—Associated with misfortune is a sense of fate—of a happening with which we have had nothing to do—"Allah's will be done." For example, when the indications are unequivocal but our actions are wrong, as when we follow a mirage to death in the desert.

II. Error—Associated with error is a sense that in some way we have had something to do with the happening, but unintentionally. For example, when the indications which we have are not sufficient for us to act with a complete sense of surety. We do the best we know how but it doesn't work out.

III. Sin—Associated with sin is a sense not only that we were responsible for the happening but that we did not do the best we knew how or did what we know we ought not to have done. For example, when in weighing multiple potential courses for purposeful action we consciously give undue weight to the fulfillment of personal purposes to the sacrifice of the accomplishment of a more integrated purpose, or knowingly we act impulsively without attempting to integrate the potential courses for purposeful action. We then have a *guilty* conscience.

IV. Misfortune, error and sin are humanistic personal factors related to situations that do not come out right. There is another superficially similar personal factor that is related to situations that do not come out right. That is frustration.

However, the conditions that give rise to the failure of accomplishment to which the sense of frustration is related are basically different from the conditions related to misfortune, error and sin, and the sense of frustration is basically different from the sense of uncontrollable fate related to misfortune, or grief related to error, or guilty conscience related to sin.

While these conditions are either neutral or negative to being and life, frustration and its conditions are its very essence. Due to the fact that nature is a becomingness and therefore always changing, "The best laid plans of mice and men" (our integrated sense and perceptual responses, our integrated purposes that disclose to us the "why to do," and our abstractions that provide us with the "how to do"), when applied to reality can never work out as expected. They must always come out wrong to a greater or less extent.

It is solely and only from the nature of the discrepancies between our purposes and their actual results, when applied, that the new becoming aspects of nature can be made known to us. But for them we would be forever static, as are some of the forms of insects and fishes that have not changed for millions of years.

The conditions attending frustration are true opportunities—maybe the only real opportunities that actually exist—for improvement. The sense of frustration instead of being dodged and avoided must be accepted as a challenge.

October 1, 1945

### SENSATIONS: THEIR NATURE AND ORIGIN

An important aspect of the Institute's work has dealt with vision in all its relations to human functioning. These investigations have been supplemented by empirical demonstrations which substantiate the central findings that have emerged. Some of the more important of these findings are as follows:

### 1. *The Nature of Sensation*

Although the human organism in its behavior acts as a result of stimuli, *these stimuli have in themselves no meaning.* The significances that are related to them in consciousness—and are experienced by the organism as sensations—*are derived* entirely *from the organism's prior experience, personal and inherited.*

COMMENT. This point of view is contrary to the prevailing lay and scientific belief that what is in consciousness has its origin either in whole or in part in the immediate externality or in the stimulus pattern.

It is apparent that there is no "meaning," for instance, in the undifferentiated light rays themselves which impinge on the cornea. Nor is there any "meaning" in the light rays as differentiated by the lens systems of our eyes that impinge on the receptors in our retinas; or in the electrical-chemical disturbances that take place between the retinal receptors and the visual center of the brain. "Meaning" is significance which has been disclosed through prior purposeful action. The significance is related to stimulus patterns existing at the time of the original experience and is reactivated when the organism is later subjected to similar stimulus patterns.

The function of sensations is not to disclose the innate character of a thing as such or its spatial position as such. It is to establish between the evolving organism and the ever-changing environment a relationship on the basis of which the organism may effectively carry out its purpose. This means that sensations are prognostic directives for purposeful action.

COMMENT. A thing as such (and its position in space) has no "meaning" except as it is related to the organism in its "now." It must be so related before the organism can sense its significances and act in regard to them.

## 2. *The Role of Purpose*

The function of sensations is to disclose alternate possible courses of action. It is the *purpose* of the organism in the "now" that determines which course will be followed.

COMMENT. Our field of visual sensations discloses multiple possibilities for action, but only certain of these possibilities will further the organism's purpose. Therefore, it is in accordance with purpose, conscious or unconscious, that the choice is made. Within the chosen course, sensations are again important in determining the effectiveness of the action. For example, if the visual sensation is "illusory" then the action, while guided by sensation, will be ineffective in carrying out the purpose.

## 3. *The Relation of Abstractions to Reality*

Abstractions, whether they are words or complex physical laws, are symbolic references. They refer to significances of reality that are relatively fixed and repeatable.

Abstractions are all characterized by the fact that of necessity they exclude the "point of view" of the organism. By "point of view" is meant his present relationship to other functional activities and his present position in his biological continuum. The organism's purpose is served by abstractions but cannot be deduced from them.

COMMENT. Because abstractions do not include the "point of view" or purpose of the organism, they in themselves are not identical with reality. Abstractions are indispensably useful in dealing with limited aspects of a situation (measuring a table to determine whether it can be carried through a door), but they can never disclose why a person would want to carry the table through the door. When the situation is one involving relationships and functional activities beyond those that can be abstracted —a normal condition in actual behavior—it is our sensations and not our abstracted knowledge that determine the nature of our actions. (Hitting a golf ball or driving an automobile cannot be successfully carried out on the basis of reasoning alone.)

## 4. *Sensation and Surety*

A sensation is not a basic unit of animal behavior (any more than a molecule is a basic unit of matter). The sensation is an integration of numerous significances related to specific characteristics of the impinging stimulus pattern.

These various significances (which in vision may be thought of for convenience as "indications" of what things are and where they are) may or may not be in agreement with what constitutes the organism's reality.

The degree of conflict among the indications is responsible for the sense of relative surety or unsurety which characterizes the organism's behavior.

COMMENT. From this it seems to follow that surety and unsurety can be brought within the field of precise scientific study and this knowledge made use of in education and training.

### 5. Sensation and Purpose

Purpose underlies the constituent parts of sensation much as energy is now known to underlie the constituent parts of the atom. Empirical evidence shows that a sensation is an experienced value resulting from purposeful action. The significance of the value therefore seems to involve purpose.

COMMENT. This makes it understandable why abstracted knowledge as such does not affect sensations. If it is purpose and not abstracted knowledge that underlies sensations, it is only through change in purpose that sensations and the behavior of the organism can be affected.

### 6. Sensation and Social Relationships

The processes that underlie our perception of our immediate external world and those that underlie our perception of social relationships are fundamentally the same.

November 1, 1945

## VALUES

"Values" can be defined as those aspects of our experiences of which we are conscious that cannot be abstracted, and therefore cannot be communicated by intellectualized abstractions.

The emotion of beauty I feel when I look at a landscape is an example of value, as is my sensation of specific "thereness" of an object before me.

It is the function of the fine arts to communicate values. The values experienced by an observer of the fine arts are not inherent in the abstractions that the arts make use of. They are the observer's memories of his experiences, or new syntheses of such memories, that he relates to the particular abstractions made use of.

There is an aspect of value in every conscious experience, from that of love to that of the understanding of the most abstract mathematical formula.

The significance of value, however, increases with the concreteness of the experience and decreases with the abstractiveness of the experience.

A completely concrete experience involves a specific person in specific relationship to other specific functional activities at a specific "when" in his specific biological continuum involving his "then" becoming purposes.

1. The concreteness becomes much less complete if what is in consciousness does not include any specific "when" in the biological continuum of a human being. Our concept of an objective material world existing in its own right and all scientific laws are based on abstractions of this nature.

2. The concreteness of the experiences becomes less complete if what is in consciousness refers to the *average* person in an average relationship to other average functional activities at a "when" of the *average* continuum involving *average* purposes. The laws of ethics are based on abstractions of this nature.

3. The concreteness becomes less complete if what is in consciousness does not include any "spatial" relationship to other functional activities. Spatial concepts, such as geographical maps, are based on abstractions of this nature.

The concreteness becomes less complete when what is in consciousness does not include any "when" relationship to other functional activities. Temporal concepts, such as periodic time, are based on abstractions of this nature.

However, even with such degrees of abstractions there still exists in consciousness an element of value. These abstractions still deal with distance and time units which are not absolute in themselves but refer to human experiential factors; that is, the distance units must refer to something humanistically significant and so must the time units.

In the final analysis all abstractions, such as the objective material world, scientific laws, words themselves, are but products of the valueful purpose of specific human organisms integrated with the value purposes of other specific human organisms.

To quote Schroedinger:

The only possible inference from these two facts is, I think, that I—I in the widest meaning of the word, that is to say, every conscious mind that has ever said or felt "I"—am the person, if any, who controls the "motion of the atoms" according to the Laws of Nature.

To quote Huxley:

The truth, however, as shown by the extension of scientific method into individual and social psychology, is that we create our own values. Some we generate consciously; some subconsciously; and some only indirectly, through the structure of the societies in which we live.

Through a fuller comprehension of these mechanisms we shall be able to guide and accelerate this process of value creation, which is not only essential for our individual lives but basic to the achieving of true evolutionary progress in the future.

December, 1945

### Consciousness and Free Will

Free Will is inconceivable unless there exists the possibility of choice of alternative action.

Free Will is inconceivable unless the alternatives are known to the chooser, that is, are in his consciousness.

January 22, 1946

### On the Illusion That a Material World Exists in Its Own Right

The fact that what we are conscious of in perception has had its origin *entirely* in past experience and does not exist in its own right in the objects we are looking at is a difficult one to believe. We subconsciously insist on believing that the various aspects of our sensations, such as size, hardness, etc., actually exist in the object in their own right and would continue to so exist if you or I or no human were there to look at it.

We can be led to an understanding of that fact by the following line of thought.

We all know that certain aspects of what is in our consciousness when we look at an object are entirely subjective and are not in the object, such as liking it or disliking it. We also know that the particular "thereness" of the object to us is not exclusively in the object itself, but only exists because of our relative position to it and therefore our point of view, ourselves, i.e., the object would have no specific thereness if we were not there. . . .

In our actual perceptual experiences such characteristics as size, weight, hardness in our sensations all depend on *our own* size. If I am a small child, I sense the table as big. If I am a grown man, I sense the table as small. That is, I am the standard against which the size of the table is related.

In science they have different arbitrarily chosen standards: one in astronomy and another in atomic physics, neither of which makes experiential sense to us. If all human standards are eliminated as is done by science, what is left? Accumulations of atoms. That's what the table is. There is no question about that. A mass of billions and billions of atoms, with distances between them relative to astronomical distances and continually changing, never the same, unpredictable and disintegrating.

That's what's there that we are looking at. But there is not the slightest resemblance between what we know is there when we eliminate all human standards and what is in our consciousness in terms of perception.

This seems to make it easier to understand why what we sense in perception is not inherently in the object we are looking at but is the significance of what we are looking at to us as human beings.

February 1, 1946

### Past Experiential Factor in Binocular Vision
#### (Most Important)

In uniocular vision, single point of view, the sense of distance exists only because of past experiential knowledge of such factors as known size, known shape, etc. Similarly, in binocular vision, double point of view, the sense of position, distance and direction exist *only* because of the *known shape* and egocentric localization of *surfaces*, i.e., whether they are flat, curved, etc.

In uniocular vision, knowledge of the shape and egocentric localization of surfaces doesn't help us at all, and we don't use it.

In binocular vision it does, and it is not necessary for us to use the uniocular factors, such as size, etc. This knowledge of the shape and egocentric localization of surfaces is not related to the geometrical characteristics of the stimulus pattern but to other characteristics to which in past experience we have related specific shapes and specific egocentric localization as, for instance, large water surfaces or surfaces whose shape is indicated by architectural detail.

January 24, 1947

### Visual Perception and Social Perception

By the term visual perception we mean all the phenomena that are dealt with in the demonstrations concerning the origin and nature of sensation.

By social perception we mean perceptions that include our relationship with other human beings.

It should be noted that, so defined, visual perception is limited to our relationship with inanimate external events. To explain: all the "things" that are looked at in our demonstrations are inanimate. It would seem apparent that the problem of social perception would immediately arise if another human being were included in the externality at which we are looking. The including of another person in the field makes the phenomenon basically a different one for the following reasons: Assume our hypothesis that sensations are prognostic directives for action in carrying out our purposes. When the "objects" in the external field are only inanimate, the prognostic reliability of our sensations will be directly related to our knowledge of the significance of these "objects" to us. The significance of inanimate external objects is determined, that is, it is either fixed, or if it is changeable, the changes are determined by fixed laws that can be known.

If, however, another person is in the field of view, this no longer holds. The prognostic reliability of our sensations will then depend upon what that other person does. That in turn is not determined by any fixed laws but solely by the other person's purposes. The prognostic reliability of our sensations will be directly related to the extent they reveal the purposes of the other person.

It follows that there is a basic difference between visual perception and social perception as defined. It is almost as if with social perception another dimension has entered into the situation, namely, the necessity of relating ourselves not only to the intellectual purposes but also to the "value-sense purposes" of another person or persons.

January 27, 1947

### CREATIVENESS: GROWTH—FORM AND FLOW

To grow one must expect the emerging unexpected. It is not enough to expect the expected.

The expected is the determined form each of us brings to the now.

The emerging unexpected is the flow without which there would be no becomingness, no growth, no creativeness, no life.

Many believe that the emerging unexpected can be found in the "extraordinary" (bizarre). But the emerging unexpected is ordinary. The "extraordinary" is not related to reality.

The emerging unexpected is born from concrete experience vivified by hope and faith.

The emerging unexpected can be recognized (1) by the quality of our "value sense" and (2) by our logic.

Our value sense will be one of (a) surety; (b) beauty; (c) humor in respect to ourselves and others who grasp the emerging unexpected, and irony in respect to those who have not grasped it.

Our logic will confirm that the emerging unexpected is real and true, first, because it does not violate or contradict any of the aspects of the expected, and, secondly, because it makes the expected more logically understandable.

January 28, 1947

### CREATIVENESS: GROWTH—FORM AND FLOW (*Continued*)

To understand the implications of the statement of January 27 on expecting the emerging unexpected, it is necessary to define the nature of the unexpected emergence which we must expect.

The concept "emergence" can mean any change in events completed in a limited duration. For example: a fire, due to lightning, that burns down our house—an unpredictable atomic event and therefore "unexpectable"—or the rising of the sun which is predictable and therefore "expectable."

The significance to us of this type of event is contained with the termination of the event. For good or bad as far as we are concerned, such phenomena are fortuitous, beyond our control. After they have happened, all we can say in regard to their significance to us is "Kismet."

It is apparent that these types of phenomena are not of a nature such that it would be possible for one to experience expectation of the emerging unexpected.

An event in which we can expect the emerging unexpected must be one that extends into the future, the future aspects of which, although unknown to us, will be significant to us.

But this alone is not enough. For instance, the thunderstorm, lightning from which burnt down our house, extends into the future, and its future aspects, though unknown, may be significant to us.

The "emergence" must also be characterized by the fact that human beings have been responsible for its significant aspects and that human beings alone are responsible for the development of its potential future aspects that will have further significance for human beings. For instance, human beings discovered that fire was significant to their uses. They were responsible for starting an emergence that included the development of fire for human use extending through human history to the present firing of atomic structure.

At any specific stage in this evolving event of fire as significant to the human race, certain individuals had the capacity to expect the emerging unexpected. They did not stop and believe the event was terminated—ended—determined—that all they knew about it, their then concepts concerning it, was all that could be known.

Convinced by concrete experience that there were more potentialities for human significance in fire than could be formulated in their abstract conceptual structures, they had a faith to expect significances beyond those that could be intellectually conceived. But for this expectation of the emerging unexpected they would neither have developed sense responses to details that had never been sensed before, nor have intuitively sensed hypotheses to confirm, nor have had the perseverance to devote themselves to what otherwise would have been a hopeless undertaking.

January 29, 1947

### CREATIVENESS: GROWTH—FORM AND FLOW (*Continued*)

In the just prior note on this matter the concrete situations in which one experiences expectation of the emerging unexpected involved external events that were of an inanimate nature.

Consider a concrete situation in which the external events involved were other persons. Under these conditions one would have to be able to expect the unexpected in the behavior of another person. This in turn means sensing another person's emerging unexpected purposes and sensed values, since it is these factors that determine his behavior.

There are two general possibilities in such a situation. You may not be in communion with the other person or you may be in communion with the other person.

If you are in communion with the other person then there may be a *mutual* experiencing of the expectation of the emerging unexpected. In other words, the *mutual* experiencing of the expectation of the emerging unexpected *is communion*.

In fact, isn't this the essence of what true lovers experience?

### SPECIFICITY OF CONSCIOUSNESS—COMPLETENESS

Under conditions where we are related to otherness by light impingements, if we are conscious at all, what is in consciousness has *complete specificity*. Consider the simple case of a point of light in completely dark surroundings, rays from which are forming an image on our retina.

If we are aware of it at all, what is in our consciousness will be of complete specificity. This specificity can be analyzed into various abstracted qualities.

It can be analyzed into the following qualities:

1. Thatness; e.g., a star, or a hole in a wall, or the shine of a polished surface.

2. Thereness:

a. in distance—in the heavens, at the end of the room, near at hand;

b. in direction—in some specific direction from us, we can't see it in two directions at the same time, or if it is moving we see it in a specific direction at a specific time.

Actually in our consciousness the "thatness" is not separated from the "thereness." If the thatness is a star, the distance is that of the heavens. If it is a hole in the wall, its distance is at the end of the room. If it is a shine off an object, its distance is at hand.

It has been shown that these specificities are the statistical averages of similar specificities with which we have had prior experience.

This in turn means that the stored memories we bring to the now from experience are not abstractions but integrated synthesized specificities.

It is apparent on consideration that the specificities of "thatness" and "thereness" are only some of the specificities that were present in our concrete prior experiences. Examples of other specificities that we know were present are (1) specific muscle tonus, (2) specific emotions, (3) specific purposes, (4) specific values, (5) specific expectancies, (6) one or more specific other "thatnesses." Related to each of these specificities in consciousness were concomitant specific physiological patterns.

The importance of these considerations seems to be that they make clear that what we record in experience are not abstractions but complete specificities in a penumbra of other specificities. Further, in concrete experiences when we are related to otherness what is in consciousness are not abstractions but complete specificities in a penumbra of other specificities.

But we must stop to consider what we mean by the word complete. As used so far it means at least an integration of (1) "specific thatness significance" to the experiencer, (2) "specific thereness significance" to the experiencer. But it is apparent that the "specific thatness significance" to the experiencer will vary according to the specific interests of the experiencer.

This means that the word "complete" must include the "now" *interests* of the experiencer. "Interests of the experiencer" means his purposes and expectations.

Further it is apparent that "the specific thereness significance" to the experiencer will vary according to the specific relative position of the "thatness" to the experiencer.

It would seem of necessity to follow conclusively that if in a concrete situation where the experiencer is related to otherness, if he is conscious at all, what is in consciousness is complete specificity including specific thatness and thereness, purposes and expectations in the specific now of the experiencer both in space and time.

March 2, 1947

CONCEPTS—ABSTRACTIONS—VALUES—PURPOSES—STATISTICAL
AVERAGES—GENERALIZATIONS

Concepts and abstractions are in their essence based on statistical averages.

Values and purposes are in their essence based on the unique specificity of an experiencing organism's "now" as determined by its own uniqueness (unique biological history) and the uniqueness of its locus (relationship) in the becomingness of the functional direction of other unique functional activities, organic and inorganic.

Statistical averages only disclose, refer to, the probability of certain factors in concrete events.

Value-purpose is an actual factor in a specific concrete occasion. (Compare Schroedinger.) Equally great error results from:

I. Conceiving concepts and abstractions as unique realities.

II. Conceiving values and purposes as having existence as statistical averages.

May 16, 1947

### MEANS AND ENDS

Can ends justify the means for accomplishing the end?

The difficulty that the above question raises is due to the fact that when we pose the question we are unconsciously abstracting. We are considering the result of a "final" action as a concreteness existing in its own right, entirely divorced from a total process.

In fact "ends" exist concretely only as parts of a total process in which there is nothing in the nature of an "end."

If one looks for the crucial part of the total process, it is apparently to be found in the conscious value choice made by a specific individual that leads to a prognosis that in turn leads to action. This conscious value choice is crucial because of its "causal efficacy." But even it is not an "end" in the sense we use the word when we raise the question "Can the end justify the means?"

The "value choice" has causal efficacy only to the extent that it is related to action altering external factors. When we speak about "means," we also refer to action that alters "external factors." We have to make a "value choice" to formulate prognoses that lead to action to bring about the means.

It would seem apparent that the quality of the "value choice" we make concerning "means" must be of the same standard as the value choice we make concerning the "end," or one will counteract the other and nothing will be gained in the direction of the emergence of value quality, either in the specific individual making the choices or in "external phenomena."

It would seem apparent from the above that in concreteness "means" and "ends" are not separate—that the "means" are part of the "ends" and that the "ends" are part of the "means." In other words, we can only justify the means by the ends on the level of abstraction, and when we do that we are not *realists*.

July 24, 1947

While we all want to believe in the ultimate reality and efficacy of values and value judgments, up to the present we have had no sound scientific basis for such an assumption. It appears now that a sound scientific basis for the assumption of the ultimate reality and efficacy of value judgments exists when we recognize that value judgments provide the most reliable prognosis for successful action in carrying out our purposes, and that value judgments alone assure us of the possibility of successful emergence.

September 4, 1947

### GUIDE TO CHOICE OF ACTION

The most reliable prognosis of the "goodness" or "badness" of our choice of action is the quality of our sense awareness (sensed value-quality).

As compared with sensed value-quality it is apparent that intellectual abstractions, i.e., concepts, are completely inadequate as reliable prognoses for action in an immediate concrete situation.

Intellectual abstractions play an indispensable role *prior* to the immediate situation. They and they alone extend and enlarge the field of factors that are integrated by the synthesizing capacity of our sensory processes, and the reliability of our sensed value-quality is directly proportionate to the number of factors that are taken account of.

But there is a further test as to the extent to which our choice and action will be "good" or "bad" for ourselves and others beyond their effect on the successful carrying out of our personal purposes having to do with our personal future and becomingness.

That is the extent to which our choices and action will be "good" or "bad" from the long-range point of view involving their effect on the direction of the emergent evolution of the race.

Or, put in the form of a question: In a concrete situation is our choice of action in conformity with, in the direction of, the becomingness of advancing evolutionary emergence or in conflict against its direction?

In fact our choice and action must be either in this current or against it or out of it. Maybe our choice and actions affect the direction of evolutionary emergence. But we have not the perspective or evidence for considering that possibility.

But we can raise the question as to whether or not we have any basis for being aware of prognostic indications as to whether our choices and actions are in this current of possibly successful evolutionary emergence or against it or out of it.

If our awareness of value-quality based on the integration of our personal experience registered in our brains provides a prognosis that our immediate choice and action will further our personal future becomingness, i.e., be in line with, in the current of, a successful personal future, it is not inconceivable that we may be able to be aware of other types of value-quality that are based on the integration of our inherited experience (registered in our chromosome structure) that provide us with prognoses that our immediate choice and action will further our evolutionary emergence, i.e., provide us with clues as to whether our choices and actions are in the current of evolutionary emergence.

September 10, 1947

### IDENTITY—SENSATIONS—CONCEPTS—SEMANTICS

As we have seen, for a sensation of a quality related to an externality ("chairness") to have a high degree of identity, it must persist from different viewpoints in space and time. To have an absolute degree of identity, a sensation of a quality ("chairness") related to an externality must persist throughout the actual use of the externality by the perceiver.

An identity, or persistence of sameness, since it serves the role of prognosticating, is a function of usefulness. Having served its purpose, there is no longer need for identity.

Since in concreteness all the factors involved, including the person's purposes, are specifically unique, it follows that the quality with whose identity the person is concerned is specifically unique.

But the moment we abstract and think of qualities unrelated to the sensations of a specific person in a concrete situation, this is no longer so. Conceptually abstracted qualities, such as "chairness," related to thinking or saying the word chair have no prognostic aspect, no relation to carrying out purposeful action.

Moreover, their persistence of identity is not affected as is the persistence of identity of a concrete sensation. Their degree of identity is unaffected by alteration of the thinker's spatial or temporal point of view and is not tested by actual use. They are not a function of our purposes.

Abstractions are effective only to the extent that their identity persists.

And what do they identify, refer to? Webster defines "chair" as "a seat, usually movable, for one person." Note he doesn't define it in terms of its use, i.e., something to sit on, but as something existing in its own right, which it doesn't, in an imaginary world which doesn't exist.

And while the "that" in which a concrete sensation is related is uniquely specific, the "that" to which an abstraction refers is a general classification.

### ABSTRACTING—SYMBOLIZING—INVOLVING KNOWNS— PROGNOSTICATIONS

I have been much confused in my understanding when using these terms. I have assumed that I was "abstracting" when in a concrete experience I focused my awareness on a part separated from the whole to which it is related. For instance, an awareness of distance ("thereness") separated from the whole of "thereness and thatness."

I have also assumed I was abstracting when I was using words, i.e., symbolizing.

On consideration it would appear that what we are aware of when we use words (i.e., symbolizing) is an entirely different aspect from an "abstracting" as above described.

When we use a word, "a naming," that which is in consciousness includes implicitly—without any "specific reference"—the total field of the significances that have been disclosed to us through our prior concrete experience with the phenomena to which the word refers.

For example, consider what is implicitly in my awareness when I use a noun—the noun "water," for instance. There is potentially in my awareness something to drown in and to slake my thirst; hot and cold; salt and fresh; blue and yellow; the sea when I was young; the Connecticut River now when I am old; everything encompassed in the "cast net" of my prior concrete experience irrespective of time or place.

What I am aware of, far from being an abstraction, is an integration or more exactly it is the "staking out of a claim" of a particular field of "togetherness," apart from other fields of "togetherness."

These "togethernesses" are, so to speak, outside of the fields of time and space, but within in the field of usefulness, purpose, value.

But what is included in these "staked-out claims"—fields—can never be the same for any two individuals, not only because their prior experiences are different, but also because the particular implicit phases that are patent in awareness, when a symbol is used, can never be exactly the same. Hence one of the difficulties in communicating by words.

So far so good, as long as I am postulating that awarenesses are "knowns-knowings," but when I take into account (as shown by our demonstrations) that awarenesses are not "knowns" but are only "prognostications," to make any sense out of the mess at all I have to reformulate my total understanding.

That awarenesses are in fact prognostic *pre*sumptions, and not *as*sumptions, appears to be of great significance. It necessitates an understanding of why our awarenesses are prognoses and not disclosures (or *pre*sumptions and not *as*sumptions). This involves explaining why we are presumers and what is prognosticated. The most sensible explanation, which is confirmed by our demonstrations, is that all awarenesses (perceptions) are patent or implicit prognostic directives for action.

Action for what? The only answer seems to be: For carrying out our purposes, and purpose involves value.

If our awarenesses are prognostic presumptions, we can only get understanding by including in the integration of a knowable whole the aspects of action, purpose, and value and also aspects of abstractions, and "namings" and what-not. But such integration seems to be beyond anyone's thinking capacity unless one does it in terms of sequences of relationships, starting with the aspect of emergent value-quality as the firmest naming we can now get hold of, and relating to it the aspects of purpose and action, abstractions and namings from the point of view of the role they play in the emergence of value-quality.

To go back to the matter of symbolizing (using for an example the noun "water"). It appears as above stated that a "naming" can be thought of as the "staking out of a claim" of a particular field of "togetherness" apart from other fields of "togetherness," and it would appear that in the "claim staked out" by the noun "water" many "phases" are implicitly included. It should be noted that the noun "water" refers to a natural phenomenon. If we use a noun that refers to an artifact made by man, such as "chair," the phases implicit in the "claim which it stakes out" are very much more limited. For instance, one has about covered the "claim staked out" by the noun "chair" in the meaning that it is something to sit on.

In fact, in naming man's artifacts it might do away with confusion if we define them in terms of their use. However, it is apparent that couldn't be done with phenomena like "water," which has a lot of "opposite" uses. To get around that difficulty, we have to use a "catch-all" naming, which apparently has caused us to overlook [the fact] that all phases in the "claims staked out" by words are in terms of usefulnesses.

So much for nouns taken by themselves as namings.

It would seem apparent, as Dewey and Bentley say, that they in themselves alone are senseless. To use Shakespeare's words, they are as

> ". . . a tale
> Told by an idiot, full of sound and fury,
> Signifying nothing."

(I am indebted to my secretary for this quotation.)

Nor does it help to add an indefinite article, such as "a," before them. However, the addition of the definite article "the," although it doesn't add any more sense, is an indication of focusing towards something that may have sense.

The addition of an adjective such as "cold" (the "cold water") only serves as an indication of more precise focusing, to direct attention to a particular part of the "staked-out claim," without really adding any sense.

We can go further in the direction of sense if we add a verb. For instance, "The cold water froze." But it is only when we add the effect of the action relative to a purpose that we really begin to get any sense. And the particular nature of the sense depends on the effect of the action on purposes. For instance, "Cold water froze my foot" is a very different sense from "Cold water froze the surface of the pond so I could go skating."

What I am trying to get at is that apparently we don't get sense ("firmness in meaning"—Dewey's and Bentley's expression) until we get a sentence. A sentence "stakes out claims" in the aspect of purpose and value. However, what is in awareness is not a disclosure of "knowns-knowings" about purposes and values but prognostications, "presumptions-presumings" for action bearing on the "realization" of emergent value-quality.

What has just been said above has to do with what one gets out of symbolizing, using words, when one so to speak is talking to oneself, i.e., when there is no attempt at communication.

But when one tries to communicate to others by words, added to the difficulties above mentioned is the fact that due to differences in individual experience the phases included in the "claims staked out" by symbols will never be the same for the communicator and the communicatee.

If we reach a higher degree of "firmness" of "naming" by using sentences, it would follow that there will also be a higher probability of communication if sentences are used. But it should be noted that when sentences are used, the significances being dealt with are purposes and values. Both parties are made aware of similar phases of value and purpose.

But again the common awareness is not a disclosure of "knowns-knowings" about value and purposes but prognostications, "presumptions-presumings," for action bearing on the "realization" of emergent value-quality.

The realization won't take place from communication alone.

Realization of emergent value-quality only comes about as the result of joint action. It might be said that when this happens the communicator and the communicatee are in *communion*.

I am dwelling on this because of my difficulty (and it may be my fault because I am a tyro in this field) in getting any sense out of considering "knowns" or "knowings" or "names" or "namings" unless one includes either patently or innately action, purposes, ultimately emergent value-quality.

And further, what is most important, it seems impossible to deal with all these factors as a whole unless we postulate that our "awareness" has to do not with "knowns-knowings" but with prognostications, "presumptions-presumings."

October 29, 1947

### The New "Gestalt"

The Gestalt hypothesis that the synthesis of elements constituted a whole that is different from their sum was epochal.

As Michotte states, the frame of the synthesis up to now has been limited to "form" which is essentially a spatial concept.

Michotte, in developing a *Gestalt* of causality, is extending the frame of synthesis to include time. But the time aspect he is including is objective time. His *Gestalt* is limited to Euclidean space plus time, not time integrated with space which is "relativity." He explicitly excludes organic "personal" time, nor does he include future time (expectancy) or emergence.

In our *Gestalt*, the frame of synthesis includes not only Euclidean space (form) and objective time (Michotte's causality) but also personal time, which includes future objective time (expectancy) and also emergence.

It would appear that the most patent lack in present *Gestalt* is that it does not include the past of the organism and that its most basic lack is that it does not include the factor of emergence.

Due to this fact it can deal only with the determined aspect of nature and on that account excludes the possibility of individual causality.

It would seem that the classic gestaltists, in dealing with causality, because they have to include "time" both objective and subjective, can no longer avoid including the past experiences of the organism in their *Gestalt*. This puts them in a difficult position because of the specific denials that past experiences have anything to do with the nature and origin of sensations and perceptions.

### EMERGENCE—FORM AND FLOW—SECURITY

Emergence of necessity implies a becomingness from "something." Let us call that "something" an "up-to-the-now base," i.e., the "take-off" relative to which the emergence is different.

The term "form and flow" has been used to describe emergence where with every increment of flow the form is altered to provide a new form for a new flow.

What is the nature of this "form" or "base" from which the flow "takes off"?

It must have a definite determined aspect. It can be thought of as static in time. But it is apparent that such a concept is too limited, that at least it must include periodic changes in time, as night and day and calendar time. This would mean that it would be based on the synthesis of all orderly expected performances of unit (abstracted) aspects, such as that an object traveling with a given velocity would continue in its direction at the same velocity and that a stationary object would remain stationary. The basis for this type of presumption is that of greatest probability.

But Michotte's work makes it clear that even that concept is not sufficiently broad. The phenomena of objective (or as he calls it, mechanical) causality have to be included.

These phenomena consist of variations in the expected performance of unit factors resulting from the effect upon them due to the expected performance of other unit factors.

This can be called objective causality. Our success in carrying out our purposes is directly related to our awareness of this type of causality. Science's great contribution has been in increasing our awareness of this type of causality.

It would appear from the above that the "determined" "base" "form" from which we emerge consists not only of the static aspects of nature but also of the periodic aspects and, what is more surprising, of the objective causality aspects.

Of course none of these aspects exist in their own right apart from us. They are only those togethernesses that have significances to us due to our unique and specific purposes. They are unique to each of us.

But they are a *sine qua non* for our most basic urge not only for continuance of being but also for our emergence.

If they are disturbed or if we are caused to doubt their reality, we cannot emerge.

They are our most primary *security*, more important to us even than our lives.

Now the hard thing to grasp is that, as important to us as this "basic form" is, we have continually to alter it, give it up, at least parts of it, in order to emerge, grow, really live.

January 16, 1948

### ACTING ON VALUE-JUDGMENTS

The most radical departure from generally accepted beliefs that we have demonstrated scientifically is that man will be more successful in carrying out his purposes if in concrete situations he bases his selection of alternative courses of action on value-judgments and not on logical intellectual mental processes.

We are not alone in this belief. Whitehead, Dewey, Julian Huxley, Herrick, Barnard, Conant, and others uphold the same hypothesis.

Granting the hypothesis is correct, its acceptance by the public would be most calamitous.

It is the generally accepted belief that mental processes are of only two kinds that are sharply divided and entirely different, namely, (a) intellectual logical thinking and (b) emotions.

It would follow that if the public accepted the above hypothesis, gave up using their intellects and acted only on their emotions, the human race would go backward and not ahead.

This dilemma can be resolved only through (I) increasing the general understanding of the nature of "value-judgments" and (II) increasing the capacity of people to be aware of and to make use of value-judgments.

*I. Increasing the General Understanding of the Nature of "Value-Judgments"*

It must first be clearly understood that conscious mental processes are not of only two sharply divided different types, namely, (a) intellectual logical thinking and (b) emotions.

It is true that in fact purely intellectual logical processes, such as $2 + 2 = 4$, can exist with a negligible amount of emotional overtones related to them, and in fact emotional processes, such as sexual emotions, with a negligible amount of intellectual overtones can exist. But in between these limits our conscious mental processes are integrations of varying amounts of intellectual and emotional processes, and this is the case under practically all normal conditions.

Further, all "emotional" non-intellectual mental processes are not the same. At one extreme we have those "emotions" that are related to the relatively determined urges, such as sexual functioning or hunger. These emotions are reflexly related to definite physiological phenomena and are very strong and uni-directional.* On the other extreme we have those "emotions" that are related to alternative possibilities of as yet undetermined emergence. This type of emotion is not reflexly related to any definite physiological phenomenon. Such emotions are ephemeral, balanced and subject to choice. As has been disclosed, at least one quality of which one is aware when he chooses one "emotion" of this type instead of another, as a directive for action, is that it has a value of greater "surety," "reality." This is due to the fact, as has been pointed out, that there is more supplementation—less conflict—among the innumerable indications or cues of which it is an integration, which in turn make it a more reliable prognosis.

It is emotions of this latter type that are involved in "value-judgments."

## II. Increasing the Capacity of People to Be Aware of and Make Use of Value-Judgments

In general, although everyone makes use of value-judgments to a greater or lesser extent, they are not aware that they are doing so.

Value-judgments fall within the definition of intuitions, and today, as the result of our so-called scientific conditioning, intuition tends to be regarded as beyond the pale—an activity made use of only by women and artists spelled with a big A.

In general people are not trained to be aware of intuitive value-judgments. Our modern educational methods, far from training in them, do not include them in their curriculum. In fact, no methodology has yet been developed for training students even to recognize value-judgments, much less how to develop them. The development of a person's capacity to be aware of and use value-judgments should be the basis of a so-called liberal arts education.

Some rather ineffective attempts are made in this direction in so-called art and cultural courses, but in fact it is only in extra-curricular activities that students partially educate themselves in this field.

For the most effective results it would appear that training in the use of value-judgments should be integrated with training in the conceptual rationalistic processes.

---

* But it must be borne in mind that in concrete circumstances even such strong impelling emotions do not come into full being out of nothingness. They are always preceded by a series of less reflexive emotions and have their origin in a condition of balanced possibilities when alternative choice is possible.

Value-judgments themselves may for convenience of consideration be divided into two classes. First, there are those that are made without conscious rationalization; for example, those that determine a tactful person's behavior in a social group. Second, there are those that have to be made as a result of frustration or doubt where action can be deferred or does not have to be taken until later.

Under such latter conditions the conscious rationalizing thought processes play an indispensable role in increasing the reliability of the prognosis arrived at. Rationalizing thought processes can go off on line excursions of investigations into different fields of relevant phenomena, thereby bringing the material so consciously conceptually considered into the matrix of material whose integration constitutes the value response. The value response will still be arrived at by subconscious integrating processes and not as the result of rationalistic conceptual conclusions, but it will have in it, so to speak, the relevant worth of the rationalizing excursions.

If the fields of relevant phenomena which are rationally investigated are known from actual concrete experience, the material brought home to the matrix (so to speak) will be more reliable than if one's knowledge of the relevant phenomena is only conceptual (abstract). For this reason conceptual education should never be substituted where experiential education is possible.

But because we cannot have actual concrete experience with many fields of relevant phenomena—those occurring in the past, for instance—education is indispensable to provide the necessary background of relevant phenomena.

Our accepted forms of education provide this in a way. But since it is not clearly understood how and to what use it is put, the material provided is often irrelevant and the whole methodology is most ineffective.

There is another field of education which should be clearly differentiated from that which is used in making value-judgments, namely, education in "how to do," that is, the "know-how" to carry out the line of action arrived at as the result of a value-judgment. This is the technical field of education.

In many instances in practice, the accepted methods of education accomplish very effective results within certain limits along the lines above pointed out.

Consider the medical education. In the medical school, a very thorough conceptual understanding is given of the phenomena relevant to the field in which the student later as a practicing doctor will have to make value-judgments. Further, this intellectual education is supplemented as far as possible by laboratory experiments.

As an intern the future doctor is trained in making value-judgments under the supervision of older doctors whose value-judgments have a more reliable prognosis.

When he goes into practice on his own, his prognoses are relatively reliable.

But unfortunately his whole education has been limited to the medical field and his value-judgments will be relatively unreliable in other fields.

And another interesting phenomenon takes place. If the doctor is successful due to the reliability of his value-judgments as concretely proved by his large percentage of successful diagnoses, he develops a high sensitivity to and faith in his sense of surety. He overlooks the fact that it exists not because of the particular nature of his ego but because of his education and training in the field in which he is successful. He therefore makes the mistake of assuming that his value-judgments have the same prognostic reliability in all other fields as in that of medicine.

To a degree all successful men make this mistake because of their lack of understanding of the origin and nature of value-judgments.

The importance of the above consideration in view of the line of action we are embarked on is as follows:

We should go easy in crying from the housetops that there is scientific evidence that value-judgments are the most reliable prognosis for successfully carrying out our purposes and must be relied upon if we are to lead successful and happy lives.

We should go easy, not because what we are saying is untrue, but because it will not be understood.

This does not mean that we can stop, but that we have got to include in our thinking a program and means of bringing about a more profound understanding of the nature of value-judgments and their relation to what we commonly call "emotions" and to our intellectual conceptual processes.

January 21, 1948

PROGRAM FOR FURTHER BASIC RESEARCH TO INCREASE OUR UNDERSTAND-
ING OF OURSELVES AND OTHERS AND OUR RELATION TO NATURE

*Foreword*

Our researches up to the present have been primarily directed to increasing our understanding of the origin and nature of the perception of static phenomena, having to do with *what* we see and *where* (in distance) we see it.

As important as it is to increase our understanding of the origin and nature of our perception of static phenomena, it is still more important that we have:

1. A better understanding of the origin and nature of our perception of change *—*motion*, for example.

2. A better understanding of the origin and nature of our perception of "consequence," i.e., those phenomena where the activity (e.g., motion) of one "thing" affects another (one billiard ball hitting another), commonly but mistakenly thought of as "causality."

3. A better understanding of the origin and nature of the phenomena that are involved when we act; for example, when we roll a billiard ball so that it hits another, that is, when we purposefully cause a "consequence."

Any increase in our understanding of *change,* "*consequence,*" and of our *purposeful actions* is most important in itself. But the acquisition of this knowledge is still more important in that it may be a steppingstone to a better understanding of true "causality," than which there is nothing more important.

The methodology and type of instrumentation that have been so fruitful in increasing our understanding of the origin and nature of our perception of static phenomena are directly applicable to a scientic investigation of the origin and nature of our perception of *change, consequence,* and the *phenomena that are involved when we act.*

Stated in general terms, the methodology consists of the determination under varying experimental conditions of the unique characteristics of the experienced sensations (or perceptions) of which normal observers are unequivocally aware, and their relationship to the characteristics of (a) the "external" (so-called physical) factors; (b) the physiological factors (so-called stimulus patterns); (c) the psychological factors (other than his immediate awareness) related to the observer's prior experiences; and (d) the observer's "point of view."

As it has been applied the procedure discloses:

1. The characteristics of the "external" factors which give rise to physiological factors to which specific sensational characteristics are related.

2. The characteristics of the physiological factors to which specific sensational characteristics are related.

3. The characteristics of sensational awareness when one or more indications (cues), to which specific sensational awarenesses are related, are combined so that they supplement each other or are in conflict with each other.

The nature of the instrumentation that will be used in these new in-

* Meaning "any variation or alteration"—Webster.

vestigations has been envisaged. In general it will be similar to that which was used in investigating the origin and nature of our perception of static phenomena, supplemented by further means to introduce controlled motion of different types of objects in the external field, and ultimately means to vary the subjective localization of the observer, consisting of rotating and tipping chairs and a centrifuge.

The exact nature of the instrumentation and the most effective order of sequence of demonstrating the various phenomena can only be determined empirically and in the carrying out of the investigation. This was true in the development of the instrumentation and procedure for demonstrating the origin and nature of our perceptions of static phenomena. Our experience in that development will greatly facilitate and expedite the successful carrying out of the proposed investigation.

## A Brief Statement of Some of the Expected Disclosures

*Perception of Change (Motion).* It is expected that the phenomena that will be disclosed by the investigations of the origin and nature of our perception of motion (an example of change) will confirm the following hypotheses:

1. That the perceived characteristics of motion, namely, (a) direction, (b) speed, and (c) acceleration, while they would not exist *but for* "external phenomena" and the stimulus patterns, do not have their origin in either.

2. That the perception of motion, among other relationships, exists only as it is related to (a) the perception of "thatness"; (b) the perception of "thereness"; (c) the observer's spatial point of view, "orientation"; (d) the observer's past and expectancies.

3. That the perception of motion like the perception of thatness and thereness is a "presumption."

## Procedure

Described more specifically, the demonstrations that have been envisaged by which the phenomena of motion can be investigated are as follows:

INTRODUCTORY DEMONSTRATION. 1. Demonstration consisting of an object moving in a constant direction (straight line) at a constant speed through a field anomalously perceived because of anomalous presumption as to "whatness" and "whereness" of the "external phenomena." The observer experiences an object as moving in different directions at different speeds and at different accelerations. He also experiences a change in the characteristics of the object.

SUPPLEMENTARY DEMONSTRATION OF EXPERIENTIAL PHENOMENA RE-
LATED TO PHENOMENA EXPERIENCED IN DEMONSTRATION. 2. Demonstration
consisting of a stationary object that is perceived to be in motion.

3. Demonstration consisting of an object that is moving in one direction that is perceived to be moving in the opposite direction.

4. Demonstration consisting of an object that is moving in a straight
line that is perceived as moving in an ellipse of circle.

5. Demonstration consisting of an object moving at a constant speed
that appears as moving at an accelerated speed.

6. Demonstration consisting of moving objects by which it is experienced that the perceived speed of motion is related to the subjectively
perceived "thereness" as affected by (a) overlay "indications" (cues),
(b) parallax indications, (c) coincidence of edge indications.

7. Demonstration consisting of moving objects by which it is experienced that the perceived speed of motion is related to the subjectively
perceived "thatness" as affected by (a) "size" indications, (b) brightness
indications, (c) softness of edge indications.

8. A series of demonstrations disclosing the variation of perceptions
when (a) the various indications (cues) as to direction, speed, and acceleration of motion are combined with (b) the various indications (cues)
of "thatness" and "thereness" so that they supplement or conflict with
each other, taking account of the experienced sense of "surety" and "lack
of surety."

9. A series of demonstrations disclosing the role that expectancy plays
in the perception of movement.*

May 8, 1948

### THE PRESUMPTIVE WORLD

This note is an attempt to think further into the phenomenon of presumptions.

It is apparent that presumptions are one of the types of phenomena
inherent in an "actual occasion" as defined by Whitehead.

It may be helpful before further considering the origin and nature of
presumptions to have in mind some of the other phenomena inherent in
an "actual occasion" and the relation of the phenomenon of presumptions
to them.

An actual occasion in which a specific person is participating as defined by Whitehead includes the following phenomena or "worlds":

* Editor's Note: Similar procedures were outlined for the perception of consequence and the perception of phenomena involved when we act.

1. The world of "externality" or "otherness" comprised of other functional activities, commonly mistakenly thought of as the "objective" or "physical world."

2. The phenomenon by which the participating person is related to the world of "externality," i.e., radiations, such as light rays, sound vibrations, etc.

3. The phenomenon of impingements on the person, i.e., physiological stimulus patterns.

4. The phenomenon of the so-called subjective world brought by the person to the "actual occasion." This world is divisible into at least the following sub-worlds:

a. The intellectually conceived world, i.e., the geographical (three-dimensional world) plus the world of events in time, etc. The aspects of these worlds are subject to voluntary recall. These worlds are also commonly mistakenly thought of as the "objective" physical world.

b. The world of specific significances of all types of so-called "objects," unique to the specific participating person, as exemplified by a person's awareness of various types of "thatnesses," oak leaves, cards, etc. These awarenesses are the statistical averages of his past experience with specific types of "objective" significances. These significances are registered only in the subconscious mind and are not subject to voluntary control. They are normally catalyzed into being only by physiological activities. It should be noted that, being statistical averages, they are in the nature of presumptions and do not correspond to anything in the external world.

c. The world of presumptions concerning the nature of the specific "objective" significances just mentioned above. It is these phenomena and processes which we have called the "Presumptive World" that we are especially interested in at this time.

These presumptions are also registered only in the subconscious mind and are not subject to voluntary control. They are normally catalyzed into being only by physiological activities. Some examples of such presumptions concerning the nature of such "objective" significances that have come to light and a consideration of their nature will be dealt with more fully as soon as the list of phenomena that are inherent in an "actual occasion" is completed.

5. The world of expectancy, hope, purposes.

6. The world of creativity by the specific person, including (a) the formation of value-judgments and (b) action in carrying out purposes resulting from such judgments.

Having completed the list of at least some of the most important phenomena that are inherent in an "actual occasion," let us turn back to a more thorough consideration of the "World of Presumptions."

Speaking in general terms, in every actual occasion where the characteristics of our stimulus patterns—hieroglyphics—are determined by impingements, we presume a specific significance concerning any and every "external event" that is related to our stimulus patterns by impingements.

Such presumed specific significances are not of a specific significance we experienced in the past, but the statistical average of similar specific significances we have experienced in the past. That is, we bring to the occasion a presumptive world of classified significances, be they "things" ("objects"), or "events," or what not ("Oak leaf" demonstration).

Some examples of the nature of the presumptions that constitute the "Presumptive World" are as follows:

1. In the first place, we presume the "thatness" significances of an external "thing" or "object," i.e., its nature, that it is a playing card, or an oak leaf, or a star.

2. We presume "things" remain constant, as to their size, for instance, as is disclosed by the size constancy demonstration, i.e., changed distance with change of angular size of object.

3. We presume that similar "things" are identical, as disclosed by the star point and line demonstrations.

4. We presume that what has happened will continue to happen, as disclosed by the motion demonstrations and consequence demonstrations (to be confirmed).

*(Continued,* May 11, 1948)

If we integrate (so to speak) even these few * examples of presumptions, it is apparent that they constitute a "world," so to speak, consisting of "objects" which retain their "normal" objective characteristics, such as size, color, etc., which are always whole. In which all similar "objects" have the same significances, i.e., are identical. Where what has happened will continue to happen, be it rate of speed, or consequence (result of one object hitting another), or "they lived happily ever afterwards."

Such a world is apparently very similar to what we think of as our "Ideal World," which we have always considered to be the creation of our wishful thinking. But this "Presumptive World," far from being based on wishful thinking, exists because it provides us with the most reliable prognosis for action for carrying out our purposes.

We would not be able to have sensations or perceptions but for this "World of Presumptions." The World of Perception is based on this

* There are countless more presumptions.

World of Presumptions. And in spite of the fact that we intellectually know that the presumptions that constitute this world are not necessarily true, nevertheless we create our sensations on the basis that they are true, i.e., in every actual occasion it is these presumptions that determine our perceptions and our actions.*

There would appear to be a most interesting and important characteristic about this "World of Presumptions," namely, that it can be identical for different individuals.

All our work to the present has apparently shown that there is no common world that can be shared even by two different individuals. The reasons for this are that no two persons can bring to the occasion the same past and experience; no two persons can have the same relation with externality (i.e., be in the same place at the same time); no two persons can have the same expectancies.

But apparently this "Presumptive World" we are considering can be shared by, can be identical to, different individuals.

Apparently everyone presumes that "similar things are identical," that objects are whole, that they remain constant in size, that what has happened will continue to happen.

Do these considerations provide the basis for a better understanding of the nature of the "We"? Is the "ideal world," the world of most reliable prognoses in the long run, common to us all? Is this the world we have to alter in ourselves to personally emerge?

Is this the field where Form and Flow take place, the field of true evolution?

May 12, 1948

### THE PRESUMPTIVE WORLD (*Continued*)

From the above considerations it appears that there does exist a "Common World" of a kind, namely, a "Form World" constituted of those presumptions that all men must make in order to formulate a judgment on which to base their course of action.

Let us try to give some further thought as to the nature of this "Common Form World." Our demonstrations disclose that all persons make

---

* The question arises as to whether or not we consciously take account of this "World of Presumptions." The necessity of demonstrations to cause us to recognize [that] they existed would indicate that we do not. On the other hand, the similarity of our "Ideal World" to this world of presumptions suggests that in one way or another we do.

presumptions, that the "objectiveness" significances they take account of are statistical averages of their past experiences with particular classes of "objectiveness," and also presumptions, such as that "things" ("objects") are whole, and constant, etc.

Such presumptions are common to all men and constitute a common world.

But it should be kept in mind that such presumptions apply to objectiveness in general, so to speak, and have nothing to do with the specific nature of the "objectiveness" that is taken account of. That is, no two persons have the same perception of a specific "object," as a chair or another person.

In other words, this "Common Form World" apparently has to do with "general laws" * concerning generalized objects and events irrespective of their specific significance.

It would further seem possible that such "general presumptions," such as that "things" are whole and remain constant and that "similar things are identical," provide the basis for our common awareness of tri-dimensional space; and still further that "general presumptions," such as that what has happened will continue to happen, provide the basis for our common awareness of periodic time.

If this is so, then all men looking at the same field of view would have a common experience as to the spatial distribution of the objects in the field. However, since every person attaches a different specific significance to every object, the significance of the objects in the field of view, as well as that of the view as a whole, would be different to every individual; that is, there would be no common world as to the specific aspects of experience.†

The same line of reasoning would apply to the happening of events. There would be a common world in relation to the general laws of the happening of events, but no common world as to the specific aspects of eventful experience.

In spite of the fact that our "common world" seems to be limited to the generalized aspect of "objectiveness" and events, it is apparently the matrix that binds the human race together and the basis of the "we."

It would also seem apparent that the degree and nature of community that could exist would vary greatly with the nature of the aspects of the "actual occasion" which the person or persons were experiencing and in which they were participating.

* It would be of importance to find out whether the capacity to take account of such general laws is inherited or only acquired through experience.

† These considerations would appear to have bearing on our understanding what is communicated by photographs and photographic paintings.

For instance, in our world of visual perception, where there has been great similarity in the past experiences as well as of identity of purpose of all men, the extent, so to speak, of the "common world" would presumably be much more inclusive than in social perception where the similarity of past experience as well as of identity of purpose is often limited to small groups.

May 25, 1948

### The Common World—Common Sense—"Presumptions" and "Assumptions"

In my notes of May 8, 11, and 12, I considered our "Form World," which is constituted of what I called our "presumptions" concerning "things" and "events," such as that "things" are whole and continue "unchanged," etc.

On reflection it would appear that the word "*pre*sumptions" * is not the proper one to describe these phenomena, for the reason that the prefix "pre" implies taking account *before*. Now while the word "presumptions" would appear to be the proper one to refer to actual sensations or perceptions, in that sensations and perceptions are prognostic † directives for purposeful action (i.e., "a forecast referring to the future") and their reliability can only be tested by future action, it does not appear to be the proper word to refer to our taking account of what is a "probability," ‡ such as that "things" are whole and "continue unchanged," etc.

These "likelihoods of recurrence of any particular form of event" exist apart from the specific nature of the event or any relationship to a specific "actual occasion" (Whitehead) or "actual transaction" (Dewey). In one sense they constitute a "Form World" continuing out of time and apart from space, a "world" which we assume,§ i.e., "take," "adopt," "take for granted," "suppose," "pretend" (although we know better),

---

* Presumption (Webster): Ground for presuming, or believing probable; probable, but not conclusive evidence; also, a conclusion based on such evidence.

† Prognostic (Webster): A portent; sign; omen; a prognostication; a forecast; (adj.) of, pertaining to, or serving as ground for, prognostication, i.e., prediction or forecast.

‡ Probability (Webster): Quality or state of being probable; likelihood; that which is or appears probable.

§ Assume (Webster): To take up, or into; receive; adopt; to take to or upon oneself; invest oneself with; undertake; to pretend to possess; feign; sham; to appropriate; usurp; to take for granted; suppose. *Syn.:* put on, counterfeit, sham, affect, pretend, simulate, feign.

from evidence of concurrence we experienced in our past. We will therefore call such a world our "Assumptive World" instead of our "Presumptive World," which latter term we will reserve to refer to our sensational perceptual world, which we are aware of as participants in an
"actual occasion" or "transaction."

As stated earlier, but for our "Assumptive World," our sensational
perceptual world would not exist.

Through his "sensational presumptive world" the participating organism is aware of the specific significance of the events in the "actual occurrence" or "transaction" to him personally (specifically) from his particular points of view both in space, so to speak, and in his biological
time, i.e., his "now" in his purposes and expectancies. Through his "assumptive world" the participating organism takes account not of *any*
specific significance to himself personally of the events of the "actual
occurrence" or "transaction," but takes account of significances of the
events that can be assumed to be common to all occurrences or transactions (all points of view in space and time); for example, that "things
are whole" and "continue unchanged." The significances in this Assumptive World have to do with what one might call the general laws of
"things" and "events," those aspects of "things" and "events" that are
significant to us as human beings that we have learned we can take for
granted in the long run.

Now an organism's perceptual (presumptive) world is unique to him,
i.e., there is no common perceptual world. However, the aspects of an
organism's "assumptive world" can be the same to all other organisms
who have had similar prior experiences. That is, there can be a common
"assumptive world."

It would appear that such a common "assumptive world" is the basis
of our world of "common sense." We are not intellectually aware of this
"assumptive world." We are not even sensorially aware of taking account
of it.* The demonstrations, however, disclose that we do take account
of it, even though we are not aware of it; we would not have perceptions
if we didn't.

Once we realize its nature and existence, we recognize its correspondence to what we think of as an "ideal" world of which we do have an
awareness. We also are intellectually aware that it is of the same nature
as the world of science, a world that we "adopt," "take for granted."
The only apparent essential difference between our assumptive world

---

* It is apparent that the aspects of this common assumptive world of which we
are not intellectually aware could have been acquired only through experience. That
is, they could not be acquired purely intellectually. This is why one can have common sense only in fields in which he has had actual experience.

and the world of science is that we are intellectually aware of the "world of science," which is a theoretical world, while we take account of the basic world of "common sense" without being either intellectually or sensorially aware that we are doing so. While this is the case in regard to those aspects of the "assumptive world" that are the basis of our visual prognostic world, it would appear that we are at least partially intellectually aware of the aspects of the assumptive world that are the basis of our social perception. Cf. the mores and ethics of a culture.

There is another similarity between the theoretical world of science and this basic "assumptive world" of common sense. We know that the theoretical world of science is at best only an approximate disclosure of the laws that govern "actual occurrences" or "transactions" which we "take for granted," "suppose," really "pretend." Likewise, we know that the basic "assumptive world" of common sense is only an approximate disclosure of the laws that govern "things" and "events." In the overlay demonstration, for instance, we can know beforehand that the nearer card is not a whole card, yet in spite of that knowledge we assume, "pretend," it is, and, because we do, we can't help seeing it behind the card that is further away and which appears to prevent us from seeing the whole of the nearer card. And the same holds for our assumption of size constancy.

This brings up possible grounds for a better understanding of the relation of wisdom to common sense.

Offhand, there doesn't seem to be much wisdom in "pretending," especially when we have knowledge that the pretense is false. However, there may in fact be wisdom in holding to a belief that will stand the test in the long run, even though we know that in a particular actual occurrence it is not trustworthy.

But in those "actual occasions" or "transactions" where it would appear that wisdom really comes into play, the situations are quite different from the demonstration just described.

In all "actual occasions" there are innumerable interrelated events, the perception of which involves taking account of innumerable different assumptive aspects of our world of common sense. Rarely, if ever, do these aspects of common sense confirm and supplement each other. Usually the different aspects are more or less in conflict. Isn't one of the roles of wisdom an awareness of the extent that the different aspects of "common sense" supplement or conflict with each other—an awareness that we recognize as a sense of "surety" or "lack of surety"?

And there would appear to be a still more transcendent role that wisdom can play. That is the taking account of, recognizing, either intuitively or intellectually, the fact that, although in the nature of things our "assumptive, idealized world" is nothing but a "supposition" or a "pretense," only by assuming and "pretending" can we carry out our destiny; and also recognizing, as participants in "actual occasions" and "transactions," we will often be betrayed * by our "pretenses" and "assumptions."

There is one further consideration. Why do we make such assumptions as that "things are whole" and "continue unchanged," etc.? It certainly doesn't make sense if we think of "things" or "events" existing in their own right apart from ourselves. But if we think of them as aspects we attribute to "otherness" because they are significant to us in our role as human beings in carrying out our purposes and destiny, it would appear that we would have to insist on their being "wholes" and "continuing." For nothing less than a whole will serve a purpose, or if it doesn't continue it won't serve a purpose. For our purposes, half an automobile is not an automobile; an automobile without even a wheel is not an automobile, and a decayed orange is not an orange. That is, to carry out our destiny we have to preserve those aspects of nature that are significant to its carrying out. As Whitehead says:

> It is the first step in sociological wisdom to recognize that the major advances in civilization are processes which all but wreck the societies in which they occur:—like unto an arrow in the hand of a child. The art of free society *consists first in the maintenance of the symbolic code;* and secondly in fearlessness of revision, to secure that the code serves those purposes which satisfy an enlightened reason. Those societies which cannot combine reverence to their symbols with freedom of revision, must ultimately decay either from anarchy, or from the slow atrophy of a life stifled by useless shadows. (*Symbolism, Its Meaning and Effect*, p. 88.) [Ames's italics.]

But at the same time recognizing that our "assumptive valueful ideal world" is also indispensable in the fulfillment of our destiny—such wisdom, no matter what befalls us, would prevent us from losing heart.†
Under such conditions doesn't true wisdom make itself evident as a sense of humor—humble humor, which one senses from a viewpoint outside of oneself and enables one to see more clearly what one always knew?

---

* Betray (Webster): To prove faithless or treacherous to, as to a trust or one who trusts; to fail or desert in a moment of need; to lead into error, sin, or danger.

† As Whitehead says: "At the heart of the nature of things, there are always the dream of youth and the harvest of tragedy. The adventure of the universe starts with the dream and reaps tragic beauty. This is the secret of the union of zest with peace —that the suffering attains its end in a harmony of harmonies. The immediate experience of this final fact, with its union of youth and tragedy, is the sense of peace. In this way the world receives its persuasion towards such perfections as are possible for its diverse individual occasions." (*Adventures of Ideas*, page 381.)

### THE "ASSUMPTIVE WORLD" AND ACTION "FORM AND FLOW"

It would appear that the nature of the "Assumptive World" can only be understood when one considers the phenomenal processes that take place (1) when in an "actual occasion" one's "perception" is such that it denies the validity of aspects of one's "assumptive world"; (2) when in an "actual occasion" one's actions (in accordance with the prognoses of his perceptions that are based on his "assumptive world") disclose the invalidity of aspects of one's "assumptive world."

Let us consider the phenomenal processes that take place when in an "actual occasion" one's actions disclose the invalidity of aspects of one's "assumptive world."

This situation is exemplified in a demonstration where there are two similar "objects" of different size at the same distance which are seen at different distances. When one takes a stick and tries to touch quickly first one object and then the other, one is unable to do so. One's inability immediately to accomplish this apparently simple action discloses that one's actions are denying the validity of one's assumptions that "similar things are identical." With practice, however, one can learn to touch first one object and then the other. But with the practice one learns to perceive the two similar objects not of the same size and at different distances but of different sizes at the same distance (where they actually are). In this process he alters his "assumption" that "similar things are identical." He comes to realize through experiential action that his assumption that similar things are identical was only an "assumption" and was not valid. That is, he has altered the "Form" of his "assumptive world." A "Flow" has taken place.

But now he is faced by a dilemma. What will he assume in the next situation? He cannot completely abandon his assumption that similar things are identical because that assumption has such a high probability of reliability that he would greatly impair the prognostic reliability of his perceptions and the probable success of his actions in carrying out his purposes.

On analogy in the field of social perception, he is in the position of a person who assumes "men are honest" but who has run up against two or three men who have, because of his assumption, badly cheated him. If he changes the form of his "assumptive world" and assumes men are crooks, he will be less successful in carrying out his purposes than if he assumes they are honest (which most men are).

Apparently the best he can do is to retain and continue to act upon that assumption that works best in the long run while accepting with such grace as is possible the misfortunes that are bound to occur.

But how is he to know what assumptions will work best in the long run, the retention of which is worth having to accept misfortune? That seems to be the $64 question.

History evidences that certain people have that capacity. Lincoln, the saints, and the prophets, for example, apparently had the capacity in spite of actual experiences which apparently denied the validity of their assumptions to continue to retain them.

The only suggestion as to what the capacity might be based on is that certain high grade personalities have the capacity to integrate more aspects of the "whole," i.e., they have a longer perspective into the past and becoming aspect of nature.

December 31, 1948

## THE ASSUMPTIVE WORLDS

In trying to clarify our understanding of what we are calling the "Assumptive World," perhaps the most important thing to try to clarify at this time is how assumptive worlds can be common (universal) for many different people while actual occasions would not exist but for assumptive worlds specifically unique to each individual, due to his unique purposes and spatial and temporal point of view.

To begin with, we must keep in mind that the unique specific aspects of the actual occasion would not exist but for the common generalized aspects of the assumptive worlds that the individual brings to the occasion; * that actually these specifically unique aspects and the common generalized aspects are by the very nature of things insolubly integrated in the actual occasion, and that when we are trying to think about them we are dealing only with abstracted parts ("but for's") out of the integrated whole of the actual occasion.

Now we can consider these unique specific and common generalized aspects in two different ways.

We can, as just mentioned, give our attention to an actual concrete occasion (transaction of living) and focus our awareness on abstracted specific parts of (i.e., "but for's" out of) the integrated whole of the total actual occasion. (We can be only dimly aware of the total actual

* As shown by our demonstrations.

occasion.) Or without reference to a specific actual occasion we can focus our awareness on *concepts* referring to abstracted parts ("but for's"). That is, we can analyze. We can also focus our awareness on putting together such analyzed concepts. That is, we can synthesize.

For example, as I sit here at my desk I can focus my awareness on specific parts of the total actual occasion, i.e., on some specific, unique "but for" of my actual perception from my present point of view in space and time (i.e., as the pencil on my desk or some other object). Or I can focus my awareness on some other type of "but for," such as my unique expectant purpose of meeting Jim Lowell, who will arrive soon, which is causing me to hurry in my writing, or on the actual common geographical world, Hanover, which I know Jim Lowell is sharing with me; or I can focus my awareness more dimly on the "I" and "we" aspects, i.e., the specifically unique and the common (universal) (assumptive aspects) of the actual occasion, and still more dimly on the whole of the actual occasion, trying to include the past and the future.

Can't we call these processes abstracting and concretizing or actualizing?

It would appear that such processes are quite different from what happens when with no awareness of my uniquely specific concrete situation I turn my attention to concepts which refer to differentiable aspects not of my present unique concrete experience but to differentiable aspects of experiences that are common to any actual experience I may have or that other people may have. And isn't this process what is commonly called analysis, and when we try to integrate such analyzed aspects, aren't we indulging in the process that is commonly called synthesis or syncretizing?

It would seem from the above that there are two paired types of awareness processes that we indulge in, in trying to understand and think about *actual occasions* which we must differentiate to avoid confusion, and in trying to think about and understand the nature and origin of our assumptive world it is imperative that we bear this in mind.

These two types of processes are:

   I. a. Analysis
      b. Synthesis (syncretizing)
  II. a. Abstracting
      b. Actualizing (concretizing)

We can be aware of our "I"-ness (uniqueness) and of our "we"-ness (assumptive worlds) either experientially by "abstracting" or conceptually by "analysis."

Whitehead says, "Synthesis and analysis require each other," i.e., they do not exist apart. Similarly, "abstracting" and "concretizing" require each other, and what is of more interest for our particular line of thought, specificity ("I"-ness—uniqueness) and generalness ("we"-ness—commonness) require each other, i.e., cannot exist apart.

February 3, 1949

### On Action and Emergence

We have not given sufficient consideration to the role that the "but for" factor of *action* plays. To explain: (a) we run up against a "hitch" in carrying out a purpose; (b) we seek an answer as to why we are thwarted; (c) we start inquiring (intellectual but in the last analysis checked intuitively by value-judgments).

This inquiry includes:

1. The framing of the proper *question.*

2. The formulation of hypotheses answering the question arrived at.

3. The conceptualizing of means to alter the conditions of the situation that gave rise to the "hitch." (The alteration may be either a change of external functional activities *or* of our *own assumptive worlds.*)

4. Personally executing actions that will alter the conditions of the situation.

5. A later taking account of the effectivity or lack of effectivity of such action in altering the conditions of the situation giving rise to the "hitch."

6. Altering our future behavior in accordance with what we have empirically learned through the above processes and again going through the same processes.

It is apparent that *action* and taking account of the effect of action are indispensable "but for's" in any "transaction of living."

Now the bearing of action on emergence is that it is the action with its consequences that constitutes, is, the emergence. The action may bring about the following types of changes: changes in "external functional activities," changes in our assumptive worlds, and thus in turn changes in our purposes, and, maybe most important, changes in our capacity to make value-judgments and the sum total of value-quality.

It is only through action that *actual real* changes are brought about. Without action nothing really happens. Perhaps most important is that unless they are acted upon, the value-quality of our value-judgments is not permanently registered or laid to account.

It would seem apparent that it is only action that brings into the picture those new factors and conditions that we spoke of yesterday that give rise to new "hitches" that never existed before which automatically lead to *continual emergence*.

There is another line of considerations that seem important to me.

As I have been thinking about "hitches" I mistakenly had in mind that we only have one "hitch" at a time. Of course actually we carry on in the midst of innumerable overlaid interwoven hitches in one and the same now. In duration and also significance they vary from the very transitory and trivial—such as being delayed in catching a train—through hitches related to our economic and social security, to those of apparently eternal duration and significance—such as being thwarted by our relations with our fellowmen or by death.

All of these hitches and the emergences related to them are all interwoven and inter-operative.

We carry them all on together. Our resolution of any one of them affects the resolution of all of the others.

It would seem apparent that the nature of our action that will have a bearing on the resolution of the different types of hitches varies as greatly as does the nature of the hitches—for example, all the way from limiting oneself to two cocktails to believing in one's guts in the "reverence for life" (Schweitzer) to passive resistance in order to change the "assumptive worlds" of others (Gandhi).

February 9, 1949

## On the Nature of "Value-Judgments"

It is believed that the demonstrations disclose that perceptions can have the following characteristics:

A. "Preciseness" and "vagueness."
B. "Unequivocalness" and "equivocalness."
C. "Surety" and "lack of surety."

To make clear just what is meant by these terms:

A. "Precise" is used in its meaning as "exactly or sharply defined." * "Vague" is used as meaning "ill defined." For example, our perception of the distance between the two star points of different brightness is vague relative to the more precise distance we experience between the end star points in a series of star points of graded brightness.

* All definitions are taken from Webster's New International Dictionary.

B. "Unequivocal" is used as meaning "not doubtful; not ambiguous." "Equivocal" is used as meaning "puzzling, perplexing, having two or more significations." For example, our perception of the large playing card in the overlay demonstration when we see it at the wrong distance is equivocal relative to the unequivocal character of our perception when we see the card at its proper distance.

C. "Surety" is used as meaning "faith, belief, assurance, confidence." "Lack of surety" is used as meaning "mistrust, doubt, misgiving." For example, our perception of the distorted window when "indications" of which we are not aware have been added that conflict with those which cause us to perceive it in a definite position is characterized by a sense of lack of surety relative to the surety of our perception of the window when there are no conflicting indications.

It should be noted that when one experiences an equivocal perception he is conceptually aware of the ambiguities. While on the other hand, when one experiences a perception characterized by "lack of surety," he is not conceptually aware of the conflicting indications.

With the above in mind we can turn to the consideration of the nature of "value-judgments." We are using the word "judgment" as meaning "a mental act involving comparison and discrimination"—"discernment and distinction"—"to distinguish by certain tokens"—"to separate by discerning differences."

More specifically we are using "value-judgment" to mean "discerning differences between the prognostic reliability of a perception in terms of sensed surety or sensed lack of surety" (the words "surety" and "lack of surety" being used in their above-defined meanings).

Value-judgments are differentiable from intellectual judgments in that in a pure value-judgment an individual discerns differences between the prognostic reliability of his perception solely on the basis of value-quality by a synthesizing-concretizing process. In a pure intellectual judgment the individual differentiates solely on a conceptual basis by an abstracting-analyzing process.

March 12, 1949

STANDARDS—QUALITIES—ASPECTS OF OUR ASSUMPTIVE WORLD

Standards are based on qualities. Qualities are aspects of "things," "objects" or "phenomena."

"Things" or "phenomena" are "but for" abstracts from the totality of an actual occasion. They only exist because of aspects of our assumptive world, such as assumptions that (a) things are whole, (b) things are constant in space and time, etc.

Such assumptions are metaphysical presuppositions that we are not even aware we are making.

The point is that the practice of science—our determined scientific world—only exists because of these man-made metaphysical presuppositions.

March 14, 1949

### SCIENTIFIC METHOD IN PSYCHOLOGY: ANALYSIS AND SYNTHESIS; QUALITATIVE AND QUANTITATIVE *

Most briefly stated, scientific methodology consists in an integration of analyzing and synthesizing. By analysis, qualitative or quantitative, a phenomenon is broken up into its parts. By synthesis the parts are put together in a relationship determined by finding out how the alterations of the parts affect each other (relevant variability).

Consider that the subject of the scientific investigation is a particular visual perception.

*Analysis*

By the method of qualitative analysis, following the analogy of qualitative chemical analysis, we would separate the visual perception into its constituent parts or elements, i.e., distinguish its component parts.

Since a visual perception is a subjective awareness, its elements are sub-

* Definitions (based on Webster):

*Analysis:* Separation of anything into constituent parts or elements; also, an examination of anything to distinguish its component parts, separately, or in their relation to the whole.

*Synthesis:* Composition or combination of parts, elements, etc., so as to form a whole; also, the whole thus formed. *Logic & Philos.* The combination of separate elements of thought or sensation into a whole, as of simple into complex conceptions, or species into genera;—the opposite of *analysis*.

*Quality:* (from *qualis*, how constituted). (1) Proper or essential being; nature (now rare). (2) Hence, an attribute; characteristic. (3) Class, kind or grade.

*Qualitative:* Relating to or concerned with quality; as *qualitative* analysis in chemistry; contrasted with *quantitative*.

*Quantity:* (from *quantus*, how much or how great). A measurable or numerable amount.

*Quantitative:* (1) That is, or that may be, estimated by quantity. (2) Concerned with the measurement of phenomena, especially with respect to its quantity; as *quantitative* analysis as contrasted with *qualitative*.

jective awarenesses, such as sense of "thatness," size, color, brightness, etc.; "thereness," near, far, above, below, etc.; "motion," speed acceleration, etc.; "consequence," interaction and its results, etc.; "causality," "purposeful causality."

Such qualitative analysis simply results in further and further abstracting and classification. In itself it discloses no relationship between the abstracted factors, nor in itself does it lead to an understanding of the nature of visual perception as a whole.

The barrenness of such a qualitative analytical approach is evident if the field of factors included in visual perception is limited to subjective factors only. So investigators extended the field to include, firstly, the objective factors related to the subjective factors in a perceptual experience and, secondly, to the physiological factors so related. The application of the methodology of qualitative analysis to this extended field led only to increasing the number of factors that could be abstracted and classified.

## Synthesis

To synthesize the abstracted fields, investigation was made of the effect on the various abstracted parts of varying other abstracted parts. It was found that variation of objective and physiological factors produced marked corresponding effects on subjective factors. This led to the assumption of correspondence between subjective factors and objective factors and physiological factors, i.e., it led to three interlocked correspondences. Moreover, since alteration of objective and physiological factors "caused" alteration of subjective factors, while the converse could not take place, it was assumed that the subjective aspects of perception had their origin in the corresponding objective factors through the relation of the physiological factors. It followed that investigators looked for an understanding of the nature of perception through further qualitative and quantitative analysis of objective and physiological phenomena.

It naturally followed that the factors that were varied were objective and physiological factors, since it was assumed that they determined the subjective factors. Furthermore, in carrying out the methodology of "significant variables" it is advantageous where possible to vary the affecting factor quantitatively, and only "objective" and physiological factors can be so quantitatively controlled.

As a result there exists today an almost universally held belief that the only sound scientific methodology for increasing our knowledge of the nature of perception must be based on quantitative measurement.

One of the effects of this point of view has been to automatically exclude from the factors that could be taken into account in trying to increase our understanding of the nature of perception any factors that were *not subject to quantitative determination.*

Strictly adhered to, this excluded the possibility of including past experience, for past experience can never be quantitatively measured. It also excluded such factors as assumptions, purpose, expectancy, emergence, values, value-judgments.

The above does not mean that many investigators have not tried to take account of these factors, but it does mean that they have had no adequate scientific methodology for so doing, as is so often evidenced by the fact that they feel the necessity of justifying their work by including in the presentation of their findings some type of *quantitative verification.*

This in turn brings us to the necessity of understanding just what quantitative verification is. Quantitative verification means proof of a finding by quantitative measurement, i.e., "how much" in terms of some standard of reference. There are any number of standards of reference, as distance, size, color, brightness, volume, weight, time, force, etc.

In the first place, a standard is "That which is set up and established by authority as a rule for the measure of quantity, weight, extent, value, or quality" (Webster). That is, every standard is set up by man in relation to his particular purposes. Even time standards (periodic time), distance standards (whether in wave lengths or light-years) are man's abstractions which he created for his purposes. No standard exists in its own right.

Secondly, standards are only useful if they are used in the field for which they were conceived, i.e., a weight standard won't disclose anything about how far one object is from another.

Thirdly, when one adopts and applies a standard to obtain measurements of a phenomenon, he limits himself as to what he will find in that phenomenon to that field of significances for which that particular standard was conceived.

For instance, in the field of perception space standards will disclose nothing in time, time standards will disclose nothing in "consequence," "consequence" standards will disclose nothing in "causality."

Sound scientific methodology does not require that an investigator be as accurate as possible but only accurate enough to provide sufficient prognostic reliability in regard to the phenomena he is investigating. This is evidenced by the different length standards that can be used. If the most accurate possible were required, only wave lengths should always be used in the quantitative determination of distance.

To return to perception: If one adopts a distance standard, say feet, it will disclose the *correspondence* between the subjective factor of sensed distance and the objective factor of measured distance, but that is all it will disclose. It will disclose nothing more about the subjective factor of sensed distance—neither its nature nor its origin.

This is made more evident if we take account of how we determine what we mistakenly assume is correspondence between sensed and measured distance. It is impossible to put a measuring stick on sensed distance. The only way a so-called "correspondence" is disclosed is by comparing the sensed distance of one kind *A*, say vision, with a sensed distance of another kind *B*, for instance touch or hearing.* We then measure the objective distance of the *B* sensed object and substitute it for the *B* sensed distance. We then assume we have determined the sensed distance *A* in measured quantitative objective distance. But actually all that has been done is to compare two sensed distances *A* and *B*, or more accurately, the same sensed distance as disclosed by two different kinds of indications related to different physiological processes. The measured objective distance which we have substituted for sensed distance *B* is of an entirely different nature from the sensed distance *B*. Sensed distances are awarenesses of specific thereness, are prognostic directives for action of the body as a whole or any part of it. Measured objective distances must be measured from some particular point, such as the uniocular nodal point, of which no account is taken in sensed distance. Moreover, the objective distance from such a point must be measured in terms of some standard of distance, such as wave length, centimeters, feet, meters, miles or light-years, which are completely foreign to the nature of sensed distances.

The assumption of any correspondence of sensations to measured objectivity prevents us from understanding the nature of sensations. William James saw this clearly and would have, as he said, no "truck" with the concept of correspondence. As said above, when one makes use of the standard of objective length in investigating the phenomena of subjective perceptual sensations, he automatically increases the field he is dealing with to include the immediate external conditions. So doing will enable him to get information as to how effectively a person could act under the particular circumstances. But that is all. It will prevent him from learning more about the origin and nature of perception.

To reiterate, this does not mean that quantitative distance measurements are not most useful *in connection* with the perception of sensed distance. Through determining the degree of correspondence between sensed distance and measured objective distance in a particular individual, we can obtain most reliable information as to the probability of the effectiveness of his actions in space. But as indispensable and valuable as information

* Or if one wants to be more accurate, to compare the sensed distance of uniocular vision to that of binocular vision.

and knowledge of this type are, they throw no light whatsoever on the nature and origin of perceptual sensations themselves.

What has been said above holds equally true in regard to quantitative physiological stimulus-pattern measurements.

It would seem apparent from the above that the use of quantitative standards devised for scientific investigation of the so-called objective world, such as objective distance, size, space, time, volume, quantity, force, etc., not only is not applicable to a scientific investigation of our subjective perceptual world, but that their use in that field prevents us from learning more about it.

Does there exist a scientific methodology applicable for increasing our knowledge of perception? The apparent answer is "yes," *if* the proper methods for analysis and synthesis are adopted and the proper standards are employed.

Let us consider a specific example. Start with an actual occasion of perception, which is an integration of all the "but for's," such as (1) "externality" (i.e., the "objective world"); (2) relating phenomena (light rays); (3) physiological stimulus patterns; (4) subjective perception (sensations), etc.

Following the accepted procedure of scientific methodology, the first step is to analyze (abstract) the total phenomenon into its phenomenal parts.

We are immediately faced by the problem of abstracting, separating, subjective perception from the external objective and physiological world. At least one way to accomplish this separation is by the use of so-called illusions, in which what is in subjective awareness is entirely different from the objective world, and which free us entirely from any type of "correspondence." Take, for instance, the example of subjectively sensed *distance*. Analyze the phenomenon of sensed distance into its constituent parts, indications, that play a role in sensed distance, such as size, brightness, overlay, parallax, etc. By making use of illusions these analyzed parts can be demonstrated as being in no "*corresponding*" relationship with the "objective world."

We are now in a position to vary systematically these abstracted phenomenal parts (indications) of the total phenomenon of sensed distance and determine *if* and *how* the other abstracted phenomenal parts (indications) are affected. This can be done by experimental setups that cause the indications to supplement each other or be in conflict, so to speak. This procedure discloses certain consistent repeatable phenomena. One then asks why? What is the explanation of these phenomena? An apparently intrinsically reasonable explanation of these phenomena is that the observer gives weight to the indications he subjectively experiences on the basis of their "prognostic reliability."

Now apparently a very important thing has happened, the disclosure of a heretofore unrecognized *standard* to make use of in determining the nature of subjective perceptions, namely, "prognostic reliability." It might be noted here that perhaps it is the disclosure of heretofore unrecognized *standards* that leads to real advances in science.*

To return to "prognostic reliability" as a standard for the scientific investigation of perception. This standard is not applicable to the effectivity of *action.* For "prognostic reliability" as a standard for the scientific investigation of perception refers only to the observer's *subjective* sense of reliability. "Prognostic reliability" has its origin in the observer's prior experience. It is the result of his empirical testing by action of the probable reliability of his sensed indications. It would seem to follow that for a sound scientific investigation of this factor, data on prior conditioning of the observer must be included.

The phenomenon of which prognostic reliability is a "quality" can be analyzed, abstracted, into at least three sub-phenomena, namely: (1) definiteness (definiteness and indefiniteness); (2) unequivocalness (unequivocalness and equivocalness); (3) surety (surety and lack of surety); each of which by its very nature is a "standard."

It would appear that the next most logical and fruitful step to develop a scientific methodology for increasing our understanding of man would be to systematically vary these abstracted phenomenal parts of the phenomenon to determine *if* and *how* the other abstracted phenomenal parts are affected.

March 22, 1949

### THE QUESTION

*What are the similarities and differences between* (a) *the form and nature of "the body of systematized scientific knowledge" arrived at from scientific inquiry and* (b) *the form and nature of the prognostic directives for action and what a person perceives and his related sensorial awareness arrived at from experiences of living ("transactions of living")?*

By (a) we mean the form and nature which "exists inherently in the arranged facts of the body of systematized scientific knowledge apart

* Cf. relativity standards which took the place of Newtonian standards.

from the ways in which the facts have been settled upon to be facts and apart from the way in which their arrangement has been secured." *

By (*b*) we mean the form and nature which exists inherently in the prognostic directives for action, including what a person perceives and his related sensorial awareness apart from the way in which these directives and sensorial awarenesses have been arrived at.

*Similarities*

The most evident basic and fundamental similarity between the nature of *the body of systematized scientific knowledge* and the nature of *the prognostic directives for action* and awareness which a person experiences is that they both *refer to* those aspects of nature that are determined and repeatable (or relatively so).†

*Differences*

They differ in the following evident ways:

BASIC DIFFERENCES IN FORM. The body of systematized scientific knowledge and the prognostic directives for action and perceptions and their related sensorial awareness that a person experiences are basically different in form.

Systematized scientific knowledge exists in the form of definite conceptual abstractions recorded in men's memories or in written or published material.

Prognostic directives for action and sensorial awareness do not exist until they are brought into being by relationship to "otherness" or externality through impingements that give rise to physiological "stimulus excitations."

VOLUNTARY RECALL. Systematized scientific knowledge can be voluntarily taken account of or not, as man wishes (i.e., he can recall it or forget it).

Prognostic directives for action and sensorial awareness are in themselves not subject to man's voluntary control. Apart from the effect of impingements he cannot recall them or forget them.

* From John Dewey's *Problems of Men* (New York: Philosophical Library, 1946), p. 211.

† When we speak of the relatively determined repeatable phenomena and laws selected and abstracted from the welter of nature by either scientific methodology or our experience in living, we subconsciously assume that they have an "objective" existence (i.e., apart from man and his purposes). It should be borne in mind that the reason that they were selected out of the welter of nature was that they were significant to man in carrying out his purposes. They in themselves have no meaning or significance apart from man's purposes.

EXTENT OF SYNTHESIS OR INTEGRATION. A person can bring into his awareness at one time only a very small part of his total fund of scientific knowledge and can be aware at one time of only very few relationships. At best his method of conceptualized thinking about his store of scientific knowledge is linear, so to speak. Only when man uses scientific laws of general form can he conceptualize broad systematic relationships, but with the sacrifice of specific concepts.

The simplest experiencing of transactions of living only exists in relation to an integrated systematized whole. That is, the simplest of such experiences exists in a continuity of biological time, past and future, and space and purpose and value.

"HOW TO DO" AND "WHAT FOR." The determined repeatable aspects of nature referred to by systematized scientific knowledge are useful to man only in disclosing to him a high probability of what he will successfully accomplish by *doing*, or *how to do*. It discloses nothing as to *why*, or *what for*, a person does or should act.

Prognostic directives for action and sensorial awareness disclose not only "how to do" but also "why" and "what for."

EFFECT ON ACTION. Scientific knowledge brought into awareness by voluntary control does not in itself directly determine action. We can act in regard to it or not, as we wish.

On the other hand, prognostic directives for action and perceptions derived from prior "transactions of living" do in themselves determine the nature of the action, provided we choose to act.

If through repeated testing by experience the prognostic directives have been found of sufficient reliability, action follows automatically (we don't have a chance to choose) from the excitations of the physiological stimulus patterns without perception or awareness (often contrary to it). We call such actions "habits." If prior experience has proved that the prognostic reliability is sufficiently reliable, determined reflex action follows the physiological excitation entirely unassociated with perception or sensorial awareness of any kind, and concerning which we have no choice.

Apparently freedom of choice and therefore responsibility is related to conscious awareness.

The greatest difference between the body of systematized scientific knowledge and the prognostic directives for action, perceptions, and their related sensorial awareness is in the way man makes use of them in operation.

Man makes use of scientific knowledge when he has come up against a hitch in his transaction of living related to some specific type of events or phenomena. To prevent the particular conditions that gave rise to the hitch from occurring, he first decides what particular phenomenon was responsible. He then turns to his body of systematized scientific knowledge and selects from it that particular knowledge that will increase his understanding of the determined predictable aspects of the phenomenon that gave rise to the hitch. He then applies that knowledge to that particular abstracted phenomenon, which application will involve *quantitative* determinations.

Man makes use of his perceptions and their related sensorial awarenesses in every moment of his wakeful living, but in quite a different way from which he uses his scientific knowledge. In using his scientific knowledge he plays a role solely as an operator. He decides what he is going to operate on and how. In making use of his perceptions and their related sensorial awareness, he is likewise an operator, *but* he is also being operated on. He carries out his activities in the midst of the occasion. He is abstracter, synthesizer, hypothesizer, in the midst of events which themselves delimit the significances he must deal with. In his immediate activity he abstracts from the immediate occasion the determined form world in which he must immediately act. But his total determined form world includes far more than the immediate occasion. His total determined form world is a continuum which includes the past and the future, the stable and the changing.

Man's total form world is the result of his purposes and the operational field for his purposes. Both the *why* and the *how* of man's existence are inherent in it. But for it there would be no reason or purpose in scientific inquiry or science, no background for its existence.

The methodologies of science are an *aping* of those man makes use of in his experience of living to disclose the relatively permanent aspects of nature. Indispensable as scientific inquiry is in providing the "how to do" to resolve the "hitches" we encounter in living, at most its operation can only be an aid to our being.

May 10, 1949

SCIENTIFIC METHODOLOGY—ANALYSIS—PHENOMENA—SUB-PHENOMENA—
ASSUMED FRAMES OF REFERENCE

In our past notes on Scientific Methodology we have described the first process in Scientific Methodology as an analysis of the phenomenon under inquiry (concerning which we want to increase our understanding) into the sub-phenomena of which it is constituted.

It appears on further consideration that an increase of our understanding concerning the sub-phenomena and their relationship to each other and to the phenomenon in itself will not increase our understanding of the *why* of the phenomenon itself.

To understand a phenomenon we must understand the hierarchy of super-phenomena of which the phenomenon in question is a sub-phenomenon and the relationships between the phenomenon in question and the hierarchy of super-phenomena.

It would follow that the term analysis is not the proper one to describe the first process in scientific methodology.

A more correct description of this process would be "a determination of all discoverable related phenomena, both super- and sub-phenomena" (related phenomena, meaning phenomenal events the variation of which affects the phenomenon in question). For example, if the phenomenon under inquiry is perception, the "objective world" is a related phenomenon, as certain variations of it affect perception, and since past experience, purpose, action, and expectancy also affect perception, they are related phenomena.*

Now individual phenomena cannot be conceived of in the abstract. They can be conceived of only as existing in a frame of reference † often unconsciously assumed. For instance, the objective-world phenomena are assumed to exist in a physical-spatial-temporal frame of reference; physiological phenomena in a chemical-electrical frame of reference. Subjective phenomena are assumed to exist in a non-spatial–non-temporal frame of reference. The phenomena of purpose exist in a biological continuum frame of reference.

Now when we relate phenomena we also relate the two frames of reference in which the phenomena exist. If the two related phenomena exist in the same frame of reference (for example, the objective phenomenon and the impinging physiological stimulus pattern phenomenon), there is no difficulty. But if they don't, as is often the case (objective phenomenon and subjective phenomenon), we are faced by a problem. Phenomena can be related to each other in terms of only one frame of reference. We can't think of them as being related in two different frames of reference

---

* The discovery of related phenomena may sometimes occur from chance or from a cut-and-try approach, but it results more often from intuitive leaps of the imagination by those of long experience in the field.

† The following are examples of frames of reference: The commonest frames of reference are space and time. So we think of the object field as related to perception as being in one place in the spatial field and perception being in another place. Or we think of the events in the object field as occurring "before" those in the perceptual phenomenon in the periodic time frame of reference, past experience as occurring prior to perception in the frame of reference of the perceiver's biological history, or of perception as occurring prior to action in the frame of reference of accomplishing purposes.

at the same time. Which of the two different frames of reference are we going to choose in which to relate the two phenomena? Apparently this difficulty can only be avoided by translating one of the frames of reference into the terms of the other frame of reference (transformation in physical terms).

For example, suppose we were dealing with the relation between "objective" phenomena and "subjective" phenomena. The frame of reference of "objective" phenomena is a temporal-spatial one. That of "subjective" phenomena is a non-temporal–non-spatial frame of reference. All psychology has been faced with the problem of what to do. If we deal with the relationship in terms of the temporal-spatial frame of reference only, we do not take account of the non-temporal–non-spatial frame of reference in which subjective phenomena exist. The answer to the difficulty is to translate (transform) the less universal frames of reference into the terms of the more universal frame of reference. In this case, to translate the temporal-spatial frame into terms of the non-temporal–non-spatial frame of reference in which subjective phenomena exist.

The more universal non-temporal–non-spatial frames of reference in which subjective phenomena exist are the frames of reference of action, purpose, value, and emergence.

For example, space can be translated into subjective functional "thereness" and time into subjective functional "earlier" and "later" and the space-time frame of reference transformed into the action frame of reference.*

* From L. Barnett, *The Universe and Dr. Einstein* (New York: William Sloane Associates, 1948), pp. 39 f:

"Along with absolute space, Einstein discarded the concept of absolute time—of a steady, unvarying, inexorable universal time flow, streaming from the infinite past to the infinite future. Much of the obscurity that has surrounded the Theory of Relativity stems from man's reluctance to recognize that sense of time, like sense of color, is a form of perception. Just as there is no such thing as color without an eye to perceive it, so an instant or an hour or a day is nothing without an event to mark it. And just as space is simply a possible order of material objects, so time is simply a possible order of events. The subjectivity of time is best explained in Einstein's own words. 'The experiences of an individual,' he says, 'appear to us arranged in a series of events; in this series the single events which we remember appear to be ordered according to the criterion of "earlier" and "later." There exists, therefore, for the individual, an I-time, or subjective time. This in itself is not measurable. I can, indeed, associate numbers with the events, in such a way that a greater number is associated with the later event than with an earlier one. This association I can define by means of a clock by comparing the order of events furnished by the clock with the order of a given series of events. We understand by a clock something which provides a series of events which can be counted.'"

May 20, 1949

### BRIEF DESCRIPTION OF CHART

*Reason for the Chart of Transactions of Living*

Each one of the demonstrations developed by the Institute discloses something about the nature of phenomena that play a role in the process of perception. It is not too difficult for a person going through the demonstrations to recognize the significance of each of the experienced phenomena considered individually. However, the real importance of the demonstrations results from a grasp of the significance of the various phenomena considered as a whole. The chart was designed in the hope that it would be helpful in gaining a grasp of the interrelation of the various phenomena.

*Description of Chart*

Because the relationship between the various phenomena is transactional and circular, and not interactional and lineal, any point on the chart is as good to start from as any other. However, it may be more understandable if we start with the square in the upper right-hand corner of the chart marked *Perception*, that which we are consciously aware of in an actual visual experience. Our perception is defined as the interpretation of our immediate environment in terms of the significance of our form world. Our *Form World*, shown in the rectangle in the lower right-hand corner of the chart, is the recorded compendium of the relatively determined and constant significances experienced in our biological and life histories. Note the lines connecting the *Form World* to our prior environmental experiences in the lower left-hand corner of the chart.

This relating of the significances of our Form World to the potential significances of the immediate environment is possible through our relationship with the immediate environment by means of light- and sound-wave impingements, our stimulus patterns, and by processes taking place in the rectangle marked *Higher Physiological Processes*. These processes can be thought of as translating the *Physiological Stimulus Pattern* "cryptograms" (see chart) produced by the impingements of light rays (*Relating Externality to Physiology* in chart) from the *Immediate Environment* (see left-hand side of chart) in terms of the significances of our Form World.

Our *Perceptions* are prognostic directives for purposeful action, which action is possible through *Physiological Motor Processes* (see chart) as

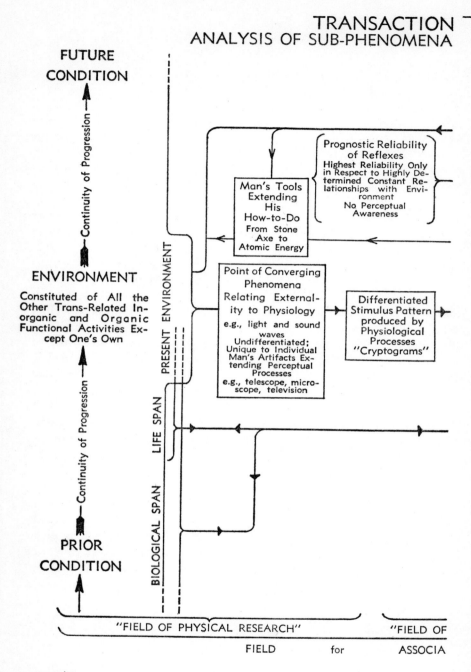

# TRANSACTION

## ANALYSIS OF SUB-PHENOMENA

FUTURE
CONDITION

← Continuity of Progression →

ENVIRONMENT

Constituted of All the Other Trans-Related Inorganic and Organic Functional Activities Except One's Own

← Continuity of Progression →

PRIOR
CONDITION

PRESENT ENVIRONMENT

LIFE SPAN

BIOLOGICAL SPAN

**Prognostic Reliability of Reflexes**
Highest Reliability Only in Respect to Highly Determined Constant Relationships with Environment
No Perceptual Awareness

**Man's Tools Extending His How-to-Do**
From Stone Axe to Atomic Energy

**Point of Converging Phenomena**
Relating External-ity to Physiology
e.g., light and sound waves
Undifferentiated: Unique to Individual Man's Artifacts Extending Perceptual Processes
e.g., telescope, micro-scope, television

**Differentiated Stimulus Pattern produced by Physiological Processes "Cryptograms"**

"FIELD OF PHYSICAL RESEARCH"    "FIELD OF

FIELD    for    ASSOCIA

A. AMES JR.
May 20, 1949

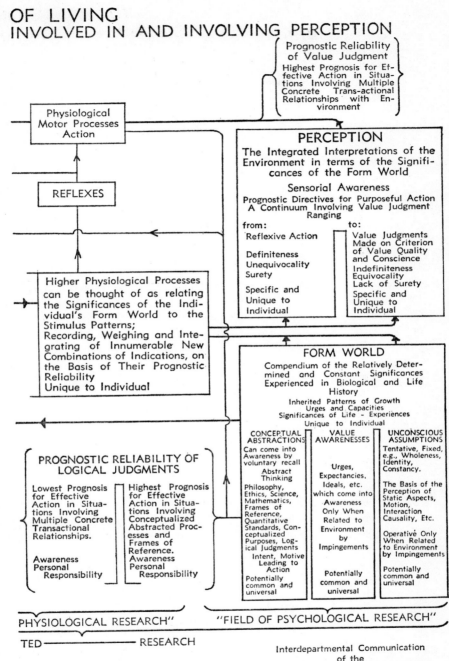

**Prognostic Reliability of Value Judgment**

Highest Prognosis for Effective Action in Situations Involving Multiple Concrete Trans-actional Relationships with Environment

**Physiological Motor Processes Action**

**REFLEXES**

**PERCEPTION**

The Integrated Interpretations of the Environment in terms of the Significances of the Form World

Sensorial Awareness
Prognostic Directives for Purposeful Action A Continuum Involving Value Judgment Ranging

from:
Reflexive Action

Definiteness
Unequivocality
Surety

Specific and
Unique to
Individual

to:
Value Judgments Made on Criterion of Value Quality and Conscience

Indefiniteness
Equivocality
Lack of Surety

Specific and
Unique to
Individual

**Higher Physiological Processes** can be thought of as relating the Significances of the Individual's Form World to the Stimulus Patterns; Recording, Weighing and Integrating of Innumerable New Combinations of Indications, on the Basis of Their Prognostic Reliability Unique to Individual

**FORM WORLD**

Compendium of the Relatively Determined and Constant Significances Experienced in Biological and Life History
Inherited Patterns of Growth
Urges and Capacities
Significances of Life - Experiences
Unique to Individual

| CONCEPTUAL ABSTRACTIONS | VALUE AWARENESSES | UNCONSCIOUS ASSUMPTIONS |
|---|---|---|
| Can come into Awareness by voluntary recall | | Tentative, Fixed, e.g., Wholeness, Identity, Constancy. |
| Abstract Thinking | Urges, Expectancies, | |
| Philosophy, Ethics, Science, Mathematics, Frames of Reference, Quantitative Standards, Conceptualized Purposes, Logical Judgments | Ideals, etc. which come into Awareness Only When Related to Environment by Impingements | The Basis of the Perception of Static Aspects, Motion, Interaction Causality, Etc. |
| Intent, Motive Leading to Action | | Operative Only When Related to Environment by Impingements |
| Potentially common and universal | Potentially common and universal | Potentially common and universal |

**PROGNOSTIC RELIABILITY OF LOGICAL JUDGMENTS**

Lowest Prognosis for Effective Action in Situations Involving Multiple Concrete Transactional Relationships.

Awareness
Personal
Responsibility

Highest Prognosis for Effective Action in Situations Involving Conceptualized Abstracted Processes and Frames of Reference.

Awareness
Personal
Responsibility

PHYSIOLOGICAL RESEARCH"

"FIELD OF PSYCHOLOGICAL RESEARCH"

TED ———————— RESEARCH

Interdepartmental Communication
of the
Institute for Associated Research
Hanover Institute Division Hanover, N. H.

shown by the lines in the upper part of the chart from *Perception* through *Physiological Motor Processes* and *Man's Tools* to *Present Environment*.

Action also occurs unrelated to *Perception*. Action may follow from purely *Logical Judgments* (see chart, lower left-hand column in *Form World*). Such action is also possible through *Physiological Motor Processes* and *Man's Tools,* as shown by the line extending upward from the lower right-hand column of the *Form World* to *Physiological Motor Processes* through *Man's Tools* to the *Present Environment*.

Action may also follow solely from *Reflex* functional activity. Such action is shown by the vertical line from *Higher Physiological Processes* through *Reflexes* and *Physiological Motor Processes* on to *Present Environment*. The results of action, i.e., whether successful or unsuccessful in furthering our purposes, play a most important *but-for* role in *Perception*. Whether the action will be successful or not is dependent on the prognostic reliability of the determinants of the action, i.e., *Perception, Logical Judgments,* and *Reflexes*. The prognostic reliability of these three different determinants of action is noted in the chart in the three brackets, *Prognostic Reliability of Reflexes* in the upper middle part of the chart; *Prognostic Reliability of Logical Judgments* in the lower middle part of the chart; and *Prognostic Reliability of Value-Judgments* in the upper right-hand corner of the chart.

There have also been noted on the chart those aspects of the total processes that are unique to the individual and those that are not.

October 25, 1949

### INQUIRY INTO THE ROLES OF ILLUSION, SURPRISE, AND FRUSTRATION IN TRANSACTIONS OF LIVING

As we carry on in our year by year, day by day, minute by minute living, we are in the midst of what we are calling continuous "transactions of living," in which innumerable events and phenomena are involved in most complex trans-relationships.

In our attempts to formulate a conceptual picture of the events involved in a "transaction of living" and their transactional relationships, however, it is only possible for us to take into account conceptually a very limited number of the phenomena actually involved and to grasp only very limited aspects of their "trans-relationships."

However, it seems possible to recognize the minimum number of processes necessary to constitute a "transaction of living," i.e., those processes but for which "transactions of living" wouldn't be.

Most briefly and generally stated they are, for the purposes of this inquiry:

1. An organism—functional activity in
2. an environment consisting of other functional activities.
3. The organism's awareness of the significance to it of its environment in
4. terms of its valueful purposes.
5. Action by organism in furthering its valueful purposes.
6. The effects of the results of such actions on itself and its environment as disclosed by
7. the effectivity of later purposeful action of the organism.

The point that is to be brought out is that a "transaction of living" must take into account not only one purposeful, valueful action by the organism and the effect of the results of the action on the organism and its environment, but also later action by the organism, which alone can disclose the nature of the effect of its prior action.

Before going on to our main inquiry it might be well here to point out that action can be differentiated into two markedly different types: firstly, action carried on by the organism in order to help him get a better perceptual grasp of the significance of his environment, i.e., to get "perceptions" that have a higher prognostic reliability; and, secondly, action by the organism in carrying out his valueful purposes *after* he has formulated his "perceptions" of his environment.

To explain: actions of the first type are those involved in ocular movements and activities such as convergence or accommodation, parallax movements of the head or by change of bodily position, moving nearer to an object to see it more clearly, or the use of the telescope or microscope, all of which are actions to get "perceptions" that have a higher prognostic reliability. And all activities involved in inquiry are of a similar nature.

Upon the formulation of a "perception" ("specification") of the probable significance of his environment, the organism decides what he "wants to do about it all" in terms of valueful purposes. That is, he makes "value-judgments" and acts accordingly. Such actions are of the second type. The effects of the results of this latter type of actions are directly trans-related to valueful purpose and its emergence.

To return to our main inquiry, i.e., the roles played by "illusion," "surprise," and "frustration" in transactions of living.

Let us first consider "illusions." It would seem apparent from our work on the origin and nature of our perception of the "whereness" and "whatness" of "objects," so-called "static aspects" of our environment, that illusions (so-called optical illusions) are something we experience in our transactions of living under the following particular circumstances:

1. The existence of sub-intellectual, unconscious assumptions of our "assumptive Form World."

2. The existence of characterized stimulus-pattern detail to which specific assumptions are related.

3. Action by the observer (sometimes other events) making evident to him that his perceptions prognosticate environmental significances different from those that actually exist.

For example, in the "chair" or "overlay" demonstrations when the observer changes his point of view (but only when he does so), he experiences an illusion, a disclosure that his perception lacks reliability as a prognosis for action. In this case it is apparent that the action by the observer which discloses the illusion is of the first type described above, i.e., action for the purpose of getting a more reliable perception of the environmental significances.

And here it may be helpful to jump ahead and consider the difference between the above-described illusions and their trans-related phenomena and frustrations and their trans-related phenomena. Frustrations, disappointments, exist when one's actions fail to accomplish the purposes for which they were undertaken. For instance, in the "distorted room" when one tries with the stick to hit the ball in the opposite corner of the room, he is frustrated (he will be disappointed) to the degree that the successful accomplishment of his purpose is important to him.

It should be noted that under these conditions no illusion exists. As far as is evident to him his perception is normal. The room appears square to him. There is no visual illusion. The only thing that bothers the observer is that his actions don't carry out his purposes.

The above seems to indicate a basic difference between illusions and frustrations and some of the differences in the conditions under which they exist.

Here the question arises as to the nature of the illusions we experience in our perception of motion (cf. Perception of Motion demonstrations).

The conditions for their existence are similar to those for the existence of illusions in the perception of the "static aspects" of our environment. In both cases the illusions are present (a) because the observer formulated his perception on assumptions that were not applicable to actual environmental significances, and (b) when through action or other events the observer discovers that his perception is not a reliable prognosis of environmental significances. The only difference in the two situations is the fact that in one case the "things" observed are static and in the other case they are in motion.

It seems that the reason why this difference is unimportant in this

particular consideration is because the nature of the environmental significances that are being taken into account in the perception of both
static "things" and motion is the same, in that they are environmental
significances that are relatively highly determined, i.e., have a high degree of constancy, continuity—functional activities we conceptualize as
existing normally in their own right unaffected by transactional relationships with other functional activities, as differentiated from those
environmental significances that have to do with changes, sequents and
consequences, the result of one functional activity's affecting or inter-
fering with what we think of as the normal behavior of another functional activity.

The geographical aspect of our Assumed Form World is an example
of the former, as is the "interaction" of the units of our solar system
in periodic time. Examples of the latter are physical, chemical and atomic
inter-actions.

This leads us to a consideration of the type of awareness that corresponds to illusions when we, so to speak, make "false" assumptions as to
the conditions involved in the perception of such sequential significances
—what Michotte has called the "perception of causality."

Sequential relations of the kind we are considering can be thought
of as consisting of four parts: two functional activities, their inter-action,
and the consequence of the inter-action.

There is an infinity of sequents * taking place in our environment—
atomic, chemical, those dealt with in classical physics, the infinitude of
sequents we think of as taking place in nature, for instance, the infinitude
of sequential situations involving inorganic matter, from grains of sand
in motion in water and air to large land masses and solar systems, and
those involving organic matter, from the infinitude of sequents involving spermatozoa to vegetable and animal activity.

In the ultimate analysis not one of these infinitudes of sequents ever
exactly repeats. But from the point of view of their significance to man,
many sequents repeat with sufficient approximation to give him a basis
for prognosis for carrying out his valueful purposes.

The quest of modern science is to increase man's knowledge of such
relatively repeatable sequents for the purpose of increasing his capacity
to prognosticate the consequences of sequents (events). But long before
man thought of science he had developed the capacity to take account
of sequents and their consequences, as he is still doing within and beyond the range of present science.

Through his recording of the significances of his past experiences as

* Sequent: "What ensues in a series of events."

related to his valueful purposes by the use of his "common sense," man, if he gets indications of the first or precedent part of a sequence, can prognosticate the consequence.

Consider the simple case of the sequents of one billiard ball hitting another. The precedent situations are: (a) One billiard ball moving with a certain velocity towards (b) another billiard ball; (c) the impact, the consequence of which is (d) the movement of the two balls after the impact.

A person observing these sequents presumes the consequence before it takes place. He makes this presumption as to the consequence from his perception of the precedent situation of one billiard ball approaching another with a given velocity. His presumption is based (a) on his assumption that the two balls are of identical weight and resilience, an assumption based in turn on the apparent similarity of the two balls both as to size and surface texture, and (b) on his expectancy, pre-assumption, based on his past experience, that if one billiard ball hits another identical billiard ball at a given rate of speed, a specific consequence will follow, i.e., the two balls will move in specific directions at specific rates of speed.

That he makes such a presumption as to the consequence of sequents, that is, expects the consequence before it happens,* is evidenced by the fact that he will be surprised if what he expects doesn't happen. For instance, suppose an observer who had played billiards and therefore had had experience with how billiard balls behave when one is hit by an-

---

* It is only in those sequential situations that (a) have a high probability of repetition and (b) with which the observer has had considerable experience that he can or will presume consequences. We all are continually experiencing sequential situations in which we are not only not surprised, no matter what happens, but are quite indifferent. We simply haven't got time to bother with the innumerable consequences of sequential situations that aren't significant to us.

The sequential situation of the billiard balls that we have used as an illustration is a most specialized and simplified example. It is a man-made situation, the result of much care and trouble, in which both billiard balls have been made, as exactly as possible, of the same size, weight, and resiliency. And great care and trouble has been taken that their interaction occurs on a surface as level as possible, having a definite uniform retardation effect. It is only under such special conditions that consequences can be presumed from the precedents in sequential situations with a high degree of reliability.

In our daily living the sequential situations we have to deal with are much more complex and involve many more trans-related factors and assumptions.

A most highly involved sequential situation exists when one observes two other people in a trans-action. The precedent aspects of such sequential situations, which is all there is upon which to base a prognosis of the consequence, necessitate innumerable assumptions on the part of the observer about both the acting parties, including their purposes and their value sense.

other was watching a friend hit a ball with his cue so that it hit another ball and that the ball which was hit, instead of moving as the observer expected, hardly moved at all, and the cue ball, instead of following the other ball, as the observer expected it to do, bounced backward towards the cue of his friend. The above consequence would follow if his friend had, unknown to the observer, substituted in place of his cue ball a light hollow plastic ball that appeared identical to a normal billiard ball.

The observer would be surprised because he had expected consequences that didn't occur. He had assumed, as he had a right to do, that the cue ball, because the texture of its surface was similar to a normal billiard ball, was of the same weight and resiliency as the ball which it hit.

From his perception of the precedent situation the observer formulated his presumption of the consequence, and when the two balls didn't do what he expected them to do, he was surprised, purely "objectively" surprised, so to speak. His surprise was in no way about himself or anything else except the peculiar behavior of the two balls.

Now the surprise that is experienced by an observer in a sequential situation is evidence that the observer has (and not necessarily because of any fault of his own) related assumptions to characteristics of his stimulus cryptogram which caused him to interpret the significance of the environmental situation as other than what it actually was. As a result the consequence of the sequential turned out to be different from what he expected.

This situation is quite different from those in which the observer experiences an illusion. To experience an illusion, the observer must be aware of the inconsistency between his perception and the significance of his environment. He is never aware of any such inconsistency in his experience with the billiard balls. To be sure, he makes a "mistaken" assumption as to the weight of the cue ball. But the incongruity between his perception and his environmental significance only becomes apparent when the consequence is not what he expected after the balls have hit each other, and at that time there is no inconsistency between the prognosis of his perception and the significance of his environment. He sees the two balls move just where they do in fact move.

There is apparently a further basis for differentiating the situations where illusions are experienced, i.e., in perception of the static or continuous aspects of our environment, and where surprise is experienced, i.e., in the perception of sequential situations.

In general in the first case the significance of our environment of which we are taking account involves egocentric relationships, i.e., relationship to our particular point of view both in space and time. For instance, our perception of "thereness" is awareness of "thereness" from ourselves. Our perception of "thatness" is awareness of "objective" significance involving its "thereness" from ourselves and our then particular purposes. If we change our point of view or if our interests and purposes change in time, the significance of the static continuous aspects of our environment also changes.

But in our perception of sequential situations our point of view, either spatial or temporal, is unrelated to the significances of which we take account. The significances we take into account in our perception of sequents are the same for any point of view at any time and place. They are general and universal in nature and are not characterized by the unique specificity that is inherent in perceptions whose significances involve the egocentric personal point of view of the observer. In a way of speaking they are relatively entirely "objective."

A compilation of all one's perceptions of sequential situations and the assumptions on which they are based would constitute what we commonly think of as the "objective world"; in our terminology it would constitute the "objective" non-personal aspect of the Assumed Form World that each of us brings to the present occasion and in terms of which certain aspects of our physiological stimulus cryptograms are translated.

June 21, 1951

### NOTES ON SURETY AND FAITH AND DOUBT AND MISTRUST

In every concrete transactional situation where we make a mistake and acknowledge it, we experience at least some degree of doubt or mistrust. The experience which disclosed the mistake empirically demonstrated to some degree the inadequacy of our Form World to provide a reliable prognosis for carrying out our purposes and enhancing our values.

The degree of the doubt will vary from a fleeting question to which we can quickly formulate an answer, as in the case of putting a trick golf ball with a misplaced center of gravity, to more profound and less easily overcome doubts, as in the case of one who has been cheated by a person he trusted, to complete mistrust and frustration, as accomplished by Soviet methods to obtain confessions.

It would seem apparent that we cannot carry out our functions as living organisms if we remain in doubt and mistrust. We could not only not make a choice; we could not act effectively. Before we can make a choice and act, some degree of surety and faith must take the place of doubt and mistrust.

An increase of our understanding of the origin and nature of surety and faith and doubt and mistrust seems very important. Surety and faith and doubt and mistrust exist only as aspects of the awareness of a particular individual in a particular concrete transactional situation.

For a start it may be helpful to consider those transactional situations where such awarenesses do not exist, are not operative.

Neither surety nor faith nor doubt nor mistrust exist or are operative in those functional activities that take place where there is no awareness, as in reflexes and habits. In these situations there is also no choice, and the behavior, action, is determined, presumably because the organism has found from long experience that under certain environmental conditions certain typical kinds of action have been found to have such a high prognostic reliability in furthering its purposes and value enhancement that in the long run they can be relied upon and accepted as determined forms. The organism is thereby freed to exercise awareness and choice under those conditions where the prognosis is less reliable.

There are other types of transactional situations where surety and faith may exist and are operative and yet where doubt and mistrust may not exist, namely, when the action is reflexly related to emotional conditions (such as sex and hunger) and the accomplishment of the purpose with emotional satisfaction. Here with awareness both of desire and satisfaction, there may be awareness of surety and faith but no awareness of doubt or mistrust. Under these conditions there is also no choice, and the behavior action is determined. The guess is hazarded that the awareness of surety and faith under such conditions is to insure the carrying on of transactional activities of particular types.

There is apparently a gradual transition from these types of transactional situations through those where there is a diminution of reflex emotional activity and awareness thereof and an increase of awareness of values. With this transition there is a decrease in awareness of surety and faith and an increase in awareness of doubt and mistrust, also a decrease in the determinative aspects of the situation and an increase in the probability of making mistakes and recognizing the nature of the mistakes and an increase in the possibility of choosing.

Up to now we have been using the words surety and faith as if they were more or less synonymous and as if they referred to only one type of awareness.

However, there are several types of transactional situations or different aspects of transactional situations, where the "that" which is in awareness that counteracts doubt and mistrust is quite different in nature.

There are three types of "afflictions," or sufferings or sorrows, that can be clearly differentiated:

1. Those following events over which man has no control (strangely enough often called "acts of God").

2. Those related to what might be called social mistakes, i.e., inadequacies of aspects of the commonly held social form world—mores, customs, etc., to which each individual is a contributor.

3. Those related to inadequacies of one's own form world, leading to individual failure to accomplish purposes because of mistakes necessitating faith and leading to emergence. It is this latter with which we are concerned in our inquiry.

While each of us has to bear and accept afflictions and sufferings of the first two types, it is through the third type that we get our real opportunity to make choices, exercise faith, and emerge. And here the mistakes have to be our own mistakes, honest mistakes made in spite of our having used our most profound wisdom and value-judgments in the expectancy of satisfaction and happiness.

We hope for success and happiness, not suffering, and usually are successful. Suffering is only real suffering when it follows from such precedents. Otherwise it is "fake" suffering, and no good can come from it.

True suffering is as hard to find as true happiness. Most of us do not have sufficiently high purposes or act on sufficiently high purposes to be able to encounter failures and real suffering.

Faith is needed to meet the first two types of afflictions and sufferings. But it is a different kind of faith. Among other reasons, because there is not the personal responsibility that causes failure to weigh so heavily upon one.

If one is sufficiently sensitive and responsible, he will be aware of his responsibility for social mistakes, and they will become his own personal mistakes and responsibility.

September 18, 1951

### Sequents—Value—Science

Action is an essential aspect of being. Action is the personal causing, by a particular individual in a particular concrete situation, of a humanly significant condition to follow after another humanly significant condition.

The following of a humanly significant condition after another humanly significant condition is only a probability.

The effectivity of a premeditated action depends upon the prognostic reliability of the prehension of the nature of the humanly significant condition that will follow the prior condition as a result of the premeditated action. In general the effectivity of action depends upon prehension of interrelated sequential events that the particular individual brings to the particular occasion.

Any increase of awareness of sequents and their interrelation increases one's potentiality for effective action.

The capacity for prehension of sequential events is derived from prior empirical experience either of the acting individual or of other persons.

Of late, science, both applied and "pure," with its empirical testing, has played a most important and indispensable role in increasing the awareness of sequents that a particular person brings to a particular concrete situation. Pure science's role is that of extending our awareness and knowledge of heretofore unrecognized sequents of a most abstract nature.

The ultimate effectivity of an action depends upon how the consequence of the action interrelates with the total interrelated sequential pattern. This is not disclosed to the acting person by his immediately intellectualized purpose for acting. Behind every such purpose is a hierarchy of other purposes which relate the immediate sequence to the total sequence pattern and of which the person is aware in terms of value. The ultimate effectivity of an action therefore depends upon the value aspect of the purpose for action, i.e., the value concretely experienced as related to the following sequential conditions, or "consequential value."

In so far as the sequents learned by science are used for non-valueful action, i.e., for consequences without value, science defeats its own ends of increasing our prehensions of sequents for action.

September 24, 1951

NOTE ON VALUES—THE VALUE MATRIX

As we have stated, a particular person in a particular concrete transactional situation is unique, due to (1) his unique position in space and periodic time (no two persons can be in the same place at the same time);

(2) his unique prehended sequential pattern; (3) his unique value purpose pattern both inherited and as developed by his unique life's experiences.

In any concrete situation it is from a person's value purpose pattern that he chooses a particular value purpose to fulfill, after which he chooses from his prehended sequential pattern the particular sequential patterns that he believes will further the accomplishment of his value purpose and then acts from his unique position in time and space to initiate the sequence.

He acts from his unique position in his time-space field of his immediate now. His action initiates unique ("how to do") sequential patterns (events) interrelated to other sequential patterns (events). The "field" of these action patterns (events) is the time-space field extending from the indefinite past to the indefinite future and indefinitely in space.

The most important question arises: "What is the nature of the 'field' in which his 'what for' valueful purposes 'operate'?" It seems apparent that it is a field of an entirely different nature from his action "field." The word "field" is inappropriate to use in referring to it due to its spatial temporal connotation. Possibly the word "matrix" would be better. As defined by Webster, "matrix" means: (1) mother—womb; (2) an enveloping element within which something originates, takes form, develops; (3) that which gives form, origin, or foundation to something enclosed or embedded in it.

As has been pointed out in some late notes, valueful purposes are characterized by their constancy, i.e., (1) they remain unchanged no matter where a person is in space; (2) they remain unchanged with the passing of time; (3) certain valueful purposes remain unchanged throughout the happening of events, sequential phenomena; others change.

It follows apparently that the matrix of valueful purposes is characterized (1) by being in the "now here," although not in the "now" of time or the "here" of space; (2) by constancy, continuous constancy, not repetitive as periodic time or as sequential events made use of in the "how to do" to accomplish purposes.

The boundaries of the matrix must include not only the "time-space" "field" and the "field" in which transactional phenomena take place, but more, and its boundaries and what happens in it are of an entirely different nature. Each person as a unique individual acting with valueful purpose in a unique concrete situation operates within his unique matrix, which "stands still," so to speak, while his sequential events, which are an aspect of his matrix and which he initiates, "flow through" it from the direction of their temporal future into that of their temporal past.

At "the same time" each person as an aspect of his social group operates within the matrix of the group, which also "stands still," while the sequential events which are aspects of the matrix of the social group and which the group initiates "flow through" it. The dynamic aspects of these matrices are values and value choices. Their operational aspects are the retention of basic forms of values and value choice, and their flow into higher quality and extension, inclusiveness, through individual and group action.

October, 1951

### More Inquiry Concerning the Named We Are Naming by "Form World"

Every individual operates in the "now" of his own unique situation. Every individual perceives from his particular unique point of view in time and space. He does this on the basis of the significance to him of his unique situation as interpreted and foreseen in terms of his stored significances derived from his prior experience both inherited and personal. What a person perceives has reality only in so far as it constitutes an aspect of his personal continuity in space-time purposes and values.

Hence there cannot exist any so-called "objective world," any "otherness-out-there," apart from the significances to unique persons operating in their unique transactional situations. The significances which every unique person assigns involve the significances to him of other "things" and of other persons together with his significances to these other "things" and persons.*

Because of certain common inherited human characteristics and certain more or less common cultural interrelationships, certain significances become common between unique persons. These shared significances in the Form Worlds of unique individuals make communication possible. Such communicable aspects are signs, laws, specifications, words. But to be communicated, they must be of continuing fixed forms. These fixed communicable forms are often mistaken for the "objective world" or "otherness" as existing in their own right apart from their significance to one's self and to other unique individuals.

Since it is only from the point of view of a unique individual's egocentric position that aspects of space, time, and sequents have any signifi-

---

* Cf. "Pour que nous percevions les choses, il faut que nous les vivions." In M. Merleau-Ponty, *Phénoménologie de la perception* (Paris: Gallimard, 1945), p. 376. The formulations of Merleau-Ponty parallel ours at many points and have been experimentally tested by Professors Buytendijk and Ratingen at Utrecht.

cance, if a person loses these aspects in some degree, he becomes separated from his environment. In extreme cases are the psychoses.

A concrete occasion of living, an experience, a "significance" for the individual is possible only because of the operational interrelationships of (1) the perceptual assumptions, (2) the prehensions, (3) the action patterns or "doings," and (4) the value forms which the individual brings to the specific occasion.

| *What an individual brings to a situation (what makes it)* | *The concrete process* |
|---|---|
| Assumptions | Perception |
| Prehensions | Sequential behavior |
| Action patterns (doings) | Transaction |
| Value forms | Valuing, value-judgment |

No one aspect would exist except for the others—i.e., there would be no perceptual assumptions established except for sequential assumptions, action patterns, and value standards. These are man's "assumptive realities." And these "assumptive realities" are the truths, the standards, the criteria through which an individual's living occurs. This total "assumptive complex" constitutes the Form World. The behavior of a unique individual follows from the unique background—Form World—he brings to the unique situation in which he finds himself.

### Behavioral Matrices

The unique situation in which an individual finds himself has to do with, among other "things," the uniqueness of his environment and the uniqueness of his position in it. He is always at a particular unique "here" and at a particular unique "now."

It becomes of importance to inquire further into what "here" and "now" refer to.

It would appear that when used to refer to the different phenomena of space and time, the words "here" and "now" are used in describing relationships in a bifurcated world; that is, the relationships of "objects" and "events" existing apart in their own right to a "subject" existing apart in its own right: the word "here" meaning that an object exists or an event is occurring at the same point in space that the "subject" is; the word "now" meaning that an object exists or an event is occurring not only at the same time the subject exists but in the subject's present existence, as differentiated from his past and future existence.

We all have an intuitive sense of what "here" refers to and what "now" refers to and of what "here-now" refers to, but when we try to conceptualize what is referred to, we run into a mass of uncertainties and contradictions.

For instance, Webster defines "here" as meaning: "In this place—opposed to there"; but he also defines it as: "at this point, now," and also as "in the present life or state." *

He defines "now" as meaning: "The present time or moment; the present; at the present time"; but he also defines it as: "in or under the present circumstances; since, at or by this time; seeing that—often with that, as 'now that the snow is melting.'"

When it has come about through common usage that the same word has different meanings and is used to refer to different and apparently conflicting referents, it does not follow that there is only one proper referent and that the other meanings of the word are not useful. The words may be quite useful, and their different referents may be quite "real." The confusion arises because we ourselves are not clear as to which of various types of operational situations we have in mind when we use the words.

We will go on to consider some of the different types of operational situations in which the words "here" and "now" have different referents and will consider the following types of operational situations.

1. Objective operational situations, i.e., those involving an abstracted (bifurcated) objective world that does not take into account the subjective, or the personal, point of view.

a. "Here" and "now" as referents in all types of inquiry, including scientific.

2. Subjective-objective operational situations (non-bifurcated), i.e., those involving an integrated subjective and objective world that includes the personal point of view.

a. "Here" and "now" as referents in the perception of objects.

b. "Here" and "now" as referents in the perception of sequential events.

c. "Here" and "now" as referents in a "transactional" situation, acting to carry out already determined purposes (when the person is faced with problems of "how" to accomplish his purpose).

d. "Here" and "now" as referents in a valueful "transactional" situation, acting to carry out valueful purposes (when the person takes into account "why" he wishes to accomplish his determined purpose).

1. OBJECTIVE OPERATIONAL SITUATIONS.

a. "Here" and "now" as referents in all types of inquiry, including scientific.

In abstracted objective operational situations, "here" has reference to

* We refer to Webster's definitions only because they are in most common use.

space—"in this place—opposed to there" (Webster), as the "here" of our world relative to the "there" of other parts of the astronomical universe, or the "here" of one atom relative to the "there" of other atoms in an atomic field. "Now" has reference to time—"at the present time or moment" (Webster) in the stream of periodic time, as the "now" of our civilization relative to past and future civilizations or the "now" of an atom's behavior relative to its past and future behavior or that of other atoms.*

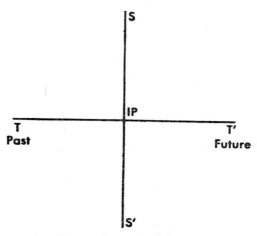

FIG. 1. INQUIRY MATRIX

If we represent three-dimensional space by the vertical line *SS′* and the flow of periodic time by the horizontal line *TT′*, the "here-now," the immediate period, would be represented by their intersection *IP* (see Figure 1).

In an abstracted "objective" world in which the subjective, personal point of view is left out operational situations can be dealt with as if there were no "here-now," no "present." We can refer to events anywhere in space and time by using the referents "there" and "then." The "there" would not be *but for* the "then," and vice versa. Such an operational situation we will refer to as an *"Inquiry Matrix."* †

These abstracted objective spatial-temporal meanings "there" and "then" are made use of in our experience as well as in quantitative sci-

---

* But it should be recognized that even in such use of the words a personal subjective egocentric point of view is *tacitly* assumed. The "here" is our world or one atom; the "now" is our present civilization or one atom.

† We are using the word "matrix" as meaning "enveloping element within which something originates, takes form, or develops" (Webster).

ences. They are, of course, indispensable to our understanding of "objective" events. They provide the coincidence of the "when" in periodic time and the "where" in metric space sequential events occur. Without these we would have no prehensions as to sequential events, i.e., "how to do."

2. SUBJECTIVE-OBJECTIVE OPERATIONAL SITUATIONS (NOT BIFURCATED).

a. "Here" and "now" as referents in the perception of objects.

Numerous examples of this type of situation are to be found in our demonstrations of the perception of "thereness" and "thatness."

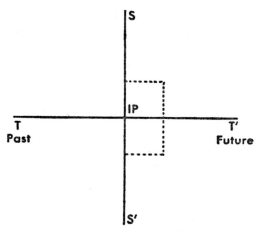

FIG. 2. PERCEPTUAL MATRIX

Our perception of objects is a prognosis of their significance to us (their "thatness"), and their direction and distance from us ("thereness") in our immediate unique present "now." Moreover, our perceptions are directives for potential action relative to objects. Thus there is inherent in their significance to us the sequential situations that would follow if we acted "on" the "object," as going to and sitting in a chair which we perceive.

It follows that our perception of objects includes other "here's" and a future aspect and therefore extends our "right here" into more inclusive "here's" and our "immediate now" into the future.

These extensions of our "right here" into other "here's" into space and our "right now" into the future vary with the nature and durations of the sequents inherent in the "objective" significance. These extensions are diagrammatically shown in Figure 2 by the dotted lines.

These spatial and future temporal extensions represent what is referred to by the words "here" and "now" when used as referents in the operational situations of perceiving objects in a non-bifurcated subjective-objective "world." Since the "here" would not be but for the "now" and vice versa, in non-bifurcated subjective-objective operational situations, the two words should be used together as in the form "here-now" (cf. "thatness-thereness").

Such an operational situation we will refer to as our *"Perceptual Matrix."*

b. "Here" and "now" as referents in the perception of sequential events.

An example of this type of sequential situation is to be found in our demonstration of a person watching a piece of bouncing putty dropped on the floor by another person. Other common examples are persons watching an athletic contest or other events in which they do not participate.

Let us consider the first case from the point of view of the observer at the instant the putty hits the floor. The observer expects the putty won't bounce because of his prehensions and the spatial-temporal events that took place *prior* to this instant. That he is surprised because it bounces shows he was taking account of spatial-temporal events he expected *would take place in the future*. That is, his "here-now" included past as well as future events.

In sequential situations we would describe what the words "here" and "now" refer to as follows.

A person's "here" embraces that area in space within which he prehends that any event in the sequence *has* taken or *may* take place.

A person's "now" includes that period in past time within which he *has* experienced prior events of the sequence and that period in future time within which he prehends that any event in the sequence *may* occur.

A person's "here-now" includes the space-time field within which the prehended sequential event *has* taken or *might* take place. Inseparable from the "here-now" are the past and prehended significances of the operational aspects of the sequential event, in other words, of the "happenings."

It is apparent that the degree of extension of the "here" and "now" varies with the nature of the sequential event from those that take place in the smallest units in space and time to the greatest.

Hence the "here-now" of these sequential situations differs from the "here-now" of the perception-of-objects situations in that the former includes aspects of the past as well as the future.

These further extensions of the "here-now" are diagrammatically shown in Figure 3 by the short-dashed lines.

These spatial and past and future temporal extensions are what is referred to by the words "here" and "now" when used as referents in the operational situation of perceiving sequential events in a non-bifurcated subjective-objective "world." Such an operational situation we will refer to as our *"Sequential Matrix."*

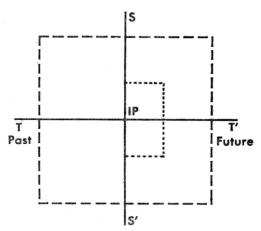

FIG. 3. SEQUENTIAL MATRIX

c. "Here-now" as referents in "transactional" situations—acting to carry out a determined purpose.

The "putting demonstration" * is an example of this type of situation involving impersonal sequents. If the action involves other people, social sequents are involved. Another example is the person driving to a town who comes to a crossroad and takes one road rather than the other.

In the putting demonstration the person has a purpose of putting a ball so that it will stop at a certain distance. To carry out his purpose he acts to initiate a sequential event, by swinging his putter, which hits the ball, which rolls along the floor and stops at a distance. The force with which he swings his putter is determined by his perception of the significances of club, ball, and floor, their "thatnesses" and "therenesses,"

---

* Editor's Note: To illustrate what was lost to experience when an individual's full participation was not involved in achieving a specific purpose, Ames devised a mechanical apparatus which, when properly set, would putt a golf ball with great accuracy.

and his prehension of the sequential events that may follow after he swings his club.

Let us consider this situation from the point of view of the person at some particular instant while the ball is rolling along the floor. His "here" at least includes the space along the floor from where he is to the mark where he wants the ball to stop. His "now" includes at least the past duration of time "from when" he formulated his purpose to hit the ball and the future duration until it stops.

In such situations, we would describe what the word "here" refers to as follows. A person's "here" at least embraces that area in space within which phenomena have occurred or can occur that the person has affected or can affect or influence in acting to further his purposes. It would follow that if the "thereness" of any phenomenon is such that a person, in acting to further his purposes, can affect or influence it, it is within his "here."

A person's "now" at least embraces those extensions in time within which the phenomena are occurring and within which the person can cause some effect or influence in acting to further his purposes. It would follow that if the "thenness" of the occurring phenomenon is such that a person, in acting to further his purposes, can affect or influence it, it is within his "now."

We would define the "here-now" as the transactional "matrix" in which he acts in furthering his purposes.

"Here" and "now" exist only from the unique point of view of a particular person and in his personal "presence" or "present." *

The "here-now" of purposes is quite different in nature from the "here-now" of sequential events. We speak of "immediate" or "present" purposes and also say "my purpose was" or "my purpose will be." We can retain the same purpose amidst continually changing events. That is, purposes have a constancy which the significances of "objects" and sequential events do not have. And we then make use of entirely different objective and sequential significances to accomplish the same purpose. While different purposes follow each other, the same purposes may keep coming back over and over again. It is as if they existed in another dimension than that of objective and sequential significances. Since the extensions of space and the durations of time within which purposefully initiated sequential events take place varies with the nature of the purposes

---

* These words as defined by Webster—"presence" meaning: "Act, fact or state of being present; the space within one's immediate vicinity; the person or personality of an individual"; "present" meaning: "Being before, in view of, or at hand; being in a certain place and not elsewhere—opposed to absent. Now existing or in process, begun but not ended, not past or future, as the present Congress."

which lead to the initiating of the sequential event, the "here-now" may vary all the way from seconds to a lifetime.

These considerations again raise the question of what "there" and "then" refer to. For it seems that there couldn't be a "here-now" if there weren't a "there-then," just as there couldn't be a "there-then" if there weren't a "here-now." It would seem that "there-then" doesn't refer simply to other abstracted "things" or "events" at other spatial positions or other times, but to *other* "presents" or "presences," to *other* "here-now's" from that of the unique present point of view of the person who experiences "thereness" or "thenness." "There" refers to other "presents" or "presences" existing some "where" else at some other "place," in the person's "here-now." "Then" refers to some other "presents" or "presences" existing some "when" else (at some other time) relative to the person's "now" at some other "time," either "past" or "future." This would include the person's own experiences as expressed by him when he says "then I was" or "then I will be." *

The above is of interest in that it seems to make evident that "being"— human behavior—can be known, understood, only from the first person's point of view; it cannot be known from the second or third person's point of view or from an historical or future point of view.†

We have been describing what a person's "here" and "now" at least embrace, when he purposefully acts. But it would appear that more is included than we have mentioned.

The constancy aspects of purpose mentioned above are of a nature that isn't elucidated, can't be referred to by terms such as "space" or "time" or objective or sequential significances. And the constancy aspect of purpose is quite different from anything words like "space," "time," or "sequential significances" refer to. It could be better referred to as "present," using the word *without* any of its spatial-temporal connotations. As has been said, "purposes" can be thought of as being in another dimension; a dimension more inclusive than sequential significances and objective significances, since these only exist because of purposes.

This dimension may possibly be suggested in Figure 4 by the area within the long-dashed line. Such an operational situation we will refer to as our "*Transactional Matrix.*"

d. "Here" and "now" as referents in a valueful "transactional" situation, acting to carry out *valueful* purpose.

An example of this type of situation is that of a person driving along a road and seeing someone ahead "thumbing" a ride. The person either

* The above seems quite evident with regard to other organic activities including those of other persons, but not so evident in the case of inorganic activities.

† Cf. Discussion of Choice in next section.

stops or drives on. In either case he acts to carry out a purpose. If he
stops, his purpose is to help the hitchhiker. If he drives on, his purpose
is to safeguard himself or not waste time. Since the person can either stop
or drive on, no question of how to act to fulfill either of his purposes is

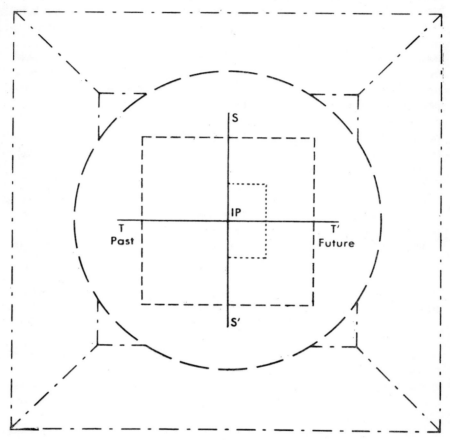

FIG. 4. TRANSACTIONAL MATRIX

involved. But he does have to make a choice between purposes. He hasn't
time to go into an "inquiry" and it wouldn't help him much if he had,
as he couldn't get the data for an effective inquiry. He acts on the basis
of a value-judgment; "why" he should do one thing rather than the other,
what he ought ("duty or moral constraint"—Webster) to do, what "feels"
right to him.

This example brings out a situation where the value, the feeling of the right thing to do, or the "what for" aspect is involved. Actually no one ever does anything just to do it; no one ever accomplishes a limited purpose just to accomplish it. While limited purposes may be involved, a person does what he does either because of the value satisfaction he experiences in doing it or because its accomplishment is of importance to him as a step towards the fulfillment of further purposes involving greater value satisfaction.

As indicated earlier, values of some kind are inherent in every purposeful action, although they may not be apparent. Values can be defined as "why" we do what we do, the "what for's" of being. In a way, they are "behind" purposes, more inclusive than purposes. If this is so, we are led to the necessity of considering what is included in the "here-now" of a transactional situation where a person is acting to carry out a valueful purpose, or more explicitly what is the "here-now" of the value aspects of our experience.

We have seen that the "here-now" of a "transactional" situation is more inclusive than the "spatial-temporal" extension of the sequential matrix. The question arises: What is the nature of the matrix when values which give rise to purposes that lead to the initiation of sequential events are included in the situation? Or the question might be phrased: How do values enter into and exist in the "here-now"? Or what is the extension of the matrix that includes values?"

We should repeat the observation that one characteristic of values is that they permeate the whole and every aspect of every "objective," sequential or transactional (purposeful) situation. Another characteristic of values is their *constancy*. Our values can remain the same, or we can hold to the values amid continually changing space and time, "thatness" and "thereness," "here-now" or the "present" or "presence," or what we are in the midst of, or in the particular sequential events we initiate, or in the particular transactional situation, or our immediate "how-to-do" purposes.

The nature of values may alter, but their alterations are not governed by changes in time and space or objects, or sequential or transactional events, or the accomplishment of particular purposes. Further, with such alteration, the basic value forms are retained. It would appear that our most basic values—those that play their role throughout our lives—were in the "code script" of our chromosome structure when we were born as human beings (cf. Schroedinger) and had their ultimate origin at least at the beginning of biological time.

The constancy aspect of values seems to be the factor that relates one's different and changing Transactional Matrices. The constancy aspect of values seems to be the factor that relates one's past "here-now's" ("past-present's") and one's future "here-now's" ("future-presents") to his immediate "here-now's" ("presents"). Values can be thought of as the "matrix" of one's "presences" or "here-now's." *

There is a further most important basic aspect of values that must be included: their "felt," sensed aspect. It is differences in this "felt" aspect of values which we use as a criterion in choosing one purposeful action rather than another. (Cf. *The "Why" of Man's Experience*, Chapter 8.) It is only when we pay attention to this "felt" aspect that values are the most reliable prognostic directives for purposeful action. It is the "felt" aspect in emotions, which can be thought of as "canned values," that determines our actions in the relatively determined aspects of our existence. It is always as "felt" that value catalyzes purposeful action.

The above brings us to still another aspect that must be considered and inquired into. That is the existence of "felt" values in concrete experiences apart from any apparent limited purposeful aspect. One example that comes to mind is one's "esthetic" experience in concrete natural situations, not involving any type of works of art, when one experiences the felt "beauty" † of the situation, whether landscape or interior, or person, or social behavior. Such all-enveloping and sometimes most poignantly felt values are what every artist tries to communicate in his works of art, what prophets and saints have so often experienced—St. Francis, for instance. Apparently they exist without any relation to limited purposes and their accomplishment.‡ They can exist, of course, in relation to the accomplishing of purposes, but when they do the outcome of the purpose becomes secondary. The person is satisfied with the valueful aspects of his effort whether they lead to success or failure. On "lower levels," so to speak, their absence in much of the competitive modern athletic activities, where the only value, if it is a true value, is related to the purpose of winning, is apparently why so much of modern athletics is decadent.

Whatever the conclusions that are reached on these points, it appears that the extension of the "Value Matrix" is more inclusive than the extension of the "Transactional" purposeful matrix and that it is more inherently present in our "here-now's"—more immanent.

An attempt has been made to indicate diagrammatically this more inclusive extension in Figure 5 by the three-dimensional cube (dot-dashed lines) called "Value Matrix" encompassing the two-dimensional circular

---

* As values permeate a social group, they can be thought of as the *"social value matrix."* So far we have been considering only "matrices" of unique individuals. But as an individual exists only as an aspect of the social whole, it would seem that what has been said would also hold for the concretely existing social group. Social values can be thought of as the "matrix" that relates the "presences" or "here-now's" of different individuals.

† Or it may have been that one's "felt" value was repulsion.

‡ Cf. Wordsworth's "emotion recollected in tranquility."

surface marked "Transactional (Purpose) Matrix" which encompasses the extension indicated by the short-dashed lines marked "Sequential Matrix," which encompasses the extension indicated by the dotted lines marked "Perceptual Matrix."

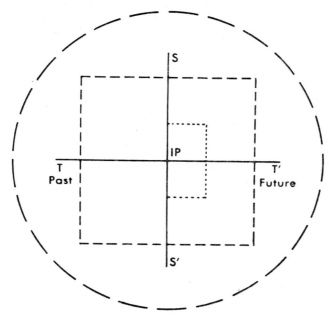

FIG. 5. VALUE MATRIX

### Concluding Observations: Emergence

In our above considerations of the "here-now" and how the various matrices "enter into" it, we have considered the "roles" of the various matrices without taking into account any possibility of alteration of their "forms," i.e., we have not included the phenomenon of emergence. The possibility for emergence exists because of the indeterminism of the "present" and what may be.

In the indeterminism of the present there is a possibility of alteration, "flow," of the "up-to-now" matrix forms. Such possibility exists where valueful purposes are *not* fulfilled (*un*successful functioning) due to inadequate prognosis. Different emotional reactions are associated with inadequate prognosis in the different matrices. For example:

With the Perceptual Matrix—illusions.
With the Sequential Matrix—surprise.

With the Transactional Matrix—frustration.

With the Value Matrix—disappointment.

Under what conditions should the feeling of guilt be associated with these different emotional reactions?

It would seem that this whole matter of emergence should be reconsidered in view of how the various matrices "enter into" the "here-now."

December 20, 1951

## LIFE

### (Some Tentative General Specifications Concerning It; with H.C.)

1. Life might be defined as a process in which an organism participates in the creation of an environment through which it can carry out its purposes.

2. In this participation, our relationship with the undetermined future is one of prognosis only, not of disclosure.

3. In every concrete situation, our prognoses as to the undetermined future are based on past experiences in similar situations.

4. This view avoids the difficulty encountered if we bifurcate reality by assuming that the various aspects of our environment are "givens" which exist "out there" in their own right apart from us and are disclosed to us by our senses.

5. In general, the success and fulfillment of our living is related to the reliability of our prognoses.

6. In every concrete situation, the reliability of an individual's prognosis is related to the number and consistency of significances that have occurred in similar situations in the past. The weighted averages of these past experiences are cues for the interpretation of the significances of the immediate situation.

7. Concrete situations, where the significances of past experiences are conflicting, provide the opportunity for an individual to choose between alternative possibilities.

8. The nature of the prognoses and choices differs in the various aspects of behavior into which the process of living may be usefully abstracted.

9. We may usefully differentiate the process of living into:

|  |  |
|---|---|
| a. Perceiving | d. Valuing |
| b. Prehending | e. Acting |
| c. Purposing | f. Emerging |

10. In life, each of these aspects is interrelated with every other. No one aspect functions except for the function it has served, serves, and will serve all the other aspects.

11. These abstracted aspects may be referred to as "matrices" (instead of "fields" or "levels")—used in the sense of "an enveloping element within which something originates, takes form, or develops" (Webster)—because of the creation taking place in each of them and because each of these matrices is more inclusive than space and time.

12. Each of these matrices involves characteristic experiences: Perceiving involves prognosis of "thatness" and "thereness"; choice between sense of surety (no conflicting indications, nonillusory) and sense of lack of surety (conflicting indications, illusory).

a. Prehending sequential events involves prognosis of following events; choice between sense of certainty that certain consequences will follow and sense of doubt that certain consequences will follow (reliability of prehension of sequents increased by scientific inquiry).

b. Purposing involves prognosis of worthwhileness of doing; choice between probable value satisfactions following the accomplishment of the intention.

c. Valuing involves weighing on basis of "conscience," "the still small voice," "rightness," "goodness," "morality," "truth."

d. Acting involves prognosis of adequacy of action patterns to insure success of intention.

e. Emerging involves results from activities by which sensed inadequacies, hitches, mistakes, or failures are overcome and which bring forth emergent value aspects of concrete behavioral situations. Such activities are the exercise of choice, admission, and recognition of mistakes, perseverance, faith.

13. Because of the unique past experience which every individual brings to an occasion and because the individual alone makes his prognoses and choices, an understanding of living and behavior is possible only from the first-person point of view.

14. From the first-person point of view, behavior occurs as follows:

a. Desire to bring forth and to experience the value aspects which are potential in every concrete behavioral situation;

b. Which effect the selection and nature of his purposing;

c. Which effect the selection and nature of his prehending of sequents;

d. Which effect the selection and nature of his perceiving;

e. Acting.

15. From the third person's point of view (the impersonal, "scientific" approach), behavior is generally studied as follows:

a. Impingements from environment;      d. Purposes;
b. Perception;      e. Action.
c. Prehension of sequents;

April 23, 1952

### ON THE "PERCEPTION AND PREHENSION OF THE INORGANIC AND ORGANIC SIGNIFICANCE—OBJECTS AND PERSONS"

A perceived person, just as a perceived "object," is an aggregate of specific differentiated characteristics, i.e., adjectives and adverbs, which define to the observer the unique potential sequential significances he can make use of as varying purposeful occasions may require. That is, every person has specific characteristics such as length, shape, and weight, etc., just as an object has, which define to the observer the unique potential sequential significances that he can make use of as varying purposeful occasion may require.

But beyond these sequential characteristics common to both objects and persons, persons have other most significant sequential characteristics that "objects" do not have, namely, those arising from the fact that persons have purposes, urges, and value desires, which objects do not have, and that persons make choices while objects do not. Moreover, the sequential significances of objects are fixed on repetitions; those of persons are constantly varying. Objects are not interested in the observer but are passive, so to speak. Still further, the observer is not significant to the perceived object. On the other hand the observer may be very significant to the perceived person; i.e., the observed person may be most interested in the observer and may be aggressive.

It follows that the specific differentiated characteristics that constitute the aggregate of a perceived "person," which the observer must be potentially able to take account of in order to behave effectively, are not only a greater number but are of an entirely different nature from those characteristics that constitute the aggregate of a perceived "object."

May 1, 1952

### On Differences in the Comprehension of Sequential Significances

The characteristic phenomena involved in the comprehension of sequential significances vary greatly with the nature of the sequents that are comprehended even when only inorganic phenomena are involved.

For instance, consider the length of durations involved from the time the consequential significances are first prehended through the taking place of the following events to the alterations in the assumptive form world. In the examples of the dropping balls this was only the matter of a few minutes.

On the one hand the corresponding duration may be much shorter—only seconds, as would be the case where an observer experiences an automobile accident, or fractions of seconds if he is observing atomic activity. On the other hand, the duration may be much longer, involving years, as where an observer experiences sequential significances of events following a hurricane, for instance, that took place early in one's life, or thousands of years following historic events, such as an ice age.

Consideration of these comprehensions of sequential significances of longer durations makes it apparent, first, that each of us is in the midst of sequential significances the consequences of which have not yet occurred; second, that many sequential significances are occurring at the same time and are inter-effective; third, that the consequences of many sequential significances are but the preceding events in a series of future sequential significances.

These future series may be emergent and therefore incapable of prehension, or [they may be] cyclical, periodic, in which case the as yet unoccurred following event is not only prehended but completely relied upon to occur, as day after night.

It would seem that periodic sequential significances are quite analogous to "objects," as we have defined them, "the same yesterday, today and tomorrow," the difference being that where "objective" significances continuously provide us with sequential possibilities for carrying out different purposes, periodic sequential significances provide us periodically with sequential significances for carrying out the same purposes. Could we say that objects are constant in the dimension of changing events and that periodic sequential significances are constant in the dimension of purpose? Is it that our various physiological periodicities—breathing, heart beats, digestive and other rhythms—are periodic sequential significances that have been found to be so efficacious in furthering a purpose that they have become reflexes?

May 2, 1952

### PERIODIC SEQUENTIAL SIGNIFICANCES AND A BIFURCATED UNIVERSE

Periodic sequential significances, which we take for granted and of which we are in general unaware, constitute the prehensive base, background of our *non*-periodic sequential significances that provide us with prognoses for carrying out particular non-continuous purposes which supplement our basic continuous purposes.

Consideration of periodic sequential significance, whether reflex physiological rhythms or periodic sequences of which we are aware, as day following night, or celestial cycles, faces one directly with the questions, first, as to whether in the last analysis cyclical following events don't exist in their own right apart from the observer, and, second, whether the bifurcation between the subjective experiences of prehension of sequential significances and what is taking place of external environmental following events be resolved into a unified whole.

We all know day will follow night with all the ensuing sequential effects, so how can we in any way be responsible for the sequences that follow? Can we do more than just prehend them because they are bound to follow? Offhand, this seems quite obvious. But is it? What do we mean by "day follows night"? What are we referring to by "the consequences that take place" when daylight follows darkness? What phenomena are we referring to when we use the word "prehending"?

When we use the words "day follows night," we are referring to an abstract generalized conception based on Greenwich time, as abstract as a spatial map which we have spoken of in our considerations of the perception of "thatnesses" at their "therenesses." At certain seasons of the year in the Arctic day doesn't follow night; light seasons follow dark seasons. Speaking exactly, day doesn't follow night in the same way at any two different points on the earth's surface and never repeats in the same way in following day and night periods.

As to the consequences that take place when daylight follows darkness, they are infinite and, speaking exactly, they are never the same on two different points on the earth's surface or on any following day and night periods.

When we use the word "prehending," we use it as referring to an abstract generalized conception relative to the understanding of a generalized average man at no particular point on the earth with no particular purposes.

Concretely, sequential significances are phenomenal processes engaged in by a particular unique human being with particular unique purposes and values at a specific point on the earth's surface at a particular time in history, whose prehension of sequential significances is specifically conditioned by the background, assumed form world, he brings to that specific situation.

It would seem from the above considerations that even in the prehension of periodic, cyclical significances the consequences prehended are not prehended just because they exist in their own right apart from the individual and are bound to follow; and [it would also seem] that there is not a bifurcation between the subjective experiences of prehension of sequential significances and the taking place of external environmental following events, but that the bifurcation which exists in abstract conceptualization resolves into a unified whole in concrete experience.

May 5, 1952

### ON THE CONSTANCY OF OBJECTS

As was pointed out earlier, it is because "objects" are the same "yesterday, today and tomorrow," i.e., because of their constancy, that "objects" have significance, are seen as "objects."

But considered as something that exists externally in its own right, we know that no object remains constant. No inanimate object, from atoms through minerals, through such things as wood or stone or pyramids or plants or solar systems, have absolute constancy. As was pointed out, the constancy aspect of objects is only an assumption, an assumption of probability of constancy, that is confirmed or altered with every visual experience.

Whether or not in a concrete situation "objects" are significant depends upon whether the duration of constancy is such that the sequential characteristics of the object can be made use of in potential following events that in turn can be made use of in the carrying out of particular purposes. For some purposes only objects having long duration of constancy are useful, e.g., a file. For other purposes only objects having short duration of constancy are useful, e.g., soap.

Because objects are characterized by being the same "yesterday, today, and tomorrow," we think of them remaining the same in time. But wouldn't it be more correct to think of objects as remaining the same in spite of, *apart* from, time and to use the word "constancy" in connection with objects as referring to their endurance in the "milieu" of following events, or in other words, to conceive of "objects" as existing in the "milieu" or dimension of events?

May 7, 1952

### Experiencing of Sequential Significances and Awareness of Sequential Significances Apart from Experiencing Them

From our earlier considerations it appeared that perception could be differentiated into stimulus perception and ultra-stimulus perception; stimulus perception being our awareness of "thatness-thereness" significances registered in our Form World, reactivated by stimulus excitations from our environment and ultra-stimulus perception being our awareness of "thatness-thereness" significances registered in our Form World reactivated by attention because of our capacity to attend to their relevance to immediate purposes (importance) ("subjective").* It was also pointed out that these two types of perception are mutually necessary and supplementary, ultra-stimulus perception providing the perspective background for the "thatness-thereness" significances of our stimulus perception, and stimulus perception continually keeping the "thatness-thereness" aspects of our Form World up to date, so to speak, with the changes in significances in our environment that are continuously taking place.

It appears that our comprehension of sequential significances can also be differentiated into two mutually necessary supplementary aspects. The sequential significances registered in our Form Worlds can be reactivated and brought into awareness either by our concrete experiencing of sequential significances or by our attention ("subjective").

To explain: My comprehension of sequential significances experienced when I watch the bouncing balls described above is an example of sequential significances registered in my Form World being reactivated and brought into my awareness by concrete experiencing of a happening (following event) that is occurring.

Examples of sequential significances registered in my Form World that are reactivated by attention would be my awareness when I give

* "The act of bringing something into clear awareness." The significances are brought into awareness because of their relevancy to immediate purposes.

my attention to happenings (following events) that may occur in the future or have occurred in the past, or that I conceive as now occurring somewhere else. To be more specific: Before I drop the ball, I can prehend the sequential significances that I will experience when I do drop it. After I have watched the bouncing putty ball drop, hit the floor, and bounce, I can reactivate that registered experience that occurred in the past by attention. Or I can envisage another person, in the laboratory upstairs, dropping the ball and the sequential phenomena that are taking place.

We are continually bringing to our awareness by attention sequential significances. I prehend that when I turn the handle of the door, it will open so I can go out of my office. I can (by attention) activate my recorded experiences that when I short-circuited the current in the laboratory, a fuse blew out. From my chair here in the office I can envisage my wife getting lunch ready at home.

I can give my attention to the sequential significances of every "object" in my "thatness-thereness" field of ultra-stimulus perception, and since such objects are "constant," "yesterday, today and tomorrow," the sequential significances of which I may be aware may be those that have taken place or may be taking place or may take place in the future. These registered past, present, and future sequential significances constitute a systematically interrelated whole within a spatial pattern which is based on my field of ultra-stimulus, "thatnesses-at-their-therenesses" significances, and perspectively structured from my immediate unique point of view both spatial and in the occurrence of events. The total structure can be thought of as the "sequential" aspect of my Form World.

It is apparent that the nature of the sequential significances that every individual registers differ markedly from those registered by any other individual. It follows that the potentially prehensible sequential means (how-to-do's) for carrying out similar purposes also markedly differ.

Just as with "thatness-thereness" significances we like to imagine an all-knowing mind that is aware in an abstracted conceptual way of a spatial map not only of all the "therenesses" of all "thatnesses" which all individuals have a knowledge of, but also of all the "therenesses" of "thatnesses" that might be discovered, so we like to imagine an all-knowing mind that is aware in an abstracted conceptual way of a complete specification integrating not only all the sequential significances ever experienced by anyone, but also all the sequential significances that might ever be discovered. It is a relief to realize that modern science has discovered indeterminancy.

With these considerations of our awareness of sequential significances as differentiated from our concrete experiencing of specific sequential significances, we will turn to a consideration, firstly, of their interdependence and, secondly, of the role played by concrete experiences of sequential significances in keeping us up to date, so to speak, with the ever-changing nature of following events that are continually taking place in our environment.

May 12, 1952

### ON PERIODIC SEQUENTIAL SIGNIFICANCES

Periodic sequential significances which we take for granted and in general are unaware of constitute the prehensive base, background, of our *non*-periodic sequential significances that provide us with prognoses for carrying out non-continuous purposes that supplement our basic continuous purposes.

Consideration of periodic sequential significances re-raises an ever-recurring question. From the foregoing considerations of *non*-periodic sequential phenomena I am quite satisfied that they "take place," so to speak, only because of my participation in them.

But when I consider periodic sequential events such as day following night, season following season, and tides following tides at periodic intervals, the question again comes to my mind whether in the last analysis periodic sequential events don't exist in their own right apart from myself or any observer experiencing them. If they do, perhaps in the last analysis non-periodic sequential events also exist in their own right apart from any observer, and in regard to both periodic and non-periodic sequential events there is a bifurcation between subjective experience and environmental conditions that cannot be resolved into a unified whole.

This question arises in respect to periodic sequential events because the aspect of repetition at specific time intervals would seem to be possible only in respect to phenomena completely impersonal in nature, existing in otherness entirely apart from any observer.

But this apparently evident conclusion is based on the assumption that such environmental events do repeat and such an assumption is contrary to all the scientific evidence that in the otherness of environmental nature no events ever repeat—"Nature never repeats"—from those that take place in millionths of seconds in atomic activity to those that take place in billions of years in the stellar universe.

This confusion apparently arises from our not being clear as to what we are referring to by the words "periodic sequential events," or more specifically, what we are referring to by such words as "the periodically repeated events of the rising and setting of the sun, day following night, with its accompanying following events."

According to our present beliefs, which are quite different from those that were formerly held and are continually changing, (1) we are referring, in regard to the sun, not to a body that is rising and setting, i.e., rotating about the earth, but to a relatively stationary body, although it is itself hurtling through space and is itself an ever-changing mass of atomic activity; (2) in regard to the earth, we are referring not to a stationary body but to a rotating mass of continually changing atomic activity rotating about a wobbling axis at continually changing rates of speed; (3) in regard to what follows the sun's rising, we are referring to what takes place on a varying limited portion of the earth's surface, due to the ever-varying impinging atomic activity from the sun; (4) this involves alteration of the atomic activity of the various collections of inorganic and organic conglomerations resulting from the impingement of the sun's radiations; (5) and what we are referring to by the words "periodically recurring" is not apparent, because nothing that occurs either in the preceding or following events ever repeats.

It would appear from the above that in purely environmental events there *is* (1) no repetition, (2) no sequential phenomena, (3) no periodicity. Consideration seems to make it evident that repetition, sequential phenomena, and periodicity are essentially products of organic activity, arising from their relation with their ever-changing non-repetitive, non-sequential, non-periodic environment. These are man-made patterns useful to him in carrying out his purposes.

Modern theories of relativity seem to provide scientific evidence that periodic time is not something that exists purely environmentally in its own right. But in spite of that evidence we still all seem to cling to a belief in the totally "objective" nature of periodic time and all the dates and calendars we live by. However, such a belief seems impossible for us to hold in regard to our periodic physiological reflex rhythms, as heart beats and breathing, through those of hunger and reproduction, through those that have been culturally developed to insure the carrying out of purposes, both innate and acquired, as exemplified by periodic repetition of exercises having to do with our personal and social material well-being and continuance. Then there are those periodically repeated exercises and forms having to do with the existence of our value aspects, the perpetuation of which is largely the responsibility of the organized religions. And beyond our personal experience and yet within our "biological" existence there is the periodicity of both birth and death. Though we have no experience to grasp the precedents of birth, we experience its consequences. We are aware of the precedents of death, but have no experience that enables us to prehend its consequences. But in spite of the fact that we cannot be aware of either the precedents or consequences of life and death, it seems they have all the characteristics of other periodic sequences of which we know and must play corresponding roles.

Collateral to these considerations it may be worthwhile to think about how "objects," sequential significances, and purposes and values, both periodic and non-periodic, come into our awareness.

"Objects" are always potentially present, coming into awareness when we open our eyes or give them our attention. In comparison, non-periodic sequential significances are not always present, but come into our awareness in general only if their particular nature is relevant to our particular varying existent purposes, with their accompanying varying value awarenesses. Periodic sequential significances related to purposes come into our awareness only periodically when the periodic purposes they play a role in carrying out need to be executed, e.g., reproduction. All such purposes, above the reflex levels, are accompanied by value awarenesses, which we also experience periodically, but only periodically.

But it would seem that beyond these values, periodic and non-periodic, which are responsible for their accompanying purposes, there is a type of value characterized by "faith" that is neither intermittent nor periodic, which is always potentially existent to be experienced. This is the type of value that sustains and directs us when purposes and their directive values have become hollow and lost their significance, as they do so often in our lives and especially "in the valley of the shadow of death."

It would appear that this constantly potential type of value is what the great prophets were capable of continuously being aware of, and it is what all of us seek in what might be called our religious activities and our searching for God.

The above consideration may seem far afield from the phenomena we are referring to by "periodic sequential events involving the inorganic aspects of nature," but it is felt that the nature of such phenomena cannot be comprehended without some understanding of the background in which they occur.

### SIMILARITIES AND DIFFERENCES BETWEEN STIMULUS AND ULTRA-STIMULUS COMPREHENSION OF SEQUENTIAL EVENTS

*Definitions*

Stimulus comprehending * of sequential events refers to awareness of registered sequential significances reactivated by impingements from environmental following events. An example of such comprehension is when I watch a ball fall, strike the surface, and rebound.

Ultra-stimulus comprehension of sequential events refers to awareness of registered sequential significances reactivated by attention † because of their relevance to immediate purposes. An example of such comprehension is when I envisage what will happen if the glass ash tray, which is dangerously near the edge of my office table, falls on the floor. (Glass bowl better example; no stimulus whatsoever.)

The word prehension is reserved to refer to awareness of what one expects the nature of the following event will be (consequence) after having experienced the preceding event of a sequence of events.

*Similarities*

1. AS TO NATURE AND ORIGIN. The sequential significances of which we are aware in stimulus and ultra-stimulus comprehension of sequential events are of the same origin and nature. They are significances of certain environmental following events that are registered in our higher mental processes and continue to exist on the subconscious level. The significances are subject to being reactivated—brought to the awareness level. They differ primarily only in that the phenomena involved in their reactivation differ. In stimulus comprehension they are reactivated by stimulus patterns given rise to by impingements from environmental following events. In ultra-stimulus comprehension they are reactivated by attention directed by purpose and value. This difference will be gone into later when we consider the differences between stimulus and ultra stimulus.

2. AS TO UNIQUENESS AND CONCRETENESS. The sequential significances of which we are aware in both stimulus and ultra-stimulus comprehension

---

* The word "experiencing" might be used in place of the word "comprehending," but it seemed better to use a word analogous to "perception" that connotes "awareness" and that could also be used both when the awareness is due to environmental impingements and when it is due to attention.

† Initiated by immediate purposes.

are similar in that they are unique, concrete and specific as differentiated from abstratced universals, either universalized assumptions or conceptualized forms. For example, my awareness of what will happen if the glass ash tray at the edge of the table falls on the floor is as unique and concrete and specific as is my awareness of the bouncing ball at which I am directly looking.

3. AS PROGNOSTIC DIRECTIVES. The prehensive aspects of the significances of which we are aware in stimulus and ultra-stimulus comprehension of sequential events have the same operational function; namely, they both provide prognostic directives for purposeful action. My prehension that the ash tray may fall provides me with prognostic directives to move it away from the edge of the table.

4. AS TO "REALITY." The significances of which we are aware in both cases are equally "real" and "important" to us, i.e., the possible breaking of the glass ash tray is as "real" and "important" to me as is my prehension that the ball will bounce. Together these two types of prehensive significances of which we are actually aware and which have the potentiality of being brought into awareness constitute what we conceptually think of as the "objective events occurring in our environment." They can also be thought of as the "sequential" aspect of our Form World.

*Dissimilarities*

1. AS TO THE PRESENCE AND LACK OF IMPINGEMENTS AND STIMULUS EXCITATION. What appears offhand to be the greatest difference between stimulus and ultra-stimulus comprehension of sequential events is that in the former our awareness is of sequential significances of "environmental following events" from which impingements from the environmental events have been or are stimulating our receptors; while in the latter our awareness is of sequential significances of "environmental following events" from which no impingements are stimulating our receptors.

For example: (1) Of a stimulus comprehension of a sequential event. My comprehension of sequential significances in watching a ball fall, hit a surface, and rebound involves (a) my perceptual awareness of the ball as an "object"; (b) after a lapse of time my awareness of the ball falling and the formulation of a prehension of how it will bounce, with associated directives as to how to act to catch it; (c) after another lapse of time my awareness of its hitting a surface; (d) after another lapse of time * my awareness of its bouncing, followed by a confirmation or alteration

* Depending upon the nature of the sequential event, these lapses of time may vary from seconds to years.

of sequential aspects of my Form World. Each of these succeeding awarenesses is activated by impingements from environmental events.

(2) Of an ultra-stimulus comprehension of a sequential event. The following example occurred yesterday. My wife and I were on our way to lunch with some friends when she remembered she had left a spherical flower vase on a table where the sun would strike it later in the day and possibly set fire to the table as it had done once before. We both at once comprehended the various following events as a single unified sequential whole. Logically the order of the following events would be (a) awareness of the sun as an object; (b) after a lapse of time its moving to a position in the sky from which its rays would come through the window; (c) after a lapse of time the focusing of the sun's rays on the table; (d) after a lapse of time the table catching fire and our house burning down. Actually we thought of the burning of the house at the very beginning. As soon as we arrived at our friends' house we telephoned home and had the shade pulled so the sun's rays would not strike the vase. Our awareness of none of these succeeding events was activated by impingements from environmental events. We all have similar comprehensions of sequential events that had already completely occurred or which would occur in the future.

With these two examples in mind we are faced by the question: What is the real difference between stimulus and ultra-stimulus comprehension of sequential events? Or a more specific question might be: In furthering effective purposeful action, what role is played by awareness of sequential significances activated by stimulus impingements beyond that played by awareness of sequential significances reactivated by attention directed by purpose?

It would appear that in all situations where the following environmental event (consequence) turns out to be what was prehended (expected), the role played by sequential awareness activated by stimulus impingements cannot be differentiated from the role played by sequential awareness reactivated by attention in respect to the effectivity of the prehension in furthering the immediate effective purposeful action.

However, in those situations where the following environmental event (consequence) turns out to be other than what was prehended, i.e., where there was misprehension, it would seem apparent that such faulty prehension could become known only through either direct stimulus relation with the nature of the environmental following event as it takes place or otherwise learning the nature of the following event after it has occurred, through external stimulus excitation by hearing, word of mouth, or reading. Apparently whether or not the registered sequential significances are reactivated by stimulus impingements or by attention makes no essential difference in my awareness of sequential significances, if, in the stimulus comprehension of sequential significances, the consequence that was prehended occurs; e.g., if, conversant as I am with the resiliency of standard tennis balls, I drop one and watch it rebound, there is no essential difference between the sequential significances I comprehend, am aware of, than there is if I shut my eyes before I drop it and envisage the sequential significances I prehend will take place.

While in the above cases there is no difference in the sequential significances of which I am aware, there is a difference in respect to what happens to the sequential aspects of my Form World. If I watch it drop and actually experience that it bounced to just the height I expected it to bounce, my prehension as to the consequence of the sequential event is confirmed, becomes more "fixed," so to speak. When I simply envisage the sequential significances without experimental confirmation of my prehensions, the sequential aspects of my Form World are simply reactivated and are in no way affected.

This may be more apparent if we consider what happens when a person who has never seen bouncing putty before drops a ball of it. If he does so with his eyes shut, his ultra stimulus comprehension, his envisagement of the sequential event, will be of one in which the ball doesn't bounce. The sequential aspect of his Form World will not be affected. If, on the other hand, he watches the ball, his stimulus comprehension of the sequential event will be of one in which, much to his surprise, the ball does bounce, and the sequential aspect of his Form World will be altered in that his assumption as to the sequential characteristics of plastic material will have been altered.

In this case where the consequence was not what was expected, the sequential significances of which one is aware are quite different with stimulus comprehension and without.

This last case also makes it clearly evident that it is only through stimulus comprehension of sequential events that our sequential Form Worlds are kept up to date, so to speak, with our ever-changing environmental conditions. Without stimulus comprehension of sequential events we would live in our own ivory halls in which the sequential significances of objects remained forever the same in a world of events forever resulting in the same consequences and, one could add, a world of determined purposes and unalterable values.

Stimulus comprehension of sequential events is also indispensable when we make use of our prehension of consequents as ends to be accomplished in carrying out our purposes.

The reliability of our prehension of the characteristics of the final consequential event that we want to take place in the future depends upon the correctness of our comprehension of a chain of sequential events involving a comprehension of the preceding events in each of the links of the consequential chain. In these steps the reliability of our comprehension of the preceding events involves the prognostic reliability of our perception of the objects involved and their sequential significances. A correct prehension of events in the "now" makes for more reliable prognostics of future events (sequents).

We might conclude these considerations by noting: When in acting to accomplish a purpose, making use of sequential events, whether or not we are successful in accomplishing our end, our "objective and sequential Form World" will have been affected, and with it our "objective and sequential" environment of objects and events.

2. AS TO VIVIDNESS. In our considerations of perception we pointed out that "in general, stimulus perception is vivid, definite, manifest, while ultra stimulus perception is hazy, indefinite, obscure." This difference apparently does not hold in respect to our awareness in stimulus and ultra-stimulus comprehension of sequential significances.

Apparently the vividness of our awareness in stimulus comprehension of sequential significances varies greatly in different situations. That is, depending upon the situation, our comprehensions of sequential significances may be far from vivid or very vivid. For instance, as I walk about in my office I prehend that each time I shift my weight the floor on which I step will support my weight, but that prehension is far from vivid. On the other hand, when walking up a stream trout fishing, my prehensions as to the consequences of taking almost every step are quite vivid.

Similarly with ultra-stimulus comprehension of sequential significances. In the circumstances above described when my wife and I left a spherical flower bowl near the window where the sun's rays might set fire to the table, our ultra-stimulus comprehension of the sequential significances was most vivid.

It would seem that the vividness of our comprehension of sequential significances is associated with at least the three factors:

1. The prognostic reliability of our prehensions. When it is sufficiently reliable we don't need to take awareness of the sequential significances. If not, we do.

2. How far in the future the consequences of the sequential significances will occur.

3. The importance to us of the consequences of the sequential significances.

It is its importance that makes it vivid.

IN REGARD TO A PARTICULAR TYPE OF CRITICISM OF OUR DEMONSTRATIONS

Certain persons, many of them psychologists, after experiencing one or more of our demonstrations, while they express an interest in their novelty, very firmly assert that all they disclose is that our past experience plays a role in what we perceive, which was discovered long ago and is now universally recognized by psychology. Although they don't explicitly say so, they imply it is too bad we are wasting our time and effort.

We have neither time nor opportuntiy to undertake the long explanations that would be necessary to communicate to such persons why we do not think we are wasting our time. Moreover, if we had they would probably not be interested in listening to us.

It does seem possible, however, that we might formulate a short statement for such persons, raising questions for them to answer that might show them that the whole matter is not quite so evident and simple as they conceive it, and that the purpose of the demonstration is to answer questions which perhaps they have not as yet formulated.

The first question to ask them might be: "How does past experience play a role in perception and what is the role that it plays?"

The second question might be: "What is the role that our environment plays in perception?"

The third question might be: "Does past experience *determine* what we perceive?"

The fourth question might be: "If past experience does *determine* what we perceive, how can you avoid the solipsistic philosophy attributed to Berkeley?"

The fifth question might be: "How can our environment play a role in perception without determining what we perceive?"

The sixth question might be: "Is our perception, in so far as it is effected by past experience, determined?"

The seventh question might be: "Is our perception in so far as it is effected by our environment, determined?"

The eighth question might be: "Is or is not our perception determined?"

The ninth question might be: "If our perception is determined, how can it be effected by purpose or choice?"

The tenth question might be: "If our perception is not determined, *how* is it effected by purpose and choice?"

This series of questions might be followed by a statement that it is these very questions and many more that the demonstrations were designed to throw some light on, and that, as far as we know, none of them have been effectively answered by any of the scientific disciplines or philosophy.

June 30, 1952

## On the "Milieu" of Sequential Events Conceptualized and Sensed Aspects

In our consideration of perception it was pointed out that the perception of a particular object, or objects—the awarenesses of the "therenesses" of "thatnesses"—apart from awareness of an extended thatness-thereness preference "field" lacks essential behavioral significance; e.g., if a person is lost in the woods, although such a person has most reliable perceptual awareness of the "objects" within his range of vision and their spatial relationship to himself and each other, he still lacks an essential for effective behavior because he has no sense of the relationship of what he is perceiving to his extended "field" of ultra-stimulus perception. We speak of such a person as having lost his *sense* of orientation.

It would be more accurate to say that he is unable to integrate his immediate perceptual awareness with his total perceptual background. What a person immediately perceives is specifically and definitely in his awareness. However, his perceptual background is at best only partly in awareness at one time. Moreover the relationship between his immediate perceptual awareness and his perceptual background is a sensed awareness and not a conceptualized one.

Similarly with the comprehension of a sequential event—the comprehension of a particular sequential event apart from awareness of an extended "milieu" of related sequential events lacks essential behavioral significance; e.g., the comprehension of the sequential event of starting an automobile apart from an awareness of where you are going to drive, or the getting to a particular town unrelated to further sequential events that will follow from your being in the town, lacks essential behavioral significance.

It is apparent that every particular sequential event in which we are involved is but a link in a chain of sequential events which extends back in experience, and forward in anticipation. The consequences of prior sequential events have occurred. The consequences of future sequential events are hoped for. The specific sequential events of which we are aware that constitute the chain of sequential events become more and more dim in awareness both as they recede into the past and extend into the future. We can take account of the immediately preceding and following sequential events conceptually. But the significance of the relationship of those further back and forward we can only sense as constituting directional flow, becomingness, unless the sequential events are periodic, in which case they will be sensed as continuity of form. This might be called a "directional" sense as differentiated from orientation sense above considered.

We can conceptualize a specific sequential event and its consequence, end. But if we focus on a specific end and have no "directional" sense of its relationship to the "temporally" extended "milieu" of sequential events, we will be as lost as the man in the woods. Further, we cannot help but believe that the end on which we are focused will justify any means and we will be unable to become reoriented again.

The above-considered extension of the "milieu" of sequential events can be thought of in abstracted terms—as "following" or "temporal."

Besides the above-described "temporal" relationship of any particular sequential event to other past and future sequential events, every particular sequential event is contemporaneously related to many other sequential events; e.g., the sequential event of starting a car by turning the key or pressing a button is concurrent with the related sequential events of bodily adjustments, pressing the clutch lever, etc., or, in the case of a participant in an athletic contest, concurrent with the chain of sequential events involved in winning the game is the chain of sequential events involved in being a good sportsman. As we carry on our lives at any one now, we are always manipulating an indefinite number of concurrent chains of sequential events, such as taking care of our health, making a living, keeping happy family relations, etc.

Effectivity of the consequences of the combined concurrent sequential events is dependent on two phenomena that are suggested by the two types of examples given above.

First, it depends upon the occurrence of the events in the various chains within the duration in which they take place, i.e., their synchronization. In lay terms this is called "timing." For example: The operator of a power shovel, to effectively operate it, must synchronize the different parts of a number of different sequential events so that they supplement each other. This is equally true for athletes (golfers, for example) and in every activity involving a multiple of concurrent sequential events. Moreover, sense of "timing" is not simply a matter of temporal sequence alone; it includes also synchronized valuation of "force" of the various sequential events, i.e., golf stroke.

The executing of any one specific sequential event apart from its synchronization or relation to the extended "milieu" of other concurrently related sequential events is not only lacking in significance but incompatible with significance.

Our awareness of the synchronic relationship of any specific sequential event to other concurrently related sequential events is in general incapable of being conceptualized. In general, conceptualization of any one sequential event prevents awareness of synchronic relationship. For example, conceptual awareness of any single sequential aspect of a golf stroke, such as when to put one's wrists into the stroke, destroys one's "timing." "Timing" can only be sensed, not thought.

The second phenomenon playing a role in the effectivity of the consequence of the combined concurrent sequential events occurs under conditions where the happening in one or more of the concurrently occurring sequential events may lead to consequences incompatible with the consequence that would follow from the happening of the other concurrently occurring events. For instance, the athlete must weigh whether, in a concrete situation, to commit a transgression of the rules of the game for the sake of winning or not to and be a good sportsman.

Under such conditions the taking account of the results of the future extension of a multiple chain of sequential events comes into play. Such a taking account is apparently what we have described as a value-judgment, which again is characterized by being sensed and not thought, i.e., conceptualized. If two such conflicting consequents are conceptualized, they are differentiated, and as differentiated they stand in an "either-or" relationship; e.g., to win *or* to be a good sportsman. But the athlete has both to want to win and at the same time to be a good sportsman. This is possible only through a sensed value frame of reference so to speak; that is, from the more inclusive perspective from which conceptually abstracted sequential events which are apparently unreconcilable can be integrated; e.g., the multiple meaning of words used in poetry.

This integrated temporal and concurrent field of related sequential events cannot be conceptualized as a whole. In its "temporal extension" apparently we can conceptualize only one link at a time of one particular sequential chain. We are unable to conceptualize the beginning or end of the chain, which involves "whys." We can be aware of the "whys" and yet unable to conceptualize them.

This coincidental relationship between two or more chains of concurrent sequential events we do not seem to be able to conceptualize at all; e.g., an athlete in a concrete situation may be aware of how far to abandon his aim to win to accomplish his aim to be a good sportsman, but he can't conceptualize the relationship between the two sequential chains.

It seems that the above consideration may give us a toe hold on the nature of values and valuing. Isn't it through our value sense that we can take account of the significances of the temporally and concurrently extended field of sequential events in relation to one or more particular sequential events of which we can be conceptually aware?

It is because such a value sense integrates far more sequential significances than can be integrated conceptually that it has a higher order of prognostic reliability in formulating judgments and as a directive for action.

The above considerations may throw some light on the nature of the extended "milieu" of sequential events which envelop every abstracted sequential event and but for which any specific abstracted sequential event is without significance.

They also make apparent that we take account of this extended "milieu" through sensed responses and not conceptually; e.g., sense of "timing" and value sense of ends of sequential chains (c.f. sense of orientation in perception of "thereness-thatness"). It is these sensed responses which can be thought of as "extra-conceptual" processes that enable us to comprehend wholes and escape bifurcations at all levels and, because they take into account more inclusive perspectives, have greater prognostic reliability.

In any concrete situation the "milieu" of sequential events which each person takes into account is an aspect of that person's Form World which he brings to the occasion. It is determined by that person's prior experience and is uniquely different from that of every other person.

The Form World is affected (confirmed or altered) by every comprehension of sequential event.

In the above analysis of the "milieu" of sequential events the sequential events that were considered involved only inorganic phenomena (repetitious natural following events significant to man or sequential events following from the use of man-made artifacts).

It is apparent that the "milieu" of sequential events in social situations involving the purposes and values of other persons would be of a more complicated and of a different nature involving not a single but a two-way reciprocal relationship between the person making use of sequential events to carry out his purposes and the other person or persons involved.

July 1, 1952

## HUMANIZED NATURE AND RAW NATURE

The hypothesis that organisms put order into unordered nature assumes the existence of a non-humanized environment, of ever-changing never-repeating following events which man humanizes in terms of sequential events, as if it were some kind of an ultimate "reality" beyond and more basic than our humanized environment.

However, it should be borne in mind that this ever-changing non-humanized "reality" is significant only as differentiated from repeatable humanized "reality," i.e., in terms of a negative definition. It seems possible that it may be definable in terms of the more ultimate reality of motives and values which we do not yet understand.

July 11, 1952

## ON BIFURCATION AND HUMANIZATION
### (With H.C.)

The "environment," the "otherness" around us, only becomes differentiated into parts or "objects" ("thatnesses" at "therenesses") in so far as we learn the potential sequential significances of aspects of the environment in order to carry out valueful, purposeful action.

And to the extent that aspects of the "environment" acquire potential human sequential significances (become differentiated into "objects"), a person can think of them as existing apart from himself just as he can think of the purposes and values of other people as existing apart from himself.

There is a great difference between this view and the usual view that "things exist in their own right." For the latter, traditional view means that things exist in their own right apart from the role they play in human living. In our view, things exist for us. We are aware of them only *in so far as* they are related to man's purposes. If you leave out human significance, you leave out all constancy, all repeatability, all form.

From this point of view, "correspondence" between aspects of the environment and subjective states is to be interpreted in terms of correspondence in potential significance, not correspondence between impingements–physiological events–subjective states.

In the "environment" there is an infinity of following (*not* sequential) events that no one person can ever know entirely. Each person picks out from these following events those particular repeatable aspects useful for his purposes. Those he picks out will depend on his capacities, training, opportunities, etc. Each person picks out the purposeful values in the environment that suit his purposes.

From the point of view of behavior, all that is available to a person is his unique Form World. In any one situation, we only get a prognosis of what will later be disclosed from further experience and action in carrying out our purposes.

Objects acquire a "human" aspect when they become differentiated out of the environment, when their potential sequential significances are learned. These sequential significances are repeatable and useful for a person.

In this sense, then, instead of having "conquered" nature, man has only "humanized" nature. There is a special "humanness" about artifacts, for man has put sequential significances into them. We give up earlier created artifacts when new ones with greater human significances are created. In this sense, man is constantly making his environment more "human."

It would seem to follow from the above that every aspect of our environment is humanized. What a person is aware of now (from first-person point of view) refers to humanized aspects of the environment which he knows exist apart from himself. "Humanizing" the environment is perhaps a preferable expression to "creating" the environment (as we have stated previously) because "humanizing" implies the personal and social use of the function described.

As individuals, we are constantly humanizing our own unique environments to carry out valueful purposes. As the environment becomes humanized, it constitutes part of our registered Form World.

The extent to which a person humanizes the immediate environment depends upon what he brings to the situation. An aspect of the environment becomes humanized above the how-to-do level when valueful purposes are brought in.

The extent to which we are aware of our environment is proportional to the extent we have been able to humanize it. We might say that the "totality" of the environment of higher organisms is more inclusive.

The word "social" refers to the human aspects of the environment when two or more people share, are aware of, the same potential human aspects of it. Mores, customs, rituals, laws are registered and preserved forms of sequential significances involving other persons as distinguished from sequential significances not involving other persons.

The above considerations appear to make intellectually acceptable both (1) why, from the behavioral point of view, all a person has available to him is what he brings to a situation—his prognosis; and (2) the existence at the same time of a humanized environment apart from the behaving individual and within which he carries out his purposive behavior.

This point of view apparently includes the essence of Berkeley's philosophy and yet avoids the sensed unreasonableness and unreality of the solipsistic view.

October 18, 1952

FIRST PERSON'S EXPERIENCE AND ANOTHER PERSON'S VIEW THEREOF

In a concrete situation: (1) "What does a person know, what is he aware of about himself and his behavior?" and (2) "What does or can another person know about a First Person's behavior which the First Person does not or cannot know?" It may be helpful to consider more specific examples of behavior as differentiated on the (a) perceptual level (matrix), (b) sequential level or matrix, (c) transactional level, purposing acting level, or matrix, (d) value level or matrix.

In the following note we will consider what the answer is to the above questions on the perceptual level.*

A more specific statement of what we are interested in would be: "On the perceptual level what is the First Person cognizant of and what is another person cognizant of both in regards to what the First Person is cognizant of and what the First Person is not cognizant of?

We will consider concrete situations in which both the First Person and the Other Person are involved from their respective operational centers.

We will use the word "cognizant" as meaning "awareness of" both significances that are experienced by each of the persons from his personal "operational center" and other types of significances they may be aware of irrespective of the where and when of their "operational centers."

First let us consider what the First Person is aware of on the perceptual level. A person is aware of the "therenesses" of the "thatnesses" within the range of his stimulus perception as significant to him from his "behavioral center."

At the same time he is taking account without being consciously aware of the "thatness-thereness" significances of his non-stimulus perceptual

---

* Editor's Note: Ames did not complete any notes considering these questions on the other three levels except for the mention of the sequential and value levels on p. 87.

field related to his stimulus perceptual field and his operational center. He is potentially capable of becoming aware of particular "thatness-thereness" significances in this field if and in so far as they may be relevant to this comprehension of sequential significances relevant to his needs and purposes.

The awarenesses of the perceptual significances in both fields are unique to First Person both because of his unique prior experience and because of his unique operational center.

Besides these "thatness-thereness" significances which are in relation to the First Person's behavioral center, there is a whole family of other "thatness-thereness" significances unrelated to his operational center of which he may be aware; e.g., when just before the kick-off in a football game I perceive the relative positions of all the players on the field. I am perceptually aware of concrete "thatness-thereness" significances relative to the "thatnesses" involved. But the "thatness-thereness" significances in themselves do not involve me personally; that is, they are not significances in relation to my operational center. For want of a better term they might be referred to as "impersonal relative perceptual significances" in an isometric frame of reference.

Beyond the above types of concrete "thatness-thereness" significance of which the First Person is or may be aware, there is still another type of "thereness-thatness" significances of which he may be aware especially when he is faced by a "hitch" and has gone into "inquiry." An example of such "thereness" significances are maps of all kinds and of such "thatness" significances are classified objects of all kinds. It is apparent that "thatness-thereness" significances of this type are neither in direct relation to any person's operational center, nor that of any existing center, nor in an isometric frame of reference. That is, they are abstracted from concreteness.

The Second Person is aware of a similar field of perceptual significances. But it is apparent that the significances of which he is aware and potentially capable of being aware are not identical to those of which the First Person is aware.

There is no possibility of their being identical, as their operational centers can never be exactly the same.

The degree of similarity of their awareness of objects they both see is directly related to the similarity of their prior behavioral experiences, which in turn depends not only on their prior environmental conditions but on their needs, purposes, and values innate and acquired.

A guide can see a deer when the tenderfoot at his side sees only a bush, and a guide knows where he is when a tenderfoot by his side does not.

It would be possible for two persons of entirely different cultures and prior experiences who stood side by side to have essentially different perceptual awarenesses, and for each of them to know that this was the case.

It would seem to follow that the extent that the Other Person can know or be aware of the awarenesses of the First Person on the perceptual level is related to his acquaintance with the nature of the perceptual awareness of the First Person. If the similarity of their mutual backgrounds is not such that he can assume its nature, he must find out by some processes similar to psychoanalysis.

It is only when the Other Person and the First Person have had similar perceptual behavioral backgrounds and their awareness of perceptual significances in relation to their operational centers are quite similar that there is a possibility for the Other Person to be aware, know, something about the First Person's perceptual significances and also what he is aware of that the First Person may not be aware of.

But even when the "Other Person" knows, has an awareness of, the perceptual significances of the First Person, such knowings and awarenesses are quite different in nature from his awareness of his own first person perceptual significances.

To explain this difference, it is necessary to consider the "First Person's" point of view of the "Other Person." This makes it evident that the terms "Other Person" and "First Person" we have been using up to now are quite inappropriate and confusing. It would seem better to use "Person A" and "Person B" and then think of either as being the "First Person" by putting ourselves in his position.

We talk about putting ourselves in another person's position, but it seems apparent that it is impossible for one to be in any other position in his extended ultra-stimulus field of "thatness-thereness" significances than the one he actually occupies.

In other words, my awareness of your awareness of perceptual significances cannot include the essential characteristics of your first person's point of view. Or in other words, your perceptual significances of which I am aware are in "impersonal" relative terms in an isometric frame of reference.

The above considerations seem to clear up two points. First, that I can be aware of what you are perceptually aware of only in so far as I am acquainted with and can assume the nature of your perceptual awareness which in turn is determined by your needs, purposes, and values. Second, that my awareness of your perceptual awareness cannot be from your first personal point of view, but only from an "impersonal" "objective" isometric frame of reference.

It seems apparent that the nearer I am to you the easier it is for me to formulate my awareness of your "thatness-thereness" significances in "impersonal-isometric" terms, but that no matter how close I am to you I cannot be aware of the "thatness-thereness" significances you yourself experience from your ego operational center.

It also seems apparent that what has been said above applies on the sequential level (matrix). That it is equally impossible for me to be able to be aware of the sequential significances that you are taking account of from your ego-operational center. That my awareness of your awareness is translation into sequential operations in an "impersonal" "objective" isometric space and periodic time field.

This would also hold true on the "valueful needs"—"valueful purpose" level (matrix). Inquiry into these more complex behavioral situations should be considered in more detail in later notes.

Bearing in mind the above-described limitations of what I can be aware of that you are perceptually aware of, let us go on to consider, first, what I can be aware of that you are perceptually aware of and, second, what I can be aware of that you are not perceptually aware of.

In regard to this latter question (what I can become aware of), it will only become apparent to me in terms of what I may be aware of relative to the efficacy of your behavior as affected by what you are not aware of.

It has been mentioned earlier that what I can be aware of that you are perceptually aware of is directly related to the degree that I can assume that the significances of which you are perceptually aware correspond, are similar to the significances of which I myself am perceptually aware.

For example, if I (who have spent a lot of time in the woods) go into the woods with a woodsman, I will expect, assume, that the significances of which he is perceptually aware in our common fields of stimulus perception will be similar to those of which I am aware. On the other hand, if I go into the woods with a person who has never been in the woods before, I will have no such assumption or expectation. This point may be more apparent if one is with a young child.

With the common run of people I can assume that the directional significance of the other person will be the same as my own. However, I cannot make such definite assumptions as to distance significances, and still less definite assumptions as to "thatness" significances.

In the field of ultra-stimulus perception, the assumptions I can make as to the correspondence of the significances of which both you and I are aware is much more tenuous than in our common fields of stimulus perception. This is because the significances of our ultra-stimulus perception of which we are aware are not reactivated by similar stimuli, have much less in common, are essentially more "private affairs," so to speak. For example, if a stranger comes to Hanover, I can't assume he has any awareness that corresponds to the significances of my ultra-stimulus perception of the "thatnesses" and their "therenesses" around Hanover of which I am aware.

Our relation with other persons is based on the assumption that we are both aware of the same perceptual significances. And at times it is based on the assumption that we are aware of perceptual significances of which they are not aware; e.g., case of guide with his sportsman who he knows can't see a deer which he sees. But in the final analysis we only know what another person is aware of, or that we are aware of what the other person is not aware of, through his behavior; e.g., as we sit beside the driver of an automobile, sometimes his driving shows that what we thought he was aware of he was not aware of and sometimes his driving shows that he was aware of what we thought he was not aware of.

The more experiences we have with a person, the more we can be sure what each of us is perceptually aware of.

October 29, 1952

## Needs and Purposes

This note is to point out that I think we have been and are giving too much attention and emphasis to that aspect of our behavior which is involved in emergence, "flow," and not enough to that aspect that is involved in maintenance of "form."

Consider the amount of our behavioral activity that is engaged in the maintenance of "form."

1. Prior to our own personal behavior form is the essence of the script code of our chromosome patterns as determined by our biological history.

2. All our reflexive physiological processes which insure the continuance and development of our bodies and their activities.

3. All our behavioral activities over which we have some conscious control which supplement our reflexes and habits in insuring the continuity of the "form" of our bodies and their activities, i.e., which provide the material necessities of life, shelter, food, clothing, exercise, etc.

4. All our behavioral activities over which we have conscious control by which we insure the continuity of our value forms.

The continuity of all these levels of forms are necessary prerequisites to emergence flow.

Could we use the words "needs" and "value needs" to refer to them as differentiated from what we refer to now by the words "purposes" and "value purposes" which we have up to now used to refer to the directives of our behavior that lead to emergent flow?

It had occurred to me that in so far as purposes refer to the future and since emergence occurs where the determined (form) of the past merges with the undetermined future that the word "purpose" (in its commonly used sense), since it involves the future, could be used to refer to emergence. But on consideration it is apparent that we use the word "purpose" to refer to behavior initiated to preserve form.

I can see that we might well use the words "needs" and "value needs" to refer to behavior initiated to preserve form. But it isn't clear to me what word or words we can use to refer to behavior initiated to lead to emergent flow.

But it does seem to me that if we continue to use the words "purpose" and "valueful purpose," we ought not to use them alone but in conjunction with the words "needs" and "value needs."

October 30, 1952

### SUPPLEMENT TO NOTE OF OCTOBER 18, 1952

On reading the typewritten copy of my note of October 18th I realized the poor job I had done in communicating the various ideas that had come to my mind. The possible importance of some of the lines of thought seems to me to be such that I should make a further effort to clarify at least three points.

1. It would seem that an understanding of the above has a direct bearing on the success of our behavior involving other persons. We have pointed out that the success of our behavior where other people are involved is directly related to our capacity to be aware of their needs, purposes, and values. In view of the above it would seem that it is equally necessary for us to be aware of what they perceive—and also their comprehension of sequential events. We might well be aware of their needs, purposes, and values, but if we were unaware of the nature of their perceptions and their comprehension of sequential events, the success of our behavior would be limited to the degree that perceptual and sequential significances play a part in the situation.

It might be said that communion and effective action were only possible where there was mutual awareness between persons on all levels (matrices).

2. It seems that another important line of thought in the note of Oc-

tober 18th is that, although one person can make effectively reliable assumptions as to what another person perceives, i.e., translations of his own perceptual awareness in terms of the other person's point of view in an isometric frame of reference, he can never experience the other person's perceptual awareness which is essentially and characteristically unique to that person.

This seems quite apparent on the perceptual level. Perhaps because the behavioral phenomena limited to this level are simpler and more comprehensible.

But I think it may be expected that with this start toward an understanding of the nature of the uniqueness of a person on the perceptual level, by following similar lines of thought on the sequential level and the purposing, transactional, and value levels, a more complete understanding of the uniqueness of a person might be arrived at.

3. Besides throwing some light on the nature of the uniqueness of a person, it would seem that the ideas considered in the note may also throw some light on the phenomena that relate a person to other persons, i.e., his social nature.

From all of the above it would seem that the relative effectiveness of a social group is related to the degree of correspondence of the perceptual awareness and comprehension of sequential significances of each of the individuals of the group. This correspondence in turn is determined by the degree of correspondence of the needs and purposes of each of the individuals of the group, which in turn is determined by the values of each of the individuals of the group.

Under different environmental conditions, social groups with the same basic needs, purposes, and values would for their carrying out and satisfaction develop different types of perceptual awareness and comprehension of sequential significances.

In any particular social group each individual person, due to his uniqueness, develops a different type of perceptual awareness and comprehension of sequential significances from other members of the group.

However, an individual does not exist by himself alone. Biologically he is the integration of many persons, and during his life the satisfaction of his value needs and value purposes is only possible through the satisfaction of the value needs and value purposes of other persons.

The social matrix is the value needs and value purposes common to all individuals of the group.

The possibility for social emergence lies in the uniqueness of the individual who, in his unique and ever-new environmental situations is aware of, can affect, both the direction of the emergence of his own individual value needs and purpose and that of his social group.

The social units of husband and wife and the family seem to provide examples where this is apparent.

When a situation arises where a person's behavior that would lead to the satisfaction of his individual value needs and purposes would prevent the fulfilling of his social value needs and purposes, or vice versa, there is a conflict between his individual and social value needs and purposes.

Such behavioral situations seem quite analogous to those on the perceptual level where there are conflicting visual indications, as uniocular and binocular when one or the other is suppressed or modified.

It would seem that such behavioral stiuations would give rise to psychiatric behavior, unconscious suppression of either individual or social value needs and purposes or their sublimation, or alteration of either the individual or social value needs and purposes.


November 10, 1952

### "First Person's Experience and Another Person's View Thereof"
#### (*Continued*)

#### (Involving Our Knowings of the Past and the Future)

In the note of October 18th it was pointed out that a better naming for this inquiry would be "A First Person's or One's Own Knowings of Another Person's Experience."

It was also pointed out that my "knowings" of your experiences (on the perceptual level), although concrete, are in "impersonal" relative terms in an isometric frame of reference.

In that note we dealt only with the situation where both one's own position and the other person's position remained unaltered. Interesting questions arise from the consideration of situations involving the change of one's own position or that of the other person.

Let us take up first the situation where the position of the other person is changed. For instance, a situation where "you" have moved to another chair in my office.

It is apparent that my knowings of your perceptual experience, after you have moved, although they will still be in impersonal relative terms in an isometric frame of reference, would be different from what they were when you were in the first position.

Among other interesting questions that arise is: "After you have moved, what are my knowings about what your perceptual experience was from your prior position?" This is not a vague academic question.

I was in an automobile accident a short time ago in which my car was stationary and another car bumped into me, and it was of primary importance to me to formulate a knowing of what was the nature of the other driver's perceptual experience of the "thatness-thereness" significances of the situation where he was in the position he was in before he hit me.

It is apparent that my first person's knowings of another person's perceptual experience when he was in a position different from the one he is now in is drastically different in nature from my knowing of another person's immediate perceptual experience. The basic difference is apparently due to the fact that in the latter case my knowings awarenesses include an experiential awareness (i.e., concrete) of the other person's from my operational center, while in the first case, as the person is no longer in his first position, I have to reconstruct his position from my memory and my knowings of the other person's position are of a much more abstract character.

The abstracted nature of my knowings of another person's prior perceptual experience becomes more apparent if both my position and that of the other person are altered. For when my operational behavioral center is altered, to have any knowings of where the other person's prior position was relative to my own present position I have to go entirely to memory and construct a completely isometric frame of reference.

Very interesting considerations arise from the above because alteration of position of either myself or the other person involves the passing of sequential events or historical time, i.e., the past and future, and seems to provide a basis for inquiry that will lead to a better understanding of the difference of the nature of our awareness and knowings of the "now" as compared with our awareness and knowings of the past and also of the future.

The primary difference seems to be that our awareness and knowings of the now are characterized by the inclusion of those awarenesses and knowings and significances relevant to our immediate unique operational behavioral centers which are not included in our awarenesses and knowings of past and future situations. And this holds equally true of our knowings and awarenesses of our own past and future perceptual experiences as it does of our knowings and awarenesses of the past and future experiences of other persons.

It might be noted here that the above is equally true of our awarenesses and knowings of our own and other person's sequential experiences —i.e., comprehension of sequential events. But this is another field of inquiry that needs to be thoroughly gone into.

### On the Reality of Perceptions

As I sit here in my office I am perceptually aware of the objects about me at which I am looking, as the chairs, table, bookcase, door, floor and walls at their particular thereness from where I am sitting—my behavioral center. I am also potentially aware of the objects in my office that are behind me, and their location from me, and also of all the objects outside of my office in the building and in the town extending into that indefinitely expanded field where I have ever been.*

All of these specific thatnesses at their specific therenesses from me constitute the unique "thatness-thereness" significances of my unique behavioral field.

They are what they are where they are, characterized by at least some degree of permanence and unalterability. They are not imagined or dream stuff. I cannot conceive of them as being other things at other places. What and where they are I sense as being actual reality. My perceptual awareness of thatnesses and their thereness from my behavioral center cannot be other than it is. It is a given that has to be as it is. I accept it as it is. My total behavioral performance is and must be based on such acceptance.

Further my perceptual awareness of thatnesses and their thereness from my behavioral center is unaltered by whether they are to my liking or not. They may be what I desire or they may destroy me, but they are as they are. They of necessity followed from what has gone before both in respect to myself and otherness. Their wherefore may be beyond my knowing and beyond my control, but they have been and they must be taken as given. In religious terms they can be thought of as divine.

That they must be accepted is evidenced by the disastrous behavioral results experienced by those who do not accept them as a take-off for their behavioral activity.

The big question is, if so, how can it be reconciled with our findings that our perceptions are not disclosures but only prognostic of the nature of the thatnesses and their therenesses from our behavioral centers?

If I believe my perceptions are only prognostic, i.e., fallible, how can I at the same time believe they could not be otherwise, are givens, that must be accepted? How can I act with the assurance that is necessary if I believe my perception is only a prognosis, is essentially fallible?

* See "Reconsideration of the Origin and Nature of Perceptions."

It would seem that this paradox arises from our thinking of the perceptual significances of thatnesses at their therenesses as something existing apart in their own right, i.e., from our thinking of thatnesses in terms of the nature of the objects and of therenesses in terms of the objects' spatial localization from the perceiving person's behavioral center.

It seems that the paradox can be resolved when we recognize that the function of our perceptual awareness is to disclose behavioral significances, behavioral possibilities of accomplishing valueful purposes. Our perceptions had their origin in prior purposeful action and indicate the nature of the action in later similar circumstances that will lead to the successful accomplishment of purposes.

In an ever-changing, undetermined cosmos where nothing repeats and no later occasion is an exact duplication of a prior occasion, our perceptions derived from the behavioral significances of prior occasions can never be an exact disclosure of the behavioral significance of a later immediate occasion. In nature they must be prognostic. Their reliability, i.e., if we act in accordance with our perceptions whether we will succeed in accomplishing our purpose, varies greatly from almost certainty to taking very long chances. But they are *all* that the unique individual, in a concrete behavioral situation, has at his disposal and his stake is accomplishment of purpose and value satisfaction. He is blessed, so to speak, by the opportunity he is given and accepts it as given.*

December 15, 1952

## ON THE NATURE OF ILLUSIONS, SURPRISES AND DISAPPOINTMENTS, FORM AND FLOW ABSOLUTES

### Illusions

Illusions, such as one experiences in the distorted room demonstration, when one has perceptual awarenesses of objects as other than they are and at other places than they are, are commonly thought of as being unreal.

---

* It seems that but for such conditions man could not be a unique responsible individual who, by exercising his choice, affects his destiny not only by determining the forms of his world but its emergence.

It might seem that it is unfortunate for man that his perceptions are only prognostic and are so often fallible, but consideration apparently makes it evident that the fallibilities of our perception are an opportunity; that if we never experienced an illusion, our "thatness-thereness" world would remain forever static. (For elaboration of this line of thought see note on "The Nature of Illusions" of December 15th.)

Certainly in one sense such illusory perceptions are unreal in that they do not correspond to most of our other indications about the environment and moreover the action they give rise to is behaviorally ineffective.

As the demonstrations apparently show, perceptions are illusory because in concrete situations we make erroneous assumptions and erroneously interpret our stimulus excitations in terms of "thatness-thereness" significances that do not exist. We think of our illusions as being false, unreal. We feel ashamed; feel that something is basically wrong that we should have related the wrong significances with stimulus excitations.

There is no question but that in illusory situations the assumptions and interpretations are mis-taken, that they do not disclose the significance of the immediate occasion; do not apply to it, so to speak. But the question that is being asked is, are they false in the sense of being unreal? Does the experiencing of illusions indicate that there is anything basically wrong in man, something to be ashamed of, possibly of the nature of a sin?

To help in answering this question, let us suppose we never experienced an illusion; e.g., that in the chair demonstration we didn't see chairs when there weren't any, or didn't see the distorted room rectangular. It is apparent that we would indeed be in trouble, for we couldn't see a real chair or a rectangular room when we were actually looking at them.

It would seem that in itself our interpretation of our stimulus excitations and the assumptions we make in so doing are always valid, real, in that it is a proper, necessary thing to do. We can't make any other interpretations or assumptions. The mistake, so to speak, in illusory perception is not in an error in interpretation and assumption in itself. The mistake is in accepting perceptions as reliable, prognostic directives for purposeful action in environmental conditions where such interpretations do not provide reliable prognostic directives. But no blame can be associated with such illusory mistakes of interpretation, and no blame should be associated with acting in accordance with our interpretation, for we can act only in accordance with our perceptions (distorted room).

Far from being in any way culpable, the experiencing of illusions are "God-sent," so to speak. It is only through illusory experience that the significances of situations, heretofore undifferentiated from other situations, are disclosed to us. If illusory situations are taken advantage of, they will enable one to alter his perceptions so that he can effectively behave in situations in which he formerly could not effectively behave; e.g., Easterner climbing mountains in the West.

The steps in the history of the evolution in the effectiveness of the perception of organisms, including man, can be thought of as those situations where the organism has taken advantage of illusory situations.

Or they can be thought of as the organism, through illusory experiences, selecting from an unordered cosmos those "thatness-thereness" significances that are significant to it for carrying out its purposes.

This humanized cosmos is what we have called the Form World of each unique individual. It is the "reality" of the highest prognostic reliability which the particular organism in its carrying out to its unique purposes has up to date been able to discover.

The evolution up to the present of an individual's perception of "thatness-thereness" significances would not have taken place but for the organism and his forebears having experienced illusions, and its evolutions in the future will not take place if the organism does not experience new illusions.

*Surprises*

As has been pointed out, an individual's perceptual awareness of "thatness-thereness" significance includes potential recognition of the sequential use to which the "thatnesses" may be available in the carrying out of his purposes. An individual will experience surprise when the consequences of sequential events he initiates to carry out his purpose turn out to be different from what he expected.

Just as a particular individual's perception of the "thatness-thereness" significances is only a prognosis for effective purposeful action, so his prehension of the consequences of sequential events he makes use of is only a prognosis for effective accomplishment of his purpose.

And just as he experiences illusions when his prognosis of "thatness-thereness" significances is mis-taken, so he experiences surprise when he mis-apprehends the outcome of sequential events.

To be surprised is also "God-sent," for it means an awareness for the first time of a sequential significance that was not heretofore known.

The evolution up to the present of an individual's comprehension of sequential significances would not have taken place but for the organism and his forebears having experienced surprise, and its evolution in the future will not take place if the organism does not experience new surprises.

*Disappointments*

Analogously, on the purposing level in any concrete behavioral situation the purposes by which an individual is motivated may or may not lead to desired value satisfaction. When they do not, he will be disappointed.* It is through disappointment that the individual learns of the

* The word "disappointment" is being used to refer to the "feelings" experienced when something we *had hoped* for doesn't occur as differentiated from the feeling

inadequacy of his purposes for furthering value satisfaction. So it would also seem that the evolution up to the present of an individual's value satisfaction would not have taken place but for the individual and his forebears having experienced disappointment and its evolution, emergence in the future, will not take place if he does not experience new disappointments.

## Absolutes

The "shock" or degree of disturbance a person experiences in an illusory situation is related to his acceptance of his perception as an unquestioned reality, an absolute, a "given," on which, under certain circumstances as driving an automobile, he continually stakes his life. In general such acceptance of one's perception is necessary for effective behavior.

Similarly the "shock" or degree of disturbance a person experiences, when he is surprised that the consequence of a sequential event is not what he expected, is related to his acceptance of his prehension of the sequential event as an unquestioned "given" reality, a surety on which we "continually" bet our lives, an absolute. In general such acceptance of one's prehension of sequential events is necessary for effective carrying out of one's purposes.

Similarly the "shock" or degree of disturbance a person experiences when he is disappointed that the value satisfaction following the accomplishment of a purpose is not what he foresaw is related to his acceptance of the "righteousness" of his purpose as unquestionable, as an absolute. In general such acceptance of the righteousness of one's purposes is necessary for effective behavior.

In other terms, for every unique individual behaving in a concrete situation there is for him, from his first person behavioral center, a hierarchy of specific absolutes but for which he could not behave effectively. These unique concrete absolutes are radically different in nature from abstracted absolutes such as scientific laws, religious dogmas and esthetic formulations, which in turn play their indispensable roles in inquiry.

The point that is to be brought out here is that these "concrete absolutes" are inherent in organic existence.

We ordinarily think of absolutes as remaining constant in time. This is true of abstracted absolutes. But these concrete "existential" absolutes vary in regard to their constancy in time.

we experience when "thatness-thereness" significances *are* different from what we believe them to be, which we refer to by illusions, and as differentiated from the feeling we experience when the consequences of sequential events *have turned* out to be different from what we prehended.

"Thatness-thereness" significance absolutes on which I bet my life vary with variations of my behavioral center. Sequential significance absolutes on which I also bet my life (as with the use of artifacts) are more constant but still variable in time. The righteousness of my purposes (absolutes on which I may also stake my life) are much more constant in time. These concrete existential absolutes also differ from abstracted absolutes in the degree to which they are shared by different individuals. The "thatness-thereness" significance absolutes are experienced only from the unique individual's unique behavioral center and cannot be socially shared. Concrete sequential absolutes can be socially shared to a greater extent. Concrete righteousness of purposes can be much more universally and socially shared.

July 10, 1953

### BEHAVIORAL POINT OF VIEW

In order to increase our comprehension of the first person behavioral point of view we have been differentiating it from the second and third person point of view.

But it would seem that to get really what we are after we should differentiate the first person's behavioral point of view from the first person's analysis of his own behavior.

For instance, consider my own immediate behavior.

When I was dressing this morning I became dimly aware, with a sense of its importance, of the differentiation between my actual behavior and my analysis of it. I immediately wanted to get a better conceptualized hold of that differentiation. I repeated it over to myself so I wouldn't forget it when I got to my office, and then went about, almost automatically with no hitches of any kind, getting my breakfast with my wife, letting the dog out, etc., and coming here.

I open the window, settle back in my chair, put my feet up on my desk, take my pad and pencil, and start writing down thoughts as they emerge in my consciousness in sequential order that is determined by an ineffable sense of significance.

I can go on and describe how I saw the "thatness-thereness" of my pencil on the desk, took account of its sequential significance as a how-to-do for my writing down my thoughts, how directed by that purpose I pick it up and start writing, how my experience of a value satisfaction (enjoyment) that what I am writing makes sense at least to me, etc.

Now what I have just been expressing is my first person analysis of my own first personal behavior, but it is certainly completely different from my behavior. No such analysis ever takes place in effective behavior. I couldn't even write if I were analyzing the therenesses of the thatnesses of my pencil marks on the paper or why I am moving my fingers and hand as I am, or why I am writing at all.

My actual first person behavior only goes on because it goes on as an undifferentiable whole.

Because of my immediate ineffable value sense of the importance of my immediate efforts I carry on enthusiastically without any absolute or definite assurance of the nature of their consequences. Come what may, this I enjoy and will to do.

I have an awareness of different aspects of my own behavior, but these awarenesses are not in terms of conceptualized abstractions.

My awarenesses of my own ongoing behavior are views of its totality but only of different "accents" of the whole. But such awarenesses are not in terms of conceptualized abstractions, differentiations, which preclude the awareness of other aspects.

It is when ongoing behavior is checked (and this is often), because of our awareness of its inefficacy for satisfaction of aims and enjoyment, that we conceptually abstract our behavior so that we can go on again behaving without abstracting.

It would seem that an immediate important task of our group is to try to get a clearer idea of the nature and character of the "accents" of our behavior of which we can be aware. Since these "accents" are never separated from the whole by "ands" but are related to it by "withs" they can be referred to only by poetic language and symbols, not by scientific formulations or specifications.

Now while we may formulate poetic references that will satisfactorily refer to "accents" of the first person's point of view of behavior, such poetic formulations can never give rise to the awareness that a first person has of his own behavior in immediacy. At best they will be static; the emergencies are not actually occurring; the choices are not those of a uniquely responsible person.

July 11, 1953

### BEHAVIORAL POINT OF VIEW (*Continued*)

It seems that some understanding of the relationship of what I have called behavioral "accents" (of which we are aware) and our ineffable behavioral "background" can be gotten from a consideration of the relation between our "stimulus perception" to our "ultra-stimulus perception."

As I sit here at my desk, my stimulus perception is of the significance of the "thatness-therenesses" of the "objects" in my field of view to my behavioral center. My ultra-stimulus perception is my sense of an enveloping field of other "thatness-therenesses" significances "but for" which my stimulus perception would have little or no significance, as is evidenced by the fact that if, after having been drugged, I came to in a strange room, I would be in a complete dilemma. I would be lost.

My ultra-stimulus perception as a whole provides my sense of "perceptual orientation," although as a whole it is ineffable, yet specific aspects of it (accents in turn) can be sensed.

It would seem that analogous relations between "behavioral accents" and "behavioral background" hold on the sequential level and also on the "purposing and valuing" levels.

As was pointed out, there is a great difference between what I take into account in behaving and my conceptual awareness of my own behavior. This of course in no way implies that my conceptual awareness of my own behavior is not real and does not play an indispensable role in behavior.

The point I want to make here is in regard to another difference; the difference between my conceptual analysis of my own behavior and my conceptual awareness of another person's behavior.

In the first case the referents of my concepts are "real" in a sense in which they are not in the latter case. In the first case I am experiencing the referents to which I am trying to conceptualize. In the latter case the best I can do is to imagine the aspects of the other person's behavior which I am conceptualizing. I myself am not experiencing them unless we assume some capacities such as telepathy.

This would seem quite apparent on the perceptual and sequential levels and on the purposing (aim) level, although it may be questioned on the value satisfaction level when the essence of the "form" approaches an absolute.

July 21, 1953

## "MOTIVATION"
### (Conceptualizations Relative To)

It would seem that the confusion that arises in our inquiries about the nature of motivation is due to our failure to recognize the multiple aspects of the phenomena referred to by the word "motivations" and the different roles they play in a concrete behavioral situation.*

We commonly think of motivations in terms of the immediate directives affecting a person's behavior as existing in a temporal frame of reference only. So we consider (1) their origin in the past, (2) their directive nature and effects in the present as in terms of purposes and (3) the consequences or ends that will occur in the future.

It seems that motivations (purposes) exist in a frame of reference more inclusive than the space-time frame of reference, i.e., have a continuity extending through yesterday, today and tomorrow, that sequential events do not have (cf. note on the different "nows").

In terms of phenomena occurring in concrete behavior, it seems that every specific motivation involves at least three differentiable aspects. The first involves and insures the preservation of form ("homeostasis"). The second is its "purposive" aspect ("directives of action"); the third the consequences of the initiated action (the occurring of the consequences that are initiated).

Each of these aspects has both its own differentiable felt significance ("importance," "value," "worth," "satisfaction") and also common felt significances. No one of the differentiable felt significances would be experienced "but for" the experiencing of the felt significances of the other aspects.

Behavior involves (1) "belief," "faith," and "satisfaction" in "form," (2) satisfaction and worthwhileness in initiating and carrying on, (3) satisfaction in ends accomplished. No one would exist but for the other two.

Without all of these three types of satisfactions there would not be continued "motivation."

It would seem that failure to bear in mind these trans-actional relationships leads us (1) to think about "motivation" apart from "form"; (2) to be unable to differentiate "purposes" from "ends"; (3) to make it difficult for us to understand the nature of the experiential phenomena that occur when we run up against hitches and frustrations; e.g., are we frustrated because of what happens to us when our "form" is jeopardized or destroyed, or when our actions are ineffective, or are we frustrated because our "aims" are at fault, or because of the nature of consequences that have occurred?

To test the validity of the above conceptualization about "motivations" we should personally, from a first person point of view, attempt to take

* Where the behaving person is "compos mentis" ("being of sound mind, memory and understanding")—acting "knowingly with intent" (law), i.e., sequentially aware.

account of and describe our own awarenesses of the various phenomenal aspects involved in a behavioral situation in which so-called "motivations" play a role.

August 29, 1953

### On Scientific Methodology: "Flow" of Orchestration on the Awareness Level

In terms of orchestration the rhythms of the basic personal emotions and their satisfactions, such as thirst and hunger, and the rhythm of the basic social emotions and their satisfactions, such as those of sex, are always going on as are the innumerable other rhythms, with their lesser and lesser degrees of prognostic reliability. Trans-acting, they constitute the symphonic harmony of being personal, social and biological.

A continuous "form" prevails which can be thought of as the relatively "homeostatic" or equilibrium aspect of orchestration.

But these felt rhythms and their symphonic value overtones never exactly repeat. We never re-experience exactly the same thirsts or hungers, or sexual passions or their value satisfactions.

There are not only continual variations of the orchestrations and symphonic harmonies taking place for each of us during our individual lives, but also continual variations taking place from generation to generation.

These variations arise from the unpredictability of the future. They will be less under more constant environmental conditions, greater under less constant environmental conditions.

These variations may be for the better or the worse as far as the continued well-being of the individual and the social group is concerned to the extent the sensed orchestration provides more or less reliable prognosis for individual and social action in concrete behavioral situations.

As these variations arise they do not affect a particular aspect of the symphonic orchestration alone. Due to the trans-actional relations between every aspect of the orchestration, a variation of a particular aspect affects the "total" orchestration.

It seems apparent that the most basic rhythms, such as our emotional thirst, hunger and sex, are most determined in nature and are less subject to alteration due to their higher prognostic reliability for biological well-being as ascertained empirically through biological history.

It also seems apparent that the aspects of the orchestration that are most susceptible to alterations are those of lesser prognostic reliability, such as those which the individual is aware of in value terms and which constitute the overtones of the symphony, harmonious or disharmonious. It would seem that it is only relative to these aspects of the orchestration that the individual is able to exercise choice, affect his own orchestration, and, through action, affect the orchestration with and of his social group.

Every such alteration of the value overtones of a symphony alters the whole symphony including the basic emotional rhythms. The basic passion rhythms continue, but they are nevertheless altered. After the individual has made his value choice, they will be "heard," sensed, differently—either more "divinely" or more "beastially."

From the above considerations it would seem that "flow" arises from the effect of processes on the value level. If so, a scientific methodology to demonstrate empirically the nature of the conditions under which "flow," either forward (emergence) or backward, takes place must deal with processes on the value level where individual choice is exercised.

October 20, 1953

RE: MANUAL FOR DEMONSTRATIONS—ON THE NATURE OF PERCEPTIONS
AND THE NATURE OF ENVIRONMENTAL PHENOMENA

CORRESPONDENCE AND LACK OF CORRESPONDENCE BETWEEN OUR
PERCEPTIONS AND "WHAT" WE ARE LOOKING AT—PROGNOSIS

The acceptance of the conclusions that what an observer is perceptually aware of is—

(1) His own unique interpretation of the significance to him of environmental conditions from his unique point of observation and behavioral center, and

(2) is different from what any other observer can be perceptually aware of, and

(3) that his perceptions are not the result of a causal chain of events originating in the environment but are his own contribution to the perceptual situation, and may or may not correspond to what he is looking at as it is perceived and known to others, or he may later discover, seems to present a new approach to the question: (a) what is the nature of perceptions? and (b) what is the nature of the environmental phenomenon that is being looked at?

Let us start our inquiry by considering two of the more generalized inferences relative to the nature of perceptions formulated from a consideration of the phenomena disclosed by the demonstration:

(1) That perceptual awarenesses are the taking into account by a person of the significances to him of environmental conditions from his unique observational and behavioral center.

(2) That our perceptual awarenesses are not disclosures to us of the nature of what we are looking at but only provide us with a prognosis as to its significance.

Relative to the first formulation—

Significance to the individual means importance to him. It is apparent that no understanding of the nature of perceptions is possible without some understanding of why what a person is perceptually aware of is of importance to him. It seems apparent that what a person is perceptually aware of is of importance to him in that it provides him with awarenesses of how to act and behave effectively, in the particular environment in which he finds himself, i.e., to carry out his purposes or, more specifically, to attain goals natural to him as a human being to fulfill his wants, wishes, desires, and experience value satisfactions.

Some purposes are rhythmic, some are not, but the particular purposes that a person is immediately desirous of carrying out are continually altering not only from babyhood to old age but from minute to minute.

In general, however, environmental phenomena remain constant and purposes vary. Although there are conditions when environmental phenomena vary while purposes remain constant.

The point that is being made is that there is no correspondence between the characteristics of environmental phenomena and the characteristics of purposes, and therefore of the characteristics of the significances of which an individual is perceptually aware.

The above applies to one and the same individual.

Between different individuals there is still less correspondence between the characteristics of purpose and the characteristics of environmental phenomena, as exemplified by the old saying—"One man's food is another man's poison."

While the above consideration may throw some light on the role that perceptions play in providing the individual with awarenesses of aspects of environmental phenomena that further or hinder him in carrying out his purposes,* they throw no light on the inherent nature of environ-

---

*To carry out their destiny, human beings have developed capacities both physiological and psychological for taking account of and making use of those fortuitous environmental phenomena that further or hinder their destiny so that they could behave more effectively. In his later evolutionary stages through scientific investigations man has greatly increased his knowledge of those environmental

mental phenomena beyond the fact that it has to be and is taken into account by the individual in carrying out his purposes.

Perhaps as far as we can go at present in answering the question "What is the inherent nature of environmental phenomena?" is to say "God knows." Certainly the findings of modern physics not only show that the answer is not as simple as it used to be thought, but that the more that is discovered, the less likelihood there is of finding the answer.

In connection with the methodology of modern physics the conclusion of these inquiries, that there are no aspects of perceptual awareness that are not significances contributed by the observer, is of interest. In the last analysis all scientific findings are based on observations, i.e., perceptions, so that they cannot avoid containing at least some aspect of human significance.

A noted modern physicist (Bridgman) has said in substance: "The shadow of the investigator is discerned in the most abstract scientific findings." An understanding of the ultimate intrinsic nature of environmental phenomena does not appear to be a necessary prerequisite for at least great advances in man's understanding the nature of his perceptions and prehension of sequential events and of his behavior.

Relative to the second formulation mentioned earlier, i.e., that our perceptual awarenesses are not disclosures to us of the significance of what we are looking at but only provide us with a prognosis as to its significance—it would seem that that staement is acceptable as it stands.*

The statement that perceptual awarenesses are prognoses only is acceptable, in that as perceptual awarenesses are made use of by the observer as immediate directions for action from his unique behavioral center, they may not lead to completely effective action. Whether or not they will he can only find out by trying.

Earlier in our writing we have considered the matter of correspondence

phenomena which recur with sufficient probability to prognosticate their repetition in the future, e.g., modern physics. But more than that, modern man, at least in the West, by harnessing the raw environmental phenomena, has created artifacts from a screw and screwdriver to atomic energy to further the carrying out of his purposes and value satisfactions.

These developments are referred to as the "conquering of nature." It would be more accurate to refer to them as modifying nature to man's purposes.

In a modern city the environmental phenomena that surround every unique individual are little else but useful artifacts.

* It should be noted that the statement would not be acceptable if the word "nature" were substituted for "significance" or if the statement said, "Our perceptual awarenesses do not correspond to 'what' we are looking at but are only a prognosis of 'what' we are looking at, for we apparently have no knowledge of the intrinsic nature of environmental phenomena, i.e., of the 'what' we are looking at apart from its human significances."

between the significances of visual awarenesses and the significance of "what" an observer is looking at, and pointed out that lack of correspondence can be perceived or known by third persons present, or by the observer later.

There is never exact correspondence, as is evidenced by the necessity of supplementing visual perception by finding with scientific instruments, where accuracy is desired, to even approximate the distances of objects and their exact nature and significance.

Marked lack of correspondence may exist because of various reasons. It may be due to abnormal so-called physical phenomena (environmental) as the bending of the light rays between the objects and the eyes, as in mirages, or where the bundles of impinging light rays are similar to bundles that have been associated with other significances, e.g., chair demonstration. Or it may be due to abnormal physiological phenomena, as abnormal lenses or retinas, as with aniseikonia, or lack of correspondence may be due to a variety of psychological phenomena resulting from lack of past experience with the particular environmental conditions, or mistaken assumptions or prehension, e.g., trapezoid window.

It is apparent that the degree of correspondence between perceived significances and the significance of environmental phenomena is related —(1) to environmental conditions, such as the constancy of the environmental conditions, and the constancy of the character of light rays and their traveling in straight lines, (2) physiological processes adapted to particular constancies of environmental conditions and the constancy of such processes, (3) psychological processes adapted to particular environmental conditions and psychological processes and the constancy of such processes.

Lack of correspondence occurs when there are variations in the constancies of any of the above types of phenomena. The apparentness of lack of correspondence is in general more marked when the lack of correspondence is due to environmental or so-called physical causes, as with mirages and in the chair demonstration. Lack of correspondence due to these causes is apparent to others and easily made apparent to the observer.

Lack of correspondence due to physiological causes is in general not immediately apparent at all to third persons, and may or may not be apparent to the observer himself; e.g., persons with aniseikonia or with refractive errors of which they are not aware.

Lack of correspondence due to psychological causes is in general not immediately apparent at all to either third persons or the observer. Such lack of correspondence can only become apparent to third persons and the observer when evidenced by the ineffective action of the observer: e.g., the Easterner in the West failing to get to the mountain he was trying to climb when he expected to.

October 23, 1953

### RE: MANUAL FOR DEMONSTRATIONS—THE NATURE OF WHAT IS IN AWARENESS WHEN WE ARE VISUALLY PERCEIVING AND WHEN WE ARE CONCEPTUALIZING

Our perceptions are our unique awareness of the significances to us from our particular viewing point of what we are looking at.

Our perceptual awarenesses differ from what we are aware of when we are conceptualizing. Our immediate perceptual awarenesses are unanalyzable sensings of the significance to ourselves of environmental conditions not necessarily involving awarenesses of abstractions. Our immediate awarenesses when we are conceptualizing are of single abstracted significances of environmental conditions not necessarily involving sensed awareness of the significances to ourselves of environmental conditions.

Perceptual awarenesses are unique to the experiencing person. Conceptualized awarenesses can be common to many persons.

Perceptual awareness does not and could not include awarenesses of conceptual abstractions referring to phenomena that play a role in perception and but for which we would not experience perceptual awareness.

Further, when we are visually perceiving, we have no awareness of the "causal phenomena" which play a role in our perceiving and but for which we would not be perceiving and of which we cannot be conceptually aware. For example, when we are perceiving visually, we are not aware of what we think of as physical and physiological processes, such as the light rays from what we are looking at that have just impinged on our eyes, or how they are refracted by the lenses in our eyes, or of the accommodation and convergence of our eyes, or of the images on our retinas, or of the disparities between the images of our two eyes, or of conducting of retinal excitations to our brain, or of the processes taking place in our brains. Nor are we aware of what we think of as psychological processes of our own contribution to what we are aware of, such as perceptual cues or taking account of them, or weighing them, and how and why we see what we are. When we are visually perceiving, we are aware only of sensing the significance to us from our particular viewing position of environmental phenomena.

We may or may not be, are not necessarily aware of purposes which our perceptual sense awareness will enable us to carry out, or of the value satisfaction that the carrying out of those purposes will fulfill. We are certainly not aware of the role that the carrying out of purposes has played in the past and is playing in the now in affecting what we are perceptually sensing, nor of the role they will play in the future in regard to what we will become.

But in spite of the lack of awarenesses of conceptual abstractions our perceptual sense awareness provides us with what awarenesses of conceptual abstractions cannot provide. Our perceptual awareness discloses to us the significances of our environment that are immediately important to us, as unique individuals in carrying out our immediate purposes.

October 28, 1953

### Re: Manual—Lack of Correspondence Between Perceptual Awareness and "What" Is Being Looked at; Illusions

Lack of correspondence between perceptual awareness and "what" is being looked at may be primarily due to (1) physical (i.e., "environmental") phenomena, (2) physiological phenomena, or (3) psychophysiological phenomena, or (4) psychological (subjective) phenomena.

### 1. *Lack of Correspondence Primarily Due to Physical ("Environmental") Phenomena*

Physical phenomena are those having to do with the characteristics of the physical events that play a role in determining the nature of the bundles of light rays that impinge on our corneas. These events involve the characteristics of the light rays impinging on the "objects" being looked at; the events determining the characteristics of the rays reflected by the "objects" towards our eyes; the events occurring to these rays between the time they leave the object until they impinge on our corneas.

There are four commonly experienced types of lack of correspondence primarily due to such phenomena:

a. Where the light rays impinging on the objects are of a character different from what the observer has been conditioned to, e.g., as when light of selected wave lengths instead of white light is used to illuminate objects; e.g., as in stage effects and pictures that change when they are illuminated by light of different wave lengths.

b. When the reflecting character of the surfaces of objects is of a character different from what the observer has been conditioned to; e.g., as by the painting of objects to camouflage.

c. When the atmospheric condition between the "objects" and the observer is different from what he has been conditioned to—(1) to cause the light rays to bend instead of traveling in straight lines; e.g., mirages, or (2) to cause the light rays to be diffused or altered in color chroma or intensity; e.g., moisture or other particles in the atmosphere.

d. Where by fortuitous chance or design the light ray bundles impinging on the corneas come from quite different environmental configurations from those to which the observer has been conditioned to relate them; e.g., men taken for deer or as the separated lines in the chair demonstration are seen as a chair.

If Michotte has been understood correctly, it is this lack of correspondence of this type which he has called the "rough of the green." It is quite commonly believed that this type of lack of correspondence is entirely due to environmental effects and that the observer plays no role whatsoever in the illusions he experiences.

While the lack of correspondence would not occur but for environmental physical phenomena, it would not occur but for what the observer contributes to the situation in the way of assumptions. Further it would not occur unless the characteristics of the light ray bundles that so impinge on his corneas were similar to those existing under situations he has been conditioned to.

To cite but two examples—(1) In the case of mirages: The curvature of the light rays is an aspect of the environmental phenomena that differs from what the observer has been conditioned to. We are all conditioned to assume that all light rays travel in straight lines. The direction from which the light rays impinge on the observer's corneas is similar to that existing under situations he has been conditioned to. So he sees the object in the direction from which the light rays are impinging on his corneas, and there is a lack of correspondence between his awareness of the direction of the objects and its actual direction. (2) In the chair demonstration, the arrangement of the separated pieces of string so that they give rise to a bundle of light rays impinging on the observer's cornea having the same characteristics as those given rise to by an actual chair give rise to a different situation from that to which the observer has been conditioned. We have all been conditioned to assume that our perception of anything as complicated as a chair could be given rise to only by a chair. However, the particularly characterized bundle of rays impinging on the observer's corneas is similar to that existing under situations he has been conditioned to when he saw chairs. So he sees a chair, and there is a lack of correspondence between what he is visually aware of and what he is looking at.

It is interesting to note here that all photographs and drawings give rise to impinging light ray bundles similar and sometimes quite identical to those given rise to by environmental situations.

In so far as the observer has been conditioned to the same or similar environmental conditions as those depicted he will be perceptually aware of environmental situations similar to those depicted.

Ordinarily the observer knows he is looking at a picture and not an actual environment. The question may arise as to the correspondence between what the observer is perceptually aware of and what is depicted, but not between what he is aware of and the environment depicted because there isn't any such environment present for the observer and he knows it. So there is no illusion.

When, as sometimes happens, the observer mistakes a photograph for an environment, he will experience an illusion and there will be a most marked lack of correspondence between what he is aware of and the environmental situation.

The above considerations throw light on the difference between symbols of and the actual presence of an environmental situation.*

## 2. *Lack of Correspondence Primarily Due to Physiological Phenomena*

Granting there were normal physical phenomena to which the observer was conditioned, lack of correspondence may exist because of physiological phenomena.

Refractive anomalies, such as near- or farsightedness or astigmatism; retinal anomalies, such as defective color sense; binocular anomalies, such as squint, or anomalous disparities between corresponding retinal points (aniseikonia) can all give rise to lack of correspondence between perceptual awareness and environmental situations.

A thorough consideration of the lack of correspondence arising from physiological phenomena would follow the same lines as those considered above arising from physical (environmental) phenomena and the same

* The above consideration also throws light on how, when there is lack of correspondence between perceptual awareness and the environmental situation, a third person can intellectually know more about a person's perceptual awareness than the person knows himself. In the foregoing described situations where there was a lack of correspondence between perceptual awareness and the environmental situation, a naïve observer might not even be aware of it, or, if he were, would not know why the lack of correspondence existed. On the other hand, a person trained in the fields of physics might in many instances not only be aware of the lack of correspondence before the naïve person was but would intellectually know why it existed.

conclusion would be reached as to the part that prior conditioning of the observer and his assumptions play in the lack of correspondence.*

October 30, 1953

RE: MANUAL—RELATION OF EFFICACY OF AN INDIVIDUAL'S BEHAVIOR TO THE
DEGREE OF CORRESPONDENCE AND LACK OF CORRESPONDENCE BETWEEN
PERCEPTUAL AWARENESS AND COMPREHENSION AND THE
ENVIRONMENTAL SITUATION

### RESOLUTIONS OF LACK OF CORRESPONDENCE

It is apparent that the efficacy of an individual's behavior in furthering his purposes is directly related to the degree of correspondence between his perceptual awareness of thatness and thereness and comprehension of sequential events and the environmental situation.

If there is such correspondence, he can be successful; if there is a lack of such correspondence, he cannot be successful.

If there is a lack of such correspondence, the efficacy of his future behavior will depend upon his capacity to resolve such lack of correspondence.

Before going on to consider how lack of correspondence can be resolved, let us first reconsider what is being referred to by the words "correspondence" and "lack of correspondence," and resolution of lack of correspondence.

If the observer is *simply observing*, the questions as to whether or not there was correspondence and the necessity of resolving the lack of

* Furthermore, from the point of view of the problem of the relative roles played by the observing person and his environment in the nature of his perceptual awareness, a person's physiology is essentially an aspect of himself, at least an essentially human aspect of reality, and all of the lacks of correspondence related to physiological phenomena throw light on what the human individual contributes to his perceptual awareness. For an example, consider the situation where the observer's eyes are crossed, either because of squint or as a result of a blow on his head or too many drinks, the directions in which he sees things, with one or maybe both eyes, will not correspond to environmental conditions. The mistaken direction in which he sees things arises from similar conditioning assumptions as exist when one sees a mirage. The difference between this and the mirage situations is that in the mirage case the light rays came from a direction the observer was not conditioned to, an environmental physical phenomenon, while in the cross-eyed case the light rays impinged on his retinas in a manner he was not conditioned to, a physiological phenomenon.

correspondence, though of great scientific interest as throwing light on the nature of perception, are irrelevant to this inquiry which has to do with the efficacy of the *behavior* of the observing individual. It is only when the observer is purposefully acting on the basis of his perception to accomplish some purpose that the matter of correspondence between his perceptual awareness and environmental conditions becomes of primary importance.

When he acts, his perceptual awarenesses are of the significance of "objects" with specific characteristics and the significance of their specific directions and distances from him.

The environmental situations to which his perceptual awareness must correspond are not any or all aspects of environmental phenomena but those particular aspects of the environmental phenomena which when affected by his actions will further his purposes.

These particular aspects or significances potentially capable of being made use of to serve human purposes exist in their own right, so to speak, in the environmental situation irrespective of the observer.*

If the observer's action as prognosticated by his perceptual awareness is in conformity with, or affects those environmental significances so that his purposes are furthered, there is correspondence; if not, there is a lack of correspondence.

The criterion of correspondence is whether or not purpose is accomplished. In the last analysis there can never be exact correspondence between perceptual awareness and environmental conditions; e.g., as perceived distance and exact environmental distance. If reliability of prognosis were based on this latter type of correspondence our apprehensions would be such that we would not dare to act at all. If reliability of prognosis is based on whether or not purpose is accomplished, then reliability can become an absolute as far as there are absolutes in life and we can have faith in our perceptual awareness without apprehension.

January 1, 1954

## New Year's Greeting—1954

Perceiving is the analyzing by a particular person, from his particular behavioral center, of the significances to him of the immediate environmental situation in terms of environmental significances which, he has

---

* But their existences are perceived only in terms of significances to the observer; e.g., the individual perceives the sun as rotating about himself as a center, though we conceptually know we are rotating relative to it.

discovered from past experiences, have furthered the purposes of his being.

Under conditions where the analysis of the significances of the immediate environmental situation in terms of the significances of prior environmental situations discloses the significances of the immediate environmental situation there is correspondence between what is in perceptual awareness and the immediate environmental situation. *Easy going.*

Under conditions where the analysis of the significances of the immediate environmental situation in terms of the significances of prior environmental situations fails to disclose the significance of the immediate environmental situation there is a lack of correspondence between what is in perceptual awareness and the immediate environmental situation. *Rough going.*

May you enjoy both.

April 21, 1954

REALITY OF ABSTRACTED ASPECTS AND SYMBOLS REFERRING TO THEM

Objects, qualities, causal phenomena, time and space are examples of abstracted aspects.

Examples of symbols referring to such abstracted objects are nouns, adjectives, sentences with subject, verb, and object.

It is a vogue of much modern thinking to deny the reality of such abstraction. For example—the semanticist's denial of the reality of and classification of objects, of symbols referring to them, and of causality; our own denials of abstractions existing in their own right; our insistence that abstractions are real only when considered in relation to all the "but for's" except for which the abstraction would not exist.

There is good reason for this vogue in so far as it is limited to the recognition of the fallacy of taking a part for the whole. But it would seem to be in error to the extent it implies that abstracted aspects cannot in themselves be real.

This error becomes apparent when one considers the concrete experiencing of a unique responsible individual carrying out his unique purposes from his unique operational center in a unique undetermined environment.

His perceptual awarenesses of differentiated "thatnesses," and their differentiated "therenesses" based on classification and the taking into account of qualitative aspects, are realities, as is their spatial relation to him.

It is not by chance that all people are perceptually aware of objects and their qualities.

The correspondence between an individual's perceptual awareness and the actual "thatnesses and their therenesses" is a reality.

When he takes account of the sequential significances of one or more differentiated "thatnesses" in terms of cause and effects furthering his purposes, the causal phenomena of which he is aware and their temporal occurrence are realities.

Whether or not he has prehended the causal effects that follow his prehending is a reality, i.e., whether or not there is a correspondence between what he foresees will happen and what actually happens.

When in a concrete situation involving others a person uses symbols as a word to initiate a chain of sequential events to carry out his purposes, the word is a reality whether or not the user had in mind the referent of the word he uses.

When a person on his own responsibility makes a choice and acts to carry out his purpose, he himself induces a chain of causal effects which alter his environment. His uniquely responsible choices and actions seem in every respect causal—the only real causal effects.

It seems that all the above-mentioned abstractions are realities in a concrete situation because of the roles they play in relation to the purposes and the enhancement of the value satisfaction of a unique responsible person in his unique undetermined situation. Purposes and value satisfaction may transcend space and time but their existence involves space and time in that they exist only through the choice and acting of unique responsible persons choosing and acting at specific instances in undetermined following events and at specific locations in such events, i.e., what we have conceptualized as specific points in space and time.

Why this is so is ineffable. Our acceptance of this belief is faith.

April 27, 1954

### Unique Individual Responsibility: Awarenesses, Perceiving, Prehending, Sensing, Conceptualizing, Valuing, Degree of Personal Control—Roles Played in Determining Purposes and Initiating Causal Action to Further Their Fulfillment

It seems apparent that there are innumerable personal sequential processes for which the individual is not responsible, such as the so-called physiological processes of which the individual is unaware.

It would appear that an individual is not responsible for sequential processes of which he has no awareness.

Conversely it would appear that an individual is responsible for sequential processes of which he is aware. Further that all awarenesses in and of themselves are partial actualities, realities, that are playing a role in the more inclusive reality of a unique responsible individual initiating action to carry out his purposes in a unique undetermined environmental situation from his unique behavioral center.

So perceived "objects" are realities. Words and symbols referring to them are realities. Prehended sequential significances are realities. Conceptualizations of such sequential significances are realities. Inquirings and specifications are realities. Sensations are realities. Valuings are realities.

One of the main points we are making here is the reality of "objects" (and of "classification," causal phenomena involving time and space, symbols, conceptualizations, words, subject, verb, object, sentences) from the perspective of every unique responsible individual from his unique behavioral center in his unique behavioral situation.

None of them are realities, i.e., exist in their own right apart from the total situation. But in the context of concreteness they are indispensable realities, whose denial can lead only to confusion and ineffectuality of personal behavior.

It would appear that there is a greater degree of personal responsibility for conceptualized symbolized awarenesses than the other abovementioned types of awareness in that conceptual awarenesses are subject to a greater degree of personal control and recall. They can be brought to awareness unrelated to an immediate unique behavioral situation, which is not the case with unconceptualized or unsymbolized perceptions, prehensions and valuings. They make it possible for us to go into inquiry to resolve hitches and frustrations.

September 25, 1954

### "GOD"

In our search for "God" we are sidetracked by our belief that what we are searching for is a static aspect of reality existing in its own right in and by itself, and that we should be able to have an ineffable sense of God when the occasion demands, even in our passivity.

On consideration it would seem that the reality to which the word "God" refers is not static but a process, "a series of actions or opera-

The "distorted room," one of Ames's perception demonstrations, in which the floor slopes sharply down to the left; also left edge of back wall is twice as far from viewing point as its right edge.

Because the room is so constructed that the retinal image it produces at the viewing point is similar to the image produced by familiar rectilinear rooms, we assume the room *is* rectilinear and we therefore make people conform to it.

tions definitely conducing to an end," "a phenomenon which shows a continuous change in time, as the process of growth" (Webster). Further, that this process occurs only with and through unique individual persons behaving in their unique positions in time and space.

The conditions for this process of growth require:

1. That the individual experiences lack of fulfillment of his well-being, ranging from feelings of inadequacy, depression, disappointment, hitches, frustration, to agony. Except for such preliminary sensing of lack of fulfillment of well-being, "God" cannot be experienced.

2. That the individual conceives or senses, through inquiry, contemplation or prayer, future conditions that may integrate or resolve such lack of fulfillment of his well-being. This may involve (a) his weighing and choosing between conflicting significances of his perceptual awareness of his immediate behavioral environment, (b) his prehension of consequences of sequential events, (c) his purposes and value satisfactions, conceptual and ineffable.

3. That the individual acts to bring about future consequences that may mitigate the lack of fulfillment of his well-being—that is, acts to bring consequences that may alter his own reality ("Form World"), i.e., that may enhance the prognostic reliability of his perception of the significance of his environment; the reliability of his prehension of sequential events; the value quality of his purposes, conceptual and ineffable.

4. The occurrence of the consequences of his action and the alteration of his "Form World" resulting from such occurrences.

In the totality of the carrying out of the conditions requisite for this process of growth, God is experienced.

Aspects of the experiencing of God may vary from those that occur in respect to the enhancement of simple perception to those that occur in respect to the enhancement of religious insight experienced by the great saints and prophets.

From the above it would appear that the experiencing of God can occur only relatively occasionally, can never be a continuous state or in our passivity.

It would also appear that the experiencing of lack of fulfillment of well-being, ranging from feelings of inadequacy, depression, disappointment, hitches, frustration, to agony, far from necessarily being calamitous, are essential preliminary processes to the experiencing of God.

They are aspects of what is in the now that have to be because of what has occurred before. What has happened, what is in "the now," is the only foundation, the only "take-off," there is from which we can enhance our future well-being and experience God.

CHOOSING AS A TRANSACTIONAL PROCESS—"FREE WILL"

*Choosing as a Process Involves*

1. A weighing on the conscious (awareness) level (as differentiated from all the weighing processes that are going on at all times in perceiving, prehending, purposing and valuing on the unconscious level) by a unique person in a unique behavioral situation, in a universe where the future is undetermined.

2. Such weighings, which involve an inquiry or contemplation or prayer or all of them, follow an awareness of a hitch or frustration, i.e., a situation where (a) an individual's unique Form World is imperiled and/or (b) there are future possibilities of the fulfillment of his well-being which he is not experiencing.

3. The conscious selection for which he alone is responsible, between two or more alternative courses of action, the consequences of which may prevent the imperiling of his Form World or enhance his future well-being, or both.

4. The initiation by action of a series of sequential events that may lead to such consequences.

5. The occurrence of such consequences.

6. The resulting effect of such occurrences on his Form World and environment, including other persons.

An example, starting on the perceiving level, would be where a hunter sees a deer with a suggestion of a splash of red on it. The situation gives rise to a perceptual conflict, hitch, of which he is aware. Does he see a deer or doesn't he see a deer? He hesitates and considers (low level inquiry). On his own responsibility he has to make a choice whether what he sees is a deer or is not a deer—possibly a man. His choice determines whether he shoots or doesn't shoot. Consequences will follow from either choice which will alter his Form World, reality and future well-being.

The choice is not a "free" choice about anything but is limited to selecting between specific alternatives—usually a single alternative—to shoot or not to shoot (on a higher level: "to be or not to be").

Under situations where a person experiences a hitch and makes a choice, doing nothing is action that starts a chain of sequential events. It is only in situations where hitches are not experienced that doing nothing is not action, i.e., does not start a chain of sequential events.

A question arises: What do we mean by the statement that a person is responsible for the choice he makes? Simply that he alone makes it. He alone is the causal factor of the consequences that follow.

He cannot necessarily be held responsible for the consequences, whether he or others deem them good or bad. Apparently all that he can be held responsible for is that he makes the best effort of which he is capable, under the specific conditions, in formulating his judgment and choice.

The further question arises: In making his choice, to what extent is a person the sole determinant of the choice he arrives at, or to what extent is his choice determined by aspects of his Form World for which he is not responsible (God or the devil)?

In the last analysis a person's judgment is always determined by his Form World.

It would seem that the role a person plays in determining (is responsible for) the choice he makes depends not upon the particular nature of specific aspects (significances) that may play a role, but upon the extent of the diverse significances on all levels that he takes into account and/or orchestrates in formulating his judgment and making his choice.

From the above it would appear that every person faced by a hitch or frustration becomes a causal factor. As we are almost always faced by hitches and frustrations on one level or another, we are almost always causal factors.

As causal factors we have a responsibility to behave to the best of our abilities.

### *"Free Will"*

What is connoted by the words "Free Will," i.e., that a person can do what he wants, would seem to have no reference to the realities considered above.

November 10, 1954

### My, Me, Myself and I

Words are pointers used by man to direct one's own or another's attention to differentiated aspects of ongoing life.

Nouns point to inanimate things; e.g., objects.

Pronouns point to specific aspects of animate beings; e.g., its or it, yours or you, my or I.

Whatever is pointed to by a word is only a particular aspect of on-going life differentiated by the pointer because of its specific significance to his well-being. Apart from its transactional relationship to the pointer's well-being it has no significance or reality.

In using nouns and second and third person pronouns, the pointer is pointing to differentiated aspects "outside" of himself.

In using first person pronouns, as "I," "myself," "me," "my," the pointer is pointing at himself, i.e., the pointer is pointing at the pointer.

If I use the words "my leg" or "my heart" or "my brain" or "my brain waves," I am pointing to differentiated aspects of my physiology.

If I use the words "I am hungry" or "I am mad" or "I am amorous," I am pointing to differentiated emotional aspects.

If I use the words "that is beautiful" or "that is good" or "that is bad," I am pointing to differentiated value aspects.

But suppose I want to point to that aspect of myself that is doing the pointing, that stands back and takes account of my above-mentioned personal differentiations and chooses which one to point at?

Apparently the only pointer I have is the word "I," possibly the words "my self."

It is apparent what an inadequate pointer these words are, not only for other persons but also for "my self."

Isn't it that the reason for their inadequacy is our commonly held belief that nouns point to "thatnesses" existing apart in their own right; our "failures" to recognize that all "thatnesses" as such don't exist but are our own classifications which we have created to take account of the potential sequential significances of our environment to further our well-being?

While the sequential significances inherent in such thatnesses as my leg or my heart or my emotions or values are apparent, it would seem that the significance of our essential "I's" or "our selves" is not apparent: that it is of a different nature from sequential significances which are characterized by their specific relation to past and future events and are affected by the choices of our essential "I's."

Isn't it that what is pointed to by "I," not being sequential in nature, cannot be isolated, cannot be pointed to by a pronoun, cannot be pointed to at all, because a pointer can't point at itself.

It would seem that these considerations throw light on the dilemma by which we are all faced when we try to follow the precept that "one must become unaware of, lose one's Self, to experience God and Reality."

It is confusing to try to understand how, by becoming unaware of an aspect of reality, we could become more aware of the total reality of God.

Further, it would seem that nothing that can be pointed at exists as a reality in its own right but only in transactional relationship to everything else that can be pointed at.

Still further, the essential "I" is not an isolated aspect of self, but is a reality in dimensions where "isolation" as we understand it in time and space does not exist.

The essential "I" isn't anything of our own that we can lose.

January 17, 1955

## On Faith and Reality from the Transactional Point of View
### (With H.C.)

Faith is "confidence in something open to question or suspicion" (Webster).

The "something" referred to is that which is necessary for our well-being and its enhancement.

What is necessary or wanted for our well-being is:

1. Continuance of the significances of static forms significant to our well-being.

2. Repetition of the significances of future events significant to our well-being (sequential events).

3. Repetition of the accomplishment of purposeful goals significant to our value satisfaction.

4. Repetition of experiencing value satisfactions.

5. Enhancement of the significances of all continuous and repetitive forms, i.e., enhancement of the significance of our well-being.

There is a hierarchy of degree of determinateness and continuance of static form and repetition of sequential events in an undetermined universe whose significances we ourselves have created.

|  | *Behavioral* | *Abstractions* |
|---|---|---|
|  | 1. Physiology | 1. Geography |
|  | 2. Sensations | 2. Science |
| Form World | 3. Prehensions | 3. Ethics |
|  | 4. Purposes |  |
|  | 5. Value responses |  |

The degree with which significances are wanted varies with their importance to our personal well-being and its enhancement. Experiences that deny the very existence of the determinateness and repeatability of the various aspects of our "Form Worlds," i.e., the continuance of its static aspects or the repetition of its sequential events, the effectiveness of purpose, the effectiveness of value-judgments in furthering our well-being, deny the existence of reality itself.

Such experiences shock us to the degree that the particular aspect of reality which is denied is significant to us. The degree of shock is related to the determinativeness and repeatability of the aspect of reality that is denied. The denial of the determinativeness of our perceptual awareness of thatnesses at their therenesses (illusions) is a minor shock; of our prehensions of sequential events (misapprehensions) a greater shock; failure to accomplish our purposes a still greater shock; the failure of our value-judgments to further our well-being (false gods) the greatest shock.

The denial of the reality of our conceptual abstractions of objects and their relations (geography), causal events in space-time (science), being impersonal, result in relatively minor shocks compared with our first-person experiences which deny reality.

Varying degrees of faith are required to carry on whenever we experience any type of shock related to the denial of our reality. The most basic want and responsibility of life is to preserve reality. It is the preservation of reality that differentiates organic from the non-determined, non-repeatable aspects of the cosmos.

However, there is another want and responsibility of life that is as basic as that to preserve reality.

That is the want and responsibility to continue our reality in an ever-changing undetermined cosmos and enhance the significance of reality. The opportunity to satisfy this want and meet this responsibility occurs only when we are shocked by experiences that deny reality.

So faith not only preserves reality but plays an indispensable role in enhancing its significance.

Every unique organism has the responsibility and want of preserving its particular reality. This is evidenced by the diversity of protecting envelopes, skins, etc., that diverse organisms have evolved to protect their total physiologies against outer effects incompatible with their particular life reality. This equally applies to the envelopes of every cell in their physiologies.

On the behavioral level the particular habits and reflexes of every organism conserve its particular life reality.

On the conscious behavioral psychological level the particular mores and customs of every higher organism conserve its particular life realities.

When an organism's life realities are affected or threatened, the organism experiences an unquestioned need and responsibility to preserve them.

When it is not apparent to the organism how its life realities can be preserved, faith is necessary.

It is in these very conditions when an organism's life realities are affected or threatened that the opportunity exists to discover heretofore unrecognized cosmic phenomena that are a hazard to the continuance of life realities and to protect its life realities against them, thereby enhancing its life's realities.

From the above it would appear that faith is an ineffable value sense of the worthwhileness of our reality.

February 7, 1955

### REALITIES—NEGATION OF TRANSCENDENCE

The words "real," "actual," "true," are all used to refer to "reality." However, their definitions are ambiguous, first because in the last analysis reality is ineffable, and, second, because they are formulated on the assumption, conscious or unconscious, of a bifurcated subjective-objective cosmos. Envisaged from the transactional point of view, a non-bifurcated reality includes all of the phenomena that are involved in the ongoing existence of living organisms, including man, and their emergence and transcendence.

It seems apparent that man has and can have no awareness, sense, or conceptual realization of the total mass of these ongoing trans-relationships; e.g., the ongoing events in the cells of our bodies.

Further, our knowing of "reality," since we can't have a knowing of anything of which we are not aware, is limited to those aspects of which we are and can be aware.

For purposes of intellectual analysis our knowing of reality can be differentiated between:

1. Significances we are aware of and take into account from our first-person point of view from our unique operational centers at which we are engaged in our ongoing behavior to maintain and enhance our well-being. In the last analysis such awarenesses are uniquely individually personal, due to the uniqueness of the behaving individual and the uniqueness of every behavioral situation. The full significances of such awareness can never be repeated *in toto* but only to the extent that ever-changing conditions may be somewhat similar. Their personal signifi-

cance can not be conceptualized or conceptually communicated to others, though they can be suggested by esthetic symbols. The nearest that others can become aware of such personally experienced significances is through sharing the same behavioral circumstances.

2. Significances we are aware of and take into account by way of specific conceptualized abstractions referred to by words or symbols or formulations which may automatically come to mind or be recalled at will. The significances to which such words and symbols refer are bifurcated and do not embrace the non-bifurcated significances experienced by a behaving person carrying out his purposes from his unique operational center. They are common for many individuals wherever and whenever they are and whatever their purposes. Examples of such conceptualized referents are (a) spatial abstractions, i.e., "thatnesses at therenesses," maps, macroscopic and microscopic; (b) temporal abstractions, historical followings; (c) sequential events, causes and effects—scientific formulations concerning inanimate nature; (d) formulations concerning animate nature, physiology, psychology, ethics and religious formulations.

The characteristic of awarenesses of such abstractions is that they are not uniquely personal but universally common, due to their referring only to the bifurcated repeatable non-emergent aspects of reality that can be commonly experienced by everyone. It follows that their significance can be experienced again and again and recalled at will and can be communicated to others *in toto*.

3. Quite similar are the abstracted significances we are aware of and take into account by way of esthetic abstractions, symbols and formulations which may automatically come into awareness or be recalled at will. The significances to which such symbols refer are similar in all respects to those just described, except that their referents are the sensed and felt aspects which, although they are common in human experience, are ineffable to the extent that they cannot be directly referred to by words or other symbols.

The above three differentiated types of non-bifurcated and bifurcated awarenesses and knowings constitute the total of "reality" for each unique person at the unique operational center at which he is engaged in ongoing behavior to maintain and enhance his well-being. There is and can be no other reality known to him.

Let us consider more specifically the non-bifurcated reality we experience in our ongoing living when we are carrying out our purposes from our unique behavioral centers. It constitutes the reality of the significance of where we are, the ground we stand on, the ground we will be standing on when we take our next step, our prehended consequences of our next action, the "why" of our purposes, our responsibilities, our choices, our well-being, our hitches and frustrations, and through their resolution the enhancement of reality itself.

Now let us consider the matter of the negation of reality. Reality is subject to negation because it is contingent. In our ongoing living, reality is being continually negated on every level of significance. The effect of its negations varies with the importance to us of the significances that are being negated. For example, sensory illusions are "low level" negations of reality that in general we take in our stride with the help of humor. Misapprehensions of the consequences of sequential events are more upsetting negations. Non-occurrence of the expected effect of accomplished purposes is a still more frustrating negation.

In general, negations of reality that we experience in personal behavior are destructive of some aspect of the uniquely determined "Form World," physiological, psychological, valueful, and religious, conceptual, that each of us brings, so to speak, to the behavioral situation and of which each of us is the sole responsible guardian and trustee. Its negation not only leaves us in a *nil* reality but also thwarts our effective behavior. And yet we must continue to carry on.

It is under these conditions that faith is necessary if we continue to live. The nature of the faith varies from our sense of surety in our perceptions to take another step, to an ineffable faith in ultimate reality and its transcendence, as when a beloved one dies or loses his mind.

The faith that sustains us when our personal reality has been negated is quite different from what sustains us when the reality of our commonly shared conceptual abstractions is negated, whether scientific, ethical, esthetic, or religious. We did not require a faith to sustain us when modern scientific discoveries negated the laws of Newtonian physics and denied the existence of matter as such and our conceptual abstractions as to the nature of time and space.

Let us now turn to further consideration of the effect that experiencing a negation of our reality has upon us. Since our personal reality is a *sine qua non* of our being, the negation of any of its significances affects our being. The negation of even a relatively insignificant aspect of our personal reality shocks us; e.g., visual illusions. The negation of more significant aspects of our reality may be so intolerable that we refuse to accept or acknowledge their occurrence, as when we refuse to accept what has occurred or what we prehend will occur if it negates our reality.

If the cause of the negation is an occurrence that is of an impersonal nature, we are convinced it is wrong, we fear it and look upon it as cruel fate.

If other persons are responsible for such negating occurrences, we condemn and become angry with them, fear them, hate them and put them out of our existence.

If our social group is responsible, we become anti-social.

If both our social group and impersonal nature are causes of the negations we create an imaginary reality.

Often it is our own behavior that negates the significances of our reality. We may then hate and fear ourselves, consider ourselves unworthy or evil, develop an inferiority or guilt complex.

In all the above we have been considering but one aspect of reality, i.e., its aspect of continuing form. The other aspect of reality is its flow, i.e., its emergence, transcendence or the opposite.

Paradoxically enough that occurs only through the negation of the form aspect of reality. And in the last analysis it only occurs through the behavior of unique individuals in unique behavioral situations who have experienced the frustration of the negating of their own personal reality and who, sustained by faith, have through inquiry, contemplation and prayer resolved the negations into a reality of more transcendent significances, or who, lacking faith, have not only failed in their responsibility to enhance reality but must continue to live in a negated reality.

The essential characteristic of our personal realities is that of established and continuing form. When we experience a negation of our reality, we experience a disruption of the continuity of form. At the same time we experience lack of surety in the effectiveness of our choosing, our purposes, and our capacity to carry them out. Under such conditions we can no longer behave effectively. Our salvation under such situations is to re-establish form. At the same time our lack of surety causes us to question the reality of our own personal reality.

So we turn to another aspect of reality that is not so subject to negation and which, because it is commonly shared by other persons, seems to have enhanced validity and which is furthermore subject to being voluntarily recalled and communicated. That is the abstracted aspect of reality above referred to, which we conceive in conceptual terms and which is the sum total of everything that we have or will have conceptual knowledge about in the fields of all the sciences, ethics, art and religion.

We might refer to this as the reality of abstracted form. The indispensable role that this reality of abstracted form plays in the enhancement and transcendence of life will be considered later, but it is entirely different from and cannot be substituted for our unique personal reality, among other possible reasons because:

1. The significances it refers to are entirely other than the ineffable significances experienced by the unique individual behaving from his unique operational center.

2. In the now it is absolute and determined and denies the contingent nature of ongoing life.

3. It denies the sacredness of the individual, his potentiality for transcendence, and the responsible role he plays in transcendence.

4. In religious terms it is a bar between the unique individual and his living God.

However, all of us sometimes, many of us all the time, to avoid the vicissitudes of our lives, substitute this "reality of abstracted form" for our own concrete personal reality. By so doing we gain the security of existence in a reality that cannot be negated. But in so doing we deprive ourselves of the opportunity to emerge and transcend.

In spite of the hitches, frustrations, and crosses we must always bear because of circumstances that continually negate our personal reality, it is only the experiencing of negations of our personal reality that make it possible for us to emerge and transcend.

And paradoxically enough it is only by our making use of the "reality of abstracted form" that we can bring about such emergence and transcendence of our personal realities. It is the humanly evolved "reality of abstracted form" that makes possible the flow of the forms of personal reality into forms of higher significances.

When an individual's personal reality is negated, his ongoing living is checked, as by a hitch or frustration; then by turning his awareness to the specific aspects of "reality of abstracted form" that refer to the specific concrete phenomena involved in the hitch or frustration, either through the mental processes referred to by inquiry, contemplation, or prayer, and experimentation, he can discover inadequacies in his up-to-the-now "personal reality" and alter them so that his reality includes more encompassing significances, and what appeared to be a negation of his reality becomes one with a more profound reality of enhanced significance.

May 5, 1955

"My World"

As I sit here in my office and ask myself what constitutes "my world," I become aware that it involves such a mass and variety of aspects, such as objects, people, motion, sequential events, purposing, valuing, choosing, acting and effect of acting, that I am at a loss as to how best to begin to conceptualize and describe it. For want of a possibly better

starting point, I will begin by thinking about "my world of objects," *
because that world is most plainly evident to me.

Since what is in my perceptual awareness concerning objects is not a
disclosure of something existing in its own right apart from me but my
own prognosis of the significance of my situation for effective behavior,
my "world of objects" is unique to me.† It follows that my most fruitful
field of inquiry must be my own personal "world of objects."

## "My World of Objects"

The objects that are most plainly evident to me are those that I
see about me, my room and its furniture and various articles and beyond
that the landscape I see out of the window.

But besides the objects I see, there are objects I take account of that
I can't see. For example, the money and keys in my pocket, my pen and
eraser and stamps in the drawers of my desk, my papers in the cabinets,
the toilet down the hall, the stairs and the door out of the building, my
home and the many other homes and buildings and roads and what not,
in and beyond the town of Hanover, extending to far countries where
I have traveled. And beyond the places I have been to I can conceptually
imagine, as on maps, countries and seas and beyond that the stellar universe. There are many, many more things in "my world of objects" that
I can't see than there are that I see.

An inseparable aspect of the objective significance of every particular
thing in my "world of objects" whether I see it or not, is where it is
relative to me. My eraser is a little to my left within reaching distance.
The wastepaper basket is close behind and a little below to the right.
My money is in my pocket. If the eraser were in the other room or the
wastepaper basket were behind the door or my money were at home, each
would have a different objective significance.

Moreover, if I change my position, where each and every thing relative to me is different, because of that difference its significance to me is
different. If I go into my other room to write, I won't use my eraser nor
will I toss wastepaper into the wastepaper basket.

And, further, the significance to me of each and every thing in my
world of objects is uniquely different to me, in varying degrees, from
what it is to any other person. In the first place, because no other person

* I am limiting my present considerations to inorganic objects only. To include
other persons as objects would necessitate considering my own taking account
of their purposes and well-being as aspects of objective significances, which is not
necessary with inanimate objects, which are without purposes and well-being.

† Empirical evidence supporting this inference has been amassed by the so-called
Transactional Psychologists.

can be just where I am, the relative position to me of things in my world of objects is different from the relative position of the same things in the other person's "world of objects."

Secondly, the significance of the things themselves in my world is different from the significance of the same things to any other person. For example, the significance to me of each of the different piles of papers on my desk or in my home is entirely different from what it would be to anyone else.

And thirdly, the things I take account of in my world of objects and also their significance are continually changing with my constantly changing purposes and interests.

While my real world of objects is unique to me because of particular past and immediate purposes and position, to the extent that other persons have had similar pasts, have similar purposes and are in the approximate positions, our real world of objects will be similar. To the extent that other persons have had different pasts, have different purposes, are at other places, our real worlds of objects will be different.

Such a conclusion seems to be in direct conflict with the universally held belief that there exists but one real world of objects in more or less fixed relative positions that exists quite apart from persons or their position in it which is disclosed by common experience and confirmed by impersonal scientific procedures.

## On the Reality of My World of Objects

The unseen things in my world of objects are as real to me as the things I am looking at and under some circumstances more important to my existence. I was once completely lost in the woods in the daytime. I could see everything about me but because I didn't know where I was I had no unseen world of objects extending out beyond my seen world. I was in danger and had difficulty in controlling my panic. On another occasion I was caught in a dark wood at nightfall without a light. I knew where I was, that is, I continued to have my unseen objective world, but I couldn't see anything. I was much annoyed but in no danger and experienced no sense of panic. In that situation I could still take into account things in my immediate objective world by my senses of hearing and touch.

An enlightening hypothetical situation would exist if, as I sat here at my desk, I were suddenly struck blind, deaf, and without sense of touch, so that I had no awareness of my immediate objective world. I might still know where I was, i.e., have an awareness of my extra-stimulus world, but that would avail me nothing. Moreover, once I had changed my position that would no longer exist.

For a person to exist there must be at least some degree of sensual awareness of one's immediate environment, objective world, and also awareness of one's extra-stimulus objective world and one's position in them.

Helen Keller, with only her sense of touch, is an interesting case to consider. Through that sense alone she developed a most fruitful immediate and extra-stimulus objective world. Moreover, the fullness of her life is evidence that it is not the so-called objective characteristics, such as color, hardness, etc., that constitute the reality of our objective worlds. The reality of things in our objective worlds is their significance to us in carrying out our individual purposes. Every baby when it is born, though it has all of its sense responses, is in the condition of the adult above considered who, through loss of her sense responses, has neither a seen nor unseen objective world. Through experience a baby creates its own seen and unseen objective world by discovering the special characteristics of environmental conditions that are significant to the furtherance of its inherited purposes and those of its social group.

To return to my world of objects. The totality of my "world of objects" of which I am potentially capable of taking account includes not only the patently evident ones that I am looking at but extends to include all those objects beyond my field of vision that I can see only with my mind's eye with various degrees of clarity. Generally speaking, I take into account the totality of the objects in my field of vision and their relation to me and to each other. But I am never aware of or take into account the totality of my world of unseen objects. My mind's eye focuses only on those particular unseen objects that are significant to the carrying out of my immediate purposes from my immediate position. For example: If my purpose is to write, my mind's eye discloses my pen in the drawer of my desk and where it is from me and not my hat on the hatrack in the other room. I am unable to take account of the "thatness-thereness" of my pen and the "thatness-thereness" of my hat at the same time.

With my mind's eye I seem to be able to take account of multiple objects only if they are together in the same field or "thereness" and not if they are at different "therenesses." My mind's eye can visualize symbols of objects that are in different locations at the same time on a map, but my mind's eye can't see objects that are in different locations from me at the same time in my actual world of unseen objects.

Besides the world of objects in spatial relation to me there is a world of objects with no spatial relation to me, tools, clothes, etc., whose "thereness" I can establish by inquiry.

My mind's eye can envisage an image of an object such as my pen as being anywhere relative to myself, as sticking on the end of my nose. But such conceptually abstracted imaginings have nothing to do with my real world of unseen objects in which my pen is in the drawer of my desk at a specific "thereness" from me, which I can use by reaching over and opening the drawer and taking it out. It is only in my real world of objects that I exist and can behave and carry out my purposes.

The essential nature of my objective world, both seen and unseen, is that I can count on its various aspects remaining the same. That is, being the same now as it was and continuing to be the same in the future, i.e., having constancy of form both as a whole and in detail. For example: I must count on my eraser being where it was in a particular compartment in my desk drawer and being pliable enough to erase pencil marks; that my home is now as and where it was when I left it this morning and will be as and where it was when I return to it this noon. If my objective worlds didn't have such constancy of form, I couldn't behave and carry out my purposes.

It is only because of the constancy of my objective world that I can carry out my purposes. Constancy has reference to the relative continuation of conditions that enable me to carry out my purposes, not to objective characteristics themselves or objective position. There is a constant mutation of both the nature and position of objects in my objective world. My eraser is continually hardening and often gets misplaced. My home is in constant need of repair, from washing windows to shingling the roof. The position of parts of it are even changing through settling. Our foods don't last, clothing wears out. Depreciation is recognized as an economic fact. Consider all the old automobiles in junk yards and abandoned houses, manufacturing plants and roads, etc., ad infinitum.

The geographical, terrestrial and material aspects of civilization are continually changing, to an unrecognizable degree in case of older ones. There is no permanence of form in the environmental world itself which can account for the permanence of form of my objective world. The permanence of form of my objective world is due to my selection from the never exactly repeating environmental world of those particular aspects whose relative continuance is of significance to me in carrying out my purposes.

The existence of a permanent world of things with objective characteristics which exists in and of itself apart from me and other persons is an imaginative fallacy.

The existence of a personal or common permanent objective world which exists in and of itself apart from me and other persons which enables me and other persons to carry out our purposes is also an imaginative fallacy.

The continuation of the form of my objective world that enables me to carry out my purposes only exists because of my own continual desires and activities to maintain it. This holds from constant alteration of what is in my visual awareness with change of seasons and the passage of years to my keeping an eraser in my drawer so that it will erase, to putting food in the ice chest, to keeping up my automobile and house, to paying taxes for repair of roads, the fire department, and what not.

The maintenance of the form of my objective world, seen and unseen, does not exist apart from but together with the personal Form Worlds seen and unseen of other persons of the social group in which I exist, from my wife and children and friends and fellow citizens, both local and world.

May 21, 1955

## MY DIFFERENT WORLDS OF ESTHETIC OBJECTS

I have also my worlds of esthetic objects, seen, unseen, conceptualized and imaginary. In general they are the same nature as my worlds of objects I have been describing.

Their difference lies in this: In the "world of objects" I have described I limited my considerations to the importances to me of the objects as disclosures of potentialities for carrying out my purposes and preserving my physical well-being, i.e., as to "how-to-do" to further my purposes and ongoing life. But besides the importance to me of accomplishing purposes and preserving my well-being, there is also the importance of experiencing value satisfaction.

I experience such value satisfaction in my worlds of seen, unseen, conceptualized and imaginary objects.

An esthetic experience is the experiencing of the imaginary worlds of value satisfactions not yet experienced but potentially capable of being experienced in the worlds of seen and unseen objects. A creative work of art is an object so designed that those who see it experience the heretofore unexperienced value satisfaction.

ON THE NATURE OF MY WORLDS OF OBJECTS

As I live along involved in my purposeful activities, I don't conceptualize the objects of my worlds of seen and unseen objects. I don't think the word *eraser* when I pick it up and use it or think the word *home* when I start to go there for lunch. When I am driving in an automobile, I carry on without conceptualizing, directed by taking into account the registered ineffable aspects of former experiences.

It is when I become aware of environmental significances with which I have had no experience and that interfere with my purposes or continued well-being that my world of abstracted conceptualized objects plays its role. If I go for a drive in my car, as long as I am on roads where I have been before I am directed, so to speak, by my world of seen objects, continually picking up known and localized objects in my world of unseen objects. But if I go beyond where I have ever been before, I must rely on my world of conceptualized objects. If the roads are marked with signs I rely on them. If there are no signs I soon get lost and to act purposefully must turn to a map—a two-dimensional conceptual abstraction of the relative relationship of abstracted objects with no personal polar relationship—and by working out where I am on the map proceed to drive as directed by my world of conceptualized objects by studying maps of the country I am going to visit.

Or if in carrying on in environmental objective significances with which I am familiar through past experience, my purposes are thwarted by an environmental objective significance I had not taken into account, I go into inquiry (as Dewey says), as when, driving automatically along a well-known road, looking at the landscape, I notice something on the road ahead. I will immediately start a train of objective conceptualization such as: Is it a skunk, or a stone, or a block of wood, or simply a piece of paper I can drive over?

In my many years of scientific research, I devoted much of my attention and activity to my world of conceptualized objects by way of consulting catalogues of scientific instruments that I might use in my research. When I got them and used them, they became part of my world of unseen objects. What success I may have attained may have been largely due to the inclusiveness of my world of conceptualized objects in that particular field and in using them, enlarging the field of my world of unseen objects.

My world of imaginary objects: An example of that world occurred when in carrying on my research I needed instrumental objects that didn't exist. By conceptually imagining, I created for myself a new world of conceptually imagined objects, the creation of which might further my purposes. When they were constructed and I used them, such imagined objects became part of seen and unseen objective worlds.

May 29, 1955

### DIFFERENT NATURE OF OBJECTIVE SIGNIFICANCES

The most obvious and easily conceptualized significances that I attribute to environmental phenomena which I characterize as objects are their sequential significances to my well-being and carrying out my purposes. In my world of experienced objects, seen and unseen, the vast majority of all the objects I look at are environmental phenomena of potential or actual sequential significance. There is nothing in my office that is not an artifact designed by man as a means for accomplishing some specific purpose. This is equally true of the objects I see as I go about the town or beyond the town—sidewalks, roads, automobiles, mail boxes, buildings, etc. And all of the objects are so designed as to indicate to me their use, sequential significance.

As I carry on my routine life, many artifactual objects in my seen and unseen worlds of objects ordinarily have only sequential significance, i.e., limited simply to potential how-to-do's. However, even then I experience a sense of surety or lack of surety in regard to the prognostic reliability of my seen object, a value sense of relative reality.

But over and beyond such sensed values very often the significance to me of the objects includes sensed values associated with the envisagement of the prehended end or the satisfaction of potential accomplishment.

And very, very often the significance to me of objects includes not only sensed reality and the sensed satisfaction of potential accomplishment, but also an awareness of the values related to and ensuing from the accomplishment of such ends.

Besides the artifactual objects designed for specific uses in my seen and unseen worlds of objects, there are many objects designed to include both sequential significances and value significances, as my home, its carpets and drapes and furniture, and in town the better designed structures, as the library and the churches.

And besides such objects of multiple significance, there are many objects in my world of seen and unseen objects that are important to me solely because of their value significance. The ornaments and objects of art in my house, my wife's flower garden and arrangements, land-scape views I especially remember, the just past unfolding beauty of spring with all its values thought of as being related to the concept of Easter.

The above hierarchy of value significances to me of objects in my worlds of seen and unseen objects are just as important and "real" to me as the sequential significances whose importance and reality we do not question. "But for" them the sequential significance of objects would have no lasting importance to me.

My above referred-to experienced value significances are an inherent aspect of my ongoing life through their transactional relationship to my uniqueness in my unique behavioral position in an undetermined environment, to my responsible choices and action, and to the consequences of my actions.

Besides such experienced value significance, I experience many value and emotional reactions that are not so transactionally related to my ongoing life. The unpleasant value and emotional reaction I often experience when I look at and smell flowers I associate with funerals is an example. I experience such values and emotions not as transactionally related significances of the object I am looking at but because of value and emotional experiences related to other circumstances that I was co-incidentally experiencing when I looked at the object. My value and emotional experiences when I look at our national flag have a coincidental origin. It is such coincidental relationships constantly repeated that modern advertising is making use of.

This brings me to a consideration of symbolic objects in general of which the above are particular examples. Symbolic objects can be defined as artifacts designed not for their use in accomplishing an end through action, as a hammer, but simply as referents to other significances in our experienced, conceptualized or sensed worlds.

Perhaps one of the simplest symbols is the objective significance of a broken branch on a trail referring only "thereness" to me from my immediate behavioral situation of an unreferred-to "thatness." A signpost with an arrow is a more specific symbolic referent. Sign languages have still more objective symbolic significance. Written words such as signs and posters have still more objective symbolic significance to me as to whatness and whereness of objects in my worlds of experienced objects, seen and unseen, and in my worlds of conceptualized objects.

Besides the symbols whose referents are significances of my worlds of objects there are all those symbols whose referents are significances of my worlds of sequential events, from catalogues to scientific literature. And beside such symbols are those whose referents are the significances of my worlds of values, from advertisements to the writings of the prophets.

In my intimate world of experienced objects, seen and unseen, as in and around Hanover, I take little or no account of symbols whose referents are objective significances. I never look at the street signs; I don't even think of the names of streets as I go about nor of the buildings nor of the stores where I am accustomed to go. But I do have to look at the signs in the supermarket and to go to the students' fraternities I have to study a college map or ask someone.

In my world of conceptualized objects, my effective behavior is dependent on objective symbolic referents.

May 30, 1955

### On the Constancy of Form of the Significances of My Worlds of Objects

The significance of an object is only the same, i.e., constant, or repeats, when it has the same sequential significance to me for carrying out the same purpose and is in the same functional position relative to my behavioral center.

As my behavioral position is always varying relative to the environmental phenomena having particular sequential significance, to make use of environmental significances to carry out my innumerable recurring purposes, I have to keep account of where (in terms of functional direction and distance) such diverse environmental significances are from my immediate egocentric behavioral center.

Such a personal "keeping account" constitutes my unique world of experienced objects, seen and unseen.

The effectivity of my purposeful behavior depends upon its continued constancy. The degree to which it is altered whether by man or natural causes reduces the effectivity of my behavior in carrying out my purpose, which in turn leads to an abandonment of many purposes themselves. A similar decrease in the effectivity of my behavior with abandonment of purpose would occur if I were permanently transported into rural China or India or Africa where the environmental sequential significances are so completely different from those that constitute my worlds of objects. The same would be true for a rural Chinese or Indian or African who was permanently transported to my environment here in Hanover.

It is the importance to me of my worlds of experienced objects, seen and unseen, as the only possible "milieu" of the fulfillment of my purposes that causes me to guard them so jealously and become aggressive and belligerent in their protection and to endow them with the aspect of ultimate reality—a reality even more real than that which I attribute to my purposes to which my worlds of objects are handmaids.

# Correspondence with John Dewey

EDITOR'S NOTE

The correspondence between Ames and John Dewey began shortly after Dewey had spent most of a day in late November, 1946, with us in New York, where a number of the demonstrations in perception had been especially set up at the suggestion of his friends Earl Kelley and William E. Kilpatrick so Dewey could experience them.

Dewey was then eighty-seven years old, and I shall never forget his excitement and almost childlike curiosity and eagerness as he shuffled from one demonstration to another.

Dewey's letters were mostly all done by him on his own typewriter without benefit of secretarial assistance; a few were in longhand.

The correspondence ended shortly after Dewey's ninety-first birthday, when his health began to fail and his interest waned. At that time Ames was sixty-eight.

John Dewey
1158 Fifth Avenue
New York 29, N.Y.

December 5, 1946

Dear Dr. Ames:

It would not be possible for me to overstate my judgment as to the importance of your demonstrations with respect to visual perception nor the importance of their being widely known. While the demonstrations themselves are in the field of visual perception, they bear upon the entire scope of psychological theory and upon all practical applications of psychological knowledge, beginning with education.

They are in line with what is best in recent psychological work. But they carry this "best" further than has yet been done, and what is more important, they provide a thorough and systematic, step by step, experimental demonstration of principles which, to the best of my knowledge, have previously been of a theoretical nature, and hence open to controversy. It is not too much to say that, in the light of the work done at the Eye Institute at Dartmouth College, this situation in psychology no longer exists.

Some years ago I wrote something about one aspect of the conclusions reached by this work, that while it was in line with observable facts, it was still in the field of theoretical discussion. The statement made had to do with the nature and function of sensory stimuli in particular and sense-perception in general. What was then lacking has now, and for the first time, received experimental demonstration of a kind as convincing as that provided in the most advanced field of physics.

In addition, these demonstrations bring together material from subjects which hitherto have been definitely isolated, and indeed often opposed to one another. The statement that is made in one of the reports of the Dartmouth Eye Institute about "Integration of Recent Developments and Hypotheses in the Sciences of Physics, Biology and Psychology" is in my best judgment fully justified. I add, on my own account, as one interested in philosophy that is capable of application to social needs and problems, beginning with those of education, that I find that this integration is capable of furnishing to philosophy the intellectual instrumentalities needed for this purpose.

Sincerely and gratefully yours,

John Dewey

December 11, 1946

Dear Doctor Dewey:

Your statement means more to us than I can express.

I am personally most greatly indebted to you for your confirmation that our disclosures are philosophically sound. It gives me a quality of assurance and faith that was heretofore lacking.

And for the furtherance of the application of our mutual point of view to social needs and problems your statement is invaluable.

Most sincerely and gratefully,

Adelbert Ames, Jr.

October 8, 1947

Dear Dewey:

I am most greatly indebted to you for sending your and Bentley's *Concerning a Vocabulary for Inquiry into Knowledge.* I have read and re-read and studied it. It is hard for me, as I am a tyro in the field.

But I know it is a great contribution. All you have to say is so pertinent to and closely related to the phenomena we are dealing with and the point of view that evolves from them.

To put it crudely, your clarification of particular names, "definitions," is the only one I have ever come across worth a damn. I have already adopted them, or am trying to. But because of my lack of background in the field there are points about your postulations that are not clear to me.

I have made a couple of attempts to write you about them, but get so long-winded and involved that I know I am not making sense.

However, the impact of your ideas has, I think, clarified for me some of my own confusions. I am sending enclosed an attempt to explain (very informally) the nature of this clarification. This explanation involves your postulations and brings out a number of important points on which I would greatly appreciate getting your reactions.

Bearing on your ideas on the "firmness" of knowings-namings, it would appear that in concrete experience our sense of "identity" corresponds to "firmness" of "knowings" in the field of knowledge. See the paper I sent you September 17 on "The Phenomena of Identity and Mistaken Identity." I am also enclosing some thoughts on "Identity, Sensations, Concepts, Semantics" which may have a bearing.

Kindest regards<br>Adelbert Ames, Jr.

October 10, 1947

Dear Ames:

Thanks for your letter. I'm not going to try to write an answer now but to say that what you send fits directly into a piece of writing for articles and ultimately perhaps for a book I've been engaged on the last few weeks. It represents a kind of reorganized culmination of my previous philosophical positions through what I got from working with Bentley, about language in general and the requirements of the transactional approach in particular, and your demonstrations re observation.

Somewhat accidentally I got a clue for starting from the dictionary —two quite different senses of the connective OF. In one sense it maintains the original English sense in which it was a variant of OFF, away from, the sense of being about, concerning. In the other sense it is not separative, but possessive—what a thing is made of, consists of. Well, the latter determines, I believe, all common sense statements of things that add *as* they enter into all the processes and affairs of living, not just physiological but human living in its widest sense, and "practical" in *that* sense, much wider of course than a narrow utilitarian sense. The *about* statements are off, away from these, but are about them—especially in terms of *how* the common sense affairs, from small to big, come into existence, the conditions of their occurrence.

These prepositions are the "scientific" ones. They react back to extend and refine, to enrich and liberate the common sense attitudes and statements. I think the application to abstraction, etc., is fairly evident. Legitimate abstraction is the *"drawing away* from." Common sense or practical prepositions in their given material is a withdrawal that isn't fine. Abstractions in the bad sense are of the kind that are so far away up in the blue or in words that they never can or do get back.

Also every common sense affair is an indissoluble union of the human and the physical. "Physics" as science draws out and forth one aspect: humanics *if* it existed would be about the other constituent. But mostly as it now exists, instead of being about the human component it takes it *as is* substantially, merely for the most part giving it a different form, which isn't the form of science but is mostly a different set of verbal clothes, which is about all physics was before Galileo, etc.

Well, if I ever get this worked out I shall owe a lot to your demonstrations. Also I think it is in line generally with your suggestions in your last letter.

Anyway, here it is for what it may suggest to you.

Yours as ever,

John Dewey

November 6, 1947

Dear Ames:

I should have written you before re your letter as to "identity, mistaken and otherwise," but I was at work on something that I hadn't seen through which I thought was worth holding up an answer for. Now I've got to where I can write about it. I have been struck with such

words as "concerns," "affairs," "care," "matter," and even "thing," *
in their idiomatic use—which I find as a rule to be more philosophical
in what it involves than formulated and philosophical senses. My conclusion is this: All perception (involving use of sense organs and motor-
vascular organs) is of "things" *as* (in their capacity, office or function)
components of a concern, affair, matter, subject, etc.; which, according
to the dictionary has in all cases to *do* with something *to be* done, an
agendum, so that what is seen, heard, or otherwise perceived is perceived as a factor (in the literal sense of a doer) in what is to be done,
treated, dealt with, etc.

That the habit-attitudes resulting from previous transactions in which
the organs of the human doer and the conditions of the *medium* (generally called environment, but which is too external a word) participate
is an important fact but secondary to the prospective reference, to the
*agendum*—the thing *adoing*. (We take our habit-attitudes for granted
at the time; only when we look back—re-flect—do we attend to them
and that, I believe, is when their operation is temporarily blocked or
suspended—as in the case of the *mistaken* identifications of your demonstrations, which operate as you say as a condition of development—at
least *should*.)

I am reasonably sure that all this has grown out of my acquaintance
with your experimental demonstrations, and I am inclined to believe that
it will be a help on the linguistic-theoretical side of formulation. It
seems to be closely allied to your comments re Identity, etc.

When I get a clean copy I'll send you a carbon of an article intended
for the Journal of Philosophy.

> Sincerely yours,
> John Dewey

> November 7, 1947

Dear Dewey:

I have delayed answering your letter of October 10 in answer to mine
about your paper on Knowledge, because I have been so absorbed in a
book, *The Perception of Causality* by A. Michotte.

I was not only delighted and reassured by what you have to say.
I was especially excited by your observations about the word "of"
("off"). They apply directly to our problem of "togetherness" and
"apartness." The very basis of our visual sensations is awareness (we

* "Thing" in dictionary: "That with which one is *concerned*" (in action, speech,
etc.) "That which is to be done."—many other uses, of course.

would not see "but for" it) of partial togethernesses apart from other partial togethernesses and these partial togethernesses only exist because of their apartness from each other.

We have, as you may remember, demonstrations of this phenomenon. They are described in the *Laboratory Manual* of our demonstrations in Chapter VI, pp. 49 *et seq.* I have some other supplementary material on Togetherness and Apartness I can send you if you would be interested to see it. This material is only preliminary and superficial, but it seems to bear directly on and confirm your line of observations as to the words "of" and "off."

But there is a further line of considerations that seems to me most important.

You and I are satisfied that it makes sense to us that the word "of" can stand for both "together" and "away from" and that it makes sense to us that perception of togetherness exists only because the perception of apartness exists and vice versa.

But it is non-sense to most other people.

Why is it sense to us and non-sense to others?

I presume because we are considering the phenomenon from a more "inclusive" "frame of reference," so to speak, than the others.

We have run into a similar situation with the phenomenon of "that-ness" and "thereness." We demonstrate that if our sense of "thatness" is altered, our sense of "thereness" is altered, i.e., "thatness" determines "thereness." But we also demonstrate that if our sense of "thereness" is altered, our sense of "thatness" is altered, i.e., "thereness" determines "thatness." Now this doesn't make sense. That is, it doesn't make sense if we believe "thatness" and "thereness" are separate phenomena existing in space in their own right.

But if we shift our point of view and recognize that actually "that-ness" and "thereness" have to do with our actions, it not only makes sense, but it couldn't be otherwise—"thatness" and "thereness" must be inseparable and interacting as we demonstrate. For we couldn't act if we were aware only of the "whatness" without being aware of "whereness" or if we were aware only of the "whereness" without being aware of the "whatness."

Doesn't this mean that if our "point of view," so to speak, is from the midst of or on the level of the phenomena we are considering, although we can recognize all sorts of relationships between the phenomena, these relationships don't make any sense? (Cf. most of present science.) The relationships make sense only when we step up, so to speak, to a higher level of reference, that is, ask another question, "What for?" in regard to the functioning of the organism. From this higher level of reference the phenomena will make sense only in terms of worth to the organism at that level.

So "thatness" and "thereness" make sense in the "what for?" of organic activity.

But there is a whole field of phenomena on the "action level" with all sorts of relationships which will only make sense from a higher level of reference of "what for?", namely, the "purpose level."

And on this "purpose level" there is a whole field of phenomena with all sorts of relationships which will only make sense from a higher level of reference of "what for?", namely, the "value level."

When we ask "what for?" on that level, we must step up to the "emergent level" and "personal causality." And so on, leading to an ever-increasing knowledge of the "what for?" of life.

Each higher level integrates more factors of the "total togetherness" than the just-preceding level.

But this integration isn't a simple adding together of factors or synthesizing them vaguely in our subconscious minds. It is a structure in which all of the factors fit in systematically and sensibly so that when we bring the structure to our attention the factors and their relationships are all apparent.

To come back to your words "of" and "off." From the point of view of three-dimensional space, it is nonsense that a "thing" could be *at* another thing and away from it at the same time. But from the point of a human being's purposeful action, a distant "off" thing may be more "of" him than the hair on his head.

What I am trying to get at, I think, is that while definitions are indispensable and the science of semantics is an invaluable contribution, we will only get out of our own confusion and be able to communicate in so far as we can consider phenomena and their symbols from levels of reference which disclose more and more of the "what for?" of the phenomena in terms of human worth.

Kindest regards,
Adelbert Ames, Jr.

P.S. I am enclosing a morning thought on "Causality" that has a bearing on the above letter which I wrote yesterday.

[Enclosure]

### Causality

When we ask the question "What for?" about a phenomenon in terms of worth to the organism, we become involved in what we mean by "causality."

This follows because the answer to the question "what for?" discloses something an organism can do which will affect the phenomenon.

For instance, the answer to the question "what for?" of "thatness" and "thereness" is that the organism is enabled to *act*, i.e., affect the spatial-temporal relationship of the phenomenon to himself or to other phenomena. This involves causality.

From the "level of reference" of action (space plus time), the causality may appear real, but in fact is very passing and trivial, nonsensical, for the organism could by reversing his action completely nullify the effect of his past action, i.e., moving one hand back and forth.

From the "level of reference" of purpose, the nature of the causality becomes more profound. But it can still be nonsensical for the organism can reverse his purpose.

This also holds true when we step up to the value "level of reference."

This seems to imply that the quality that characterizes "causality" is *endurance*. In personal terms we are only satisfied that we are causal in so far as we can sense the permanence of the results of our "activity."

But whether an organism experiences this enduring quality depends directly on his point of view, i.e., on the "level of reference."

November 12, 1947

Dear Ames:

You have covered, actually taken into a single scheme, a lot of considerations in yours of the 7th. It may take me some time to take it all in. As I see the order you present, "what for" is the actual use, usefulness, of our behavings without respect to, so intended, or deliberate; the latter constitutes the level of purpose, aim, intent. Then there is the higher, or wider (?) or deeper (?) reference of *value*. I agree with that fully, though I had never put things together that way before. But I am a little squeamish about the *word* "personal," although with recognition that we are persons, legally and morally, only because of memberships in bodies of which others are also members, I fully agree. The implication of this last clause is factual, but in lots of recent philosophical literature "person" and "personal" are affected by the individualistic movement so as to stand for something private. However, that manner of understanding the words can be easily avoided. Independently I had come to the conclusion that there is no such thing as value confined to an individual in his severalty—which is the way they are treated in most of the current discussions in philosophical writings, which are badly under the influence of an individualistic not a social psychology. Economic theory recognized that economic values are socially determined—i.e., through the togetherness of persons, and in that way economics is ahead of a good deal of philosophical theory. As a matter of fact I suppose that when a person professes a value that is not of the togetherness order, it is treated as a symptom of intellectual disorder.

I am not telling you anything in the preceding. I am stating it for my own benefit. I am quite confident that you now have hold of the culminating formulation of the significance of your experimental demonstrations so that we have before us just what you say—the structure in which all the factors fit in systematically and *sensibly* (italicizing the last word since it includes verified, or capable of demonstration of the scientific kind).

Incidentally I think your "levels of reference" is a helpful addition to the "frames of reference"—which I think was one of Whitehead's valuable contributions to understanding.

I shall add a study, via the Oxford dictionary, of *for* in addition to *of* and *about*.

I am not at all expert in technical scientific knowledge. But as I see the combined effect of relativity and of sub-atomic physics, there is now an inclusive space-time togetherness instead of the separateness of atoms and of space and time in the Newtonian system. We shall be lucky if the conclusion * drawn isn't that this particular otherness is directly *of* instead of being an aboutness in which to locate what-fors, purposes, and values in which human beings are involved.

I hope in a few days to send you the carbon of an article I've written on the respective concerns and affairs of common sense and science. It grew out of the "of" and "off" business—common sense being *of* and science *off* and therefore liberative by enabling longer and calmer views to be taken when off gets together with of. I have got more intellectually excited than for years; first by Bentley and now in a climactic way by your work.

Sincerely yours,
John Dewey

* Physical subject matter and "physical world" is a *level* of reference—*within* and *below* the what-for level. . . . Physiological subject matter, the same, but togetherness on a higher level than physical—closer to the what-for level.

November 16, 1947

Dear Ames:

Here is a carbon of the paper * I mentioned the other day. In the copy I am sending to the *Journal of Philosophy*, I have rewritten some passages, but I am sending it to you in the raw, as I think that while the passages changed are an improvement in wording, the main sense can be had from the text as I send it.

I think I have mentioned before how Bentley's use of "transaction" seems to me to fit in with a generalized formulation of the results of your work.

Sincerely yours,
John Dewey

May 26, 1948

Dear Dewey:

Thanks for the reprint of *Common Sense and Science*. I have been doing so much thinking since I read your original manuscript that it all seemed fresh and new to me.

It is splendid. Have you had any reactions to it? We would like at least a dozen reprints. How can we best get them?

I am especially interested in restudying and reconsidering what you have to say, because since our last contact consideration of the phenomena disclosed by our demonstrations has brought to light what may be a most important unrecognized aspect of what we have called a "concrete experience"—what Whitehead calls an "actual occasion" and what you so lucidly present as a "transaction of living." And interestingly enough this new aspect has to do with three of the points you bring out in your paper, namely, (1) that common sense is a name for the "general sense, feeling, judgment of mankind or of a community"; (2) that it is also a name for the general sense, feeling and judgment of the specific individuals that constitute the community; (3) the relation between common sense and science.

This heretofore unrecognized aspect that has come to light in general confirms and supports the position you take on all three of these points and it appears to increase our understanding of "common sense" both

* Editor's Note: The paper, entitled "Common Sense and Science: Their Respective Frames of Reference," was subsequently printed in the *Journal of Philosophy*, 1948, Vol. XLV, 197-207.

group and individual and also the relation of "common sense" to science. I think you would be interested in hearing about it. I could communicate what I have in mind much better if we could talk it out, but as that is not possible I will make a try at it in writing.

All of the phenomena disclosed by all of our demonstrations are of the nature of illusions. The observer's visual sensation does not correspond to the "externality" as disclosed to him by later action. Now in every case his illusion is due to specific assumptions the observer makes that he is not aware he is making. For examples: In the overlay demonstration, where he sees a nearer card back of a more distant card, he sees it back of the more distant card only because he assumes not only the shape of the nearer card but also because he assumes that *the nearer card is whole*. That his assumption is one about "wholeness" is demonstrated by the fact that if the nearer object cannot be interpreted as a whole, he won't see it behind the farther object. In the balloon demonstration, where he looks at stationary balloons at the same distance, and sees them at different distances when their relative sizes are altered, he sees them at different distances only because he assumes they remain *constant in size*. In the star point and line demonstration, where he looks at two star points or lines of different brightness or length which are at the same distance, he sees them at different distances only because he assumes that *being similar they are identical*.

In our later demonstrations on the nature and origin of the perception of motion, the observer assumes that motion that he has experienced will continue. And in demonstrations we have conceived to investigate the origin and nature of the perception of "consequence," such as one billiard ball hitting another, it can be shown that the observer assumes so-called "causative" sequence.

All the other demonstrations disclose that in every case the observer's illusory sensations only exist because of assumptions of various kinds that he makes.

Let us consider the nature of these assumptions that the observer takes account of.

In the first place, all observers make the same assumptions. That is, they are "common" to everyone.

In the second place, without exception in these assumptions the significances that the observer takes account of are not of the significance to him of the particular "thing" or "event" he is looking at. For instance, in the overlay demonstration his assumption is not about the playing card; he would make the same assumption of "wholeness" if it were a dollar bill. The significances he takes account of are what might be called "general laws" concerning "things" or "events" from all points of view in space and time, such as that "things" are whole, remain constant in size, etc. This "assumptive world" is constituted of those aspects of "things" and "events" that are significant to us as human beings that we have learned to take for granted in the long run.

In other words, this "assumptive world" is common sense.

It is apparent that the assumptions we would take account of in connection with our perception of our geographical world, so to speak, would be characteristically different from those we would take account of in our social perceptions, or from those we would take account of in our perception of the mechanical world. But in their essential nature they would all be the same.

Thirdly, these assumptions are inherently different from the sensations of which we are aware in an actual occasion or "transaction of living." Sensations and perceptions are *pre*sumptions, i.e., prognostic.

Sensations and perceptions are specifically unique to the experiencing organism, related to his unique point of view in space and time. It follows from the above that the "assumptive world" is a *common* world, while the sensational, perceptual world is an individual world.

Fourthly, at least in the case of visual sensations and in unanalyzed perceptions, the observer is completely unaware that he is making "assumptions" or that an assumptive world is a factor in his "transaction of living." Yet, but for such an "assumptive world" he could not have sensations or perceptions.

It would seem that these considerations throw considerable light on your understanding of "common sense." It makes clear how "common sense" can both be "the general sense, feeling, judgment of mankind or of a community" and at the same time "the general sense, feeling, judgment" of a specific individual.

It also apparently throws more light on the relation between common sense and science. It would seem to follow from the above that "theoretical science" is that aspect of the "assumptive world" which deals with the most generalized assumptions, i.e., those assumptions that are common to the most generalized conceptual point of view.

On the possibility that this matter may be of real interest to you, I am enclosing some notes which I have written in an effort to try to clarify my own thinking. They approach the matter from different points of view and may possibly throw further light on it.

Very kindest regards,
Adelbert Ames, Jr.

May 28, 1948

Dear Dr. Ames:

Many thanks for mss.—I'll write later.

This is to thank you and say how much satisfaction it is to me as always that I am working from a different angle of approach on lines reasonably similar to yours.

I think it would have been well if I used occasionally Whitehead's name "occasion" for the immediacy of a given case.

Sincerely,
John Dewey


June 5, 1948

Dear Dr. Ames:

I'm not ready to write about your last paper yet, but there is one point that it may be pertinent to touch upon. To *assume* is to take *to* (even *into*) one's self; I find in the Oxford dictionary an early usage (illustrated with quotations) "to adopt into partnership, service, use." Obviously an active usage, where the act is outgoing, not an intellectual usage; then there is the sense of appropriating as a right or possession —appropriating in a bad sense—which may throw some light upon the cases in which the assumption works out badly—not that the adopting into self is intrinsically bad, but it is made absolute—exclusive—i.e., without respect paid to conditions; habit using *us*, instead of *our* using the habit. (Then, historically to pretend, to make believe.) Finally, the intellectual usage: "To take for granted as the basis of an argument"— instead of as the basis of an act.

I mention this chiefly because my first reaction to your paper was (doubtless because of my habits) to weight the word too heavily in its intellectual use. The fact that the word shades off from adoption into exclusive possession—usurpation being given as a synonym—seems instructive. (Few people, even scientists when they are outside their own specialty, seem to have learned the scientific lesson of hypothesis—on trial, where trial is trying out, proving, testing.)

As to *pre*sume, the *pre* gives of course the key. But I thought I'd look it up. The first historical use is seizing *without right*, usurping; then to take upon oneself without authority—then to dare, venture; passing into the intellectual sense—to take for granted; to take as proved till the contrary is proved—to be presumptuous is to take liberties.

I have found by consulting the dictionary (Oxford) that the main trouble with traditional philosophical terminology is that it has dropped out the primary active sense and left a thinned-out intellectual usage as if it were exclusive. That is the reason that in the article I sent I have given a good deal of attention to the idiomatic sense of some words; *sense* and *usage* are synonyms.

Sincerely yours,<br>
John Dewey

June 9, 1948

Dear Dewey:

I was delighted to have your short letter dealing with the meaning of the words "assume" and "presume." I had recognized their inadequacy for the use to which I had put them and was dissatisfied with them, but could not think of any better words to use.

Your letter starts a train of thought that may be helpful. Let us go back and reconsider the nature of the "phenomenal processes" which constitute what I called the "assumptive world" and those that constitute what I called the "presumptive world." First consider them from the point of view of the nature of our awareness concerning them.

Let us start with a visual sensation of a specific "thatness" at a specific "thereness" in an "actual occasion" or "transaction of living." It is "based," so to speak, among other assumptions, on our assumption of "wholeness" and "constancy." Apparently we are not only not intellectually aware of such assumptions, we are not even sensorially aware of them—can we say not even "intuitively" aware of them? These assumptions are effective processes that exist below the awareness or conscious level.

Since the word "assumption" as ordinarily used implies at least a conscious if not an intellectual * awareness, it would seem inappropriate to use to refer to these phenomena unless the adjective "subconscious" was added to it—but I don't like that.

On the other hand, in what I have called our "presumptive world" we are at least sensorially *aware* of the specific "thatness-thereness" to ourselves. However, the word "presumption" is objectionable because as commonly used it implies intellectual awareness, i.e., when we are in-

---

* These assumptions continue to exist and to be effective even though we intellectually know they are false. For example, we continue to assume the balloons are constant in size and because of that see them move back and forth even after we know they are actually varying in size.

dulging in intellectual processes we *"presume"* even though we are not participating in "actual occasions" or "transactions of living."

Consider another type of difference between the phenomenal processes of what I have called the "assumptive" and "presumptive" worlds, namely, that our "assumptive world" is not directly related to the possibility of action, while our "presumptive world" is.

Our "assumptive world" apparently exists apart from our direct relationship to the specific "otherness" of the now. On the other hand, our "presumptive world" only exists when we are in direct relationship to a "specific otherness" from a specific unique personal point of view in "space" and "time."

This apparently brings out a most important difference between the two worlds. That is, the "assumptive world" by itself provides no possibility for *action*, while the "presumptive world" does. It is the "presumptive world" that provides the possibility for "action" in your word trans-*action*, which you use to refer to an actual concrete occasion.

Then there apparently is another great difference between the so-called "assumptive" and "presumptive" worlds, which for me is a harder one to describe clearly, but which yet seems most important. That is that the presumptive world (world of sensations) is not a disclosure but only a prognosis, i.e., "sensations are potential *prognostic* directives for furthering purpose by action." It has to do with "expectancy" (future) from the point of view of a specific "now." (A knowing beforehand.) Before what? Apparently before *action*, because only action will test and disclose the correctness of the assumed knowing.

The objection to the word prognostic is the *gnostic* part of it, which is to *know*, and we don't yet know.

The word "presume" seemed to be better because *sumere* means simply to "take" whether we know it or not.

However, the objection to both "prognostic" and "presumptive" is that in themselves they don't give any suggestion of *action*, which is the very essence of the phenomena.

Now while action, specificity, personal uniqueness, indeterminateness (until related to expectant purpose) are characteristic of the so-called "presumptive world," apparently none of these aspects are characteristic of the so-called "assumptive world."

The significances in the "assumptive world" in themselves do not provide a basis for action; they are "general," not specific; they are "common," not personally unique; they may not be correct but they are not indeterminate.

What has been said is limited to the phenomena involved in visual sensations (perception) of the static aspects of otherness (thatness and thereness), but it apparently applies to the perception of motion and also consequence (Michotte's causality).

It would also apparently apply to Social Perception, though there the situation is much more involved and complicated and the two "worlds" seem more closely integrated.

            •     •     •

Kindest regards,
Adelbert Ames, Jr.

Hubbards, Nova Scotia

July 18, 1948

Dear Ames:

Mainly on account of my hospitalization I never got around to reply to your note about my report on the dictionary account of assumption-presumption. If I had, about all I should have said is that it seemed to me to be in line with what you had written before, not opposed. For while the traditional philosophical-logical treatment deals with them as if they were cognitive from the start and inherently, the idiomatic usage makes the "practical" sense primary—that is, treats them as attitudes or dispositions which give *direction* to subsequent so-called responses; or, better, to the course of behavior or life conduct already entered upon and engaged in.

This particular philosophical-logical distortion is, I believe, typical of the basic error or mistaking of modern epistemological theory. The tradition makes the cognitive primary throughout the whole theory of knowledge, thereby throwing everything out of gear, beginning with knowings-knowns themselves, since it closes the door to seeing the latter in their position and office in the ongoing of the life-undertaking and enterprise.

Regarding your very interesting paper dated June 9th. All I have to suggest is a reason for the *position* (assumption and position and positings being two names for the same thing) that the *social* perceptive system is primary, inclusive and determining of the geographical perceptual organization. I can only state here the lines of evidence which if I developed would warrant this view or position (way of viewing). One of them is anthropological. That primitive cultures interpreted the geographical "world scene" in terms of the organization of their respective community lives seems to me to have been demonstrated by the students of primitive cultures. When psychology was written wholly in subjective mentalistic terms, the theory of *animism* flourished. It was all wrong because of this mentalistic twist; stated in terms of interpretation of the geographical perceptual systems, it makes sense. I think your term "geographical" is a valuable and much needed contribution—"physical" is too limited and "natural" seems to imply that the human (social) isn't natural. As far as I am concerned *geographical* fills a great need.

The other line of evidence is the intellectual crisis that arose when "modern" physics cut off the physical subject matter from the "spiritual" setting by which it was dominated in the Christian theological version of Plato and Aristotle, itself a rationalization of the (genuine) earlier animism. The dualisms that have determined the course of modern philosophies (as problems if not as solutions) are records of this crisis. To put the geographical world back into the human scene—in the place it actually, functionally, exercises there, is the only way I see to a philosophy at all in tune with the facts of life as now lived.

Sincerely yours,

John Dewey

Hubbards, Nova Scotia

July 27, 1948

Dear Ames:

Instead of writing in a way *directly* relevant to the papers of June you kindly sent me, I am going to write about a theme which has chiefly occupied my own reflections of late, as I think it is sufficiently congruous with the line you are working on to possess some measure of relevancy.

Beginning with the thesis which for a long time has determined my conclusions, psychological and logical, about inquiry ("thinking," reflection, etc.), I have recently been especially impressed with considerations that appear to me to *locate* more specifically the *source* of the condition involved in that thesis. The latter, roughly stated, is that the occasion of reflective, all definitely "intellectual," processes is the occurrence of some hitch, some block or obstacle in the course of the carrying on of life-transactions—that last phrase being tautological, since living *is* a course of continuity. This "hitch" or blockage is then primarily "practical" in the sense that it tends to evoke the forms of behavior called fear, rage, which, as specifically seen in animal behavior, are respectively withdrawing and aggressive, and in less intense instances curiosity, a kind of ambivalent mixture of an attacking movement with readiness to withdraw. In the *human* animal conditions are such (I would imagine because communication with others of the species takes the form of language) that curiosity becomes *directed* inquiry in which the "hitch" in question becomes *stated*, i.e., a problem, the articulated formation of which is all one with the movement toward what is taken as its resolution—and hence the restoration of the ongoing continuity of behavior which has temporarily been *diverted* into reflective or intellectual processes: inquiry, examination, observation, reasoning out, search, tentative following of clues (a process *logically* called hypothesis), etc., the practical aspect of behavior turning into manipulation of conditions to improve observations and thereby providing better clues for reasoning to follow, while the direct emotion of curiosity becomes an interest (which in some persons becomes so intense as to be a passionate ardor) in finding out; that is, an inquiry-discovery as itself amounting primarily to a life-concern. (Making "scientists" as far as it is a passion and not a conventionally adopted occupation.)

The foregoing is, however, the background of what seems to me to be possibly relevant to the work you have been doing. In human beings the occasion or source of the hitch that is converted into an inquiry-finding diversion seems to be a conflict between the old and the new—that is, behavior *habits* formed on the basis of *prior* life-behaviors and the expectations, intentions, outlooks, directed to the future, to an *in*coming and an *out*going as these involve some break, or divergence and reconstruction in the working of the resources previously at disposal.

Incidentally, I think this is the "reality" of Hegelian-Marxian dialectic, only as you said about the Gestaltists, it is taken by them as fixed and uniform instead of in process, and hence changing in content.

Sincerely yours,

John Dewey

I hope I am not out of the way in believing that you use the word "perception" in a much wider way than is current in most psychological treatises—in a way which makes it virtually a synonym of conscious apprehendings—which take in of course the *subject matter* grasped, while the "consciousness" of nineteenth century psychology was an entity by itself, not a laying hold *of*.

Hubbards, N.S.

August 9, 1948

Dear Ames:

The enclosed was sent me by Horace Fries, a professor of Philosophy at the University of Wisconsin.* It is a copy of something he wrote for a special purpose. I am sending it to you because it states one aspect of my position better I believe than I would have stated it myself which seems to have relevancy to the matter discussed by yourself and Barnard. As I have been occupied with my paper to forward to the International Congress of Philosophy at Amsterdam, I'm sending it as a kind of interim report.

Here I add that the subject of "intuition" is so important it needs some verbal explanations. The idiomatic use of the word is very different from that which is current in philosophical writings. In the latter it is supra- not sub-intellectual and "rational." Some of the nature of Kant's *a priori* was itself a refined version of what Locke attacked under the caption of "innate ideas," and, like the latter doctrine, has been used to exempt certain belief attitudes from critical examination. The common sense use of the word is very different and in general we know what it is intended to stand for. But I don't know of any clear-cut *statement* of just what it is intended to refer to. Consequently the word lends itself to ambiguous use, and is taken advantage of for obscurantist ends. It seems to be that what it stands for is the direct sense we have of our active practical ways of dealing with conditions. Strictly speaking it is of our *active*-way-of-dealing-with-things, but since what is practically important for us is what we intend and expect will proceed from the transaction, it is taken to be (correctly enough from a practical point of view) an intuition of the thing or situation involved in dealing —a kind of shorthand that does no harm till philosophy converts it into a special kind of *intellectual* performance, either of a rather low ordinary kind or of a high supra-rational nature. The intuitions work all right where preformed habit-attitudes are flexible as with an expert in a given line, but are mistaken or even the source of illusion when one is not expert or in very unusual conditions even with the latter.

As I have finished my Amsterdam paper I'll expect to read the sections in Barnard carefully very soon. The impression I got from a hasty

* Editor's Note: The short paper by the late Horace Fries was titled "The Cultural Function of Art Relative to the Conceptualization of Novel Problems."

reading was that he took the current psychological-philosophical use of "intellectual" as descriptive of the latter. I would say the sort of thing he sets over against "intellectual" is actually one form of the latter—that is, intellectual and intellect do not stand for anything structural but for something which is done or accomplished, something functional. This reifying or hypostatizing of what in fact is operational and functional is, I would say, the great vice of current psychology-philosophy and then leads others than philosophers astray.

But in the main I believe the great value of Barnard's discussion is that it is one of those rare cases in which a man of affairs, an experienced executive, also has a genuine intellectual curiosity and wisdom.

Yours sincerely,<br>John Dewey

In respect to the present theme, the reification mentioned is responsible for the separation of the "intellectual" from the "emotive-practical" or the volitionally intended. Anticipation and expectation, while functionally "intellectual," cannot be understood, as you have demonstrated, apart from the emotive-practical and vice versa.

April 27, 1949

Dear Dewey:

. . .

There are so many matters I would like to commune with you about. Of late we have been much occupied with the matter of Scientific Methodology. Many so-called authorities take the position that our work is not scientific because it is not checked by quantitative measurements. . . . We have found the ideas you have presented in your "Problems of Men" of the greatest help. We have climbed up your back, so to speak, and have the temerity to believe through the integration of lines of thought arising from our disclosures that we are adding still more clarification to that generally little understood matter.

Your criticism on our thinking to date would be invaluable. I hesitate to send you our preliminary notes and writings because of the unorganized state of the material and because this letter may not be in line with your present interests, but on the chance I am sending you a compilation of the material under separate cover.

The particular lode star that is pulling me at present is the disclosure of our various demonstrations that the simplest perceptions (in a transaction of living) are an inseparable integration of specifically unique aspects involving specific unique purposes and value-qualities and trans-actions (in "time and space") and specific unique undetermined con-vergence *with* universal common aspects involving universal purposes and value-qualities out of "time and space," so to speak.

This follows from the disclosure that the unique aspects of our per-ceptions would not exist were it not for our assumptions, which are unspecific and universal in nature, and vice versa.

Does this give a toe hold that might help to understand (without the necessity of a mystical presupposition) how sacred and profane love exist in the same reality and why fulfillment can be found neither in escape from nor in total emergence in worldly affairs (transaction)?

Kindest regards,
Adelbert Ames, Jr.

1158 Fifth Avenue
New York 29, N.Y.

May 27, 1949

Dear Ames:

This is just to acknowledge yours of a month ago. . . . I was in good shape when I came back but for the last three weeks I've spent more time in bed than out—which is the cause of the long delay in writing you. Tuesday I had a blood transfusion and I think it is going to do the job.

I have been convinced for a long time that the obsession of psycholo-gists with *quantity* is both a cause and an effect of the backwardness of that subject. A quantitative statement with no theory to determine *what* is being measured would justify calling the "measuring" of all the cracks in the plaster of my wall "science" if it were done with elaborate statisti-cal technique. To hell with it—but unfortunately they hoodooed the Foundations' Directors, who have little idea of what *Scientific Method* is, joined with a superstitious respect for what they think is Science—with an extra big capital letter.

Well, I've got that off my chest. I hope to write you before very long.

As ever yours,
John Dewey

The backwardness of philosophy in this generation is largely the back-wardness of the *psychology* prevailingly used.

Dear Dewey:

Our great difficulty is communicating our point of view to others. As an aid in that effort I have made a chart in which I have attempted to represent diagrammatically the "phenomena" we are dealing with and their trans-relationships.

I am enclosing it for your consideration.*

I am taking this liberty for the following reasons. As you will see, I have drawn heavily on you. Firstly, I want to be sure that the presentation does not do violence to your point of view (or in other words that we have not misquoted you). Secondly, you have so much wisdom in this field in which we find ourselves involved that it would be invaluable to us if you could let us know whether or not we are going astray in our thinking.

Thirdly, we have adopted your thinking about "hitches" and "inquiry."

I have been re-studying your and Bentley's writings and am most excitingly impressed by their importance and the foundation they provide for our evolving thinking. And if I am not mistaken it seems as if our material (chart) provides evidence of the correctness of your position and point of view.

Specifically, your whole exposition of "Knowings and Knowns" opens up unlimited vistas.

It seems to me that it may be of some importance that our work shows that "knowings" are essentially prognostic in nature. If that is so, "knowings" are not "contemporary," so to speak, with the "knowns." Doesn't that throw further light on the nature of the "milieu" (field) in which "trans-actions" take place?

Further questions come to mind.

If "knowings" are personal awarenesses that only exist because of the "knowns," then "seeings" are personal awarenesses that only exist because of the "seens." Then what corresponds to "knowns" and "seens" when we experience "feelings"? What are the "felts"? And when we experience "value quality," i.e., "valuings," what are the "values"?

Further, "knowings," "namings," "seeings," etc. are all in awareness. How about what we call "assumptions" which operate on a "sub-sensorial basis"? What is "the other end" of their "trans-action"? It appears to exist entirely in the "past," so to speak.

* Editor's Note: See pages 68 and 69.

Further, might it not be fruitful to separate conceptually those aspects where personal awareness exists from those where it doesn't exist, in that in the former case personal responsibility seems to be involved in a way in which it is not involved in the latter case (cf. "knowingly" in law).

Does any of this make sense?

Kindest regards,
Adelbert Ames, Jr.

May 31, 1949

Dear Ames:

I am not yet up to writing you at length but there is a sentence in yours of April 27th, bottom of first page, I want to ask about—or rather the last clause of that sentence, as I have no difficulty about the first part of the sentence. It's the passage reading ". . . *with* universal common aspects involving universal purposes and value qualities 'out of time and space' so to speak."

I thought that, while of course I had not followed and kept in mind all the details of your demonstrations and conclusions, I had understood and found myself in practical agreement with all their leading features. But I found I wasn't able to place the "universal common aspects involving universal purposes and values," while, even with the "so to speak" qualification, I should certainly have to undergo a good deal of re-education before I could understand the "out of time and space" feature. I must have missed something which I shouldn't have missed. I do not want to tax you to make a long restatement of what I have missed; but if you can refer me to specific passages in the material I have already received which bear on this point, together with a brief statement of just where and how it comes into your demonstrations and conclusions, I'll be grateful to you.

With regards,
Sincerely yours,
John Dewey

June 1, 1949

Dear Dewey:

Your letter of May 27 arrived yesterday just after I had mailed to you the letter and chart which you have probably now received. I was

delighted with what you had to say, but am much disturbed that you
have not been well.

I continually use you as an example both for myself and for others
that one does not have to be old just because he has lived a lot of years;
that as we live more years we should become more contemporary, more
in the midst of the transactions of living. That is what you have done,
and God give you good health because you have so much to give all
of us that we all need so much.

I am now at work and very excited in trying to understand and
write about the Trans-action of Illusionings *-Illusions. I find I am continually getting myself into a muddle because of inadvertently thinking
in terms of inter-actions instead of trans-actions, and not keeping clearly
in mind the nature of the "field" (poor word), "milieu" of the transaction. But I hope with practice I will do better.

It seems to be coming out that Illusionings-Illusions are the *sine qua
non* to emergence; going one way round the "space-time" circle to the
"perfecting," so to speak, of our Form World (see chart), and going
the other way round the same circle to more successful purposeful action and the creation of enhanced value-quality.

Kindest regards,<br>
Adelbert Ames, Jr.

June 3, 1949

Dear Dewey:

Just received your letter of May 31 expressing your difficulty with
my "universal common aspects involving purposes and value qualities
out of time and space."

I am most grateful, for you have put your finger on the weakest link
in our formulation, so to speak, where we are most beyond our depth
and where I have felt most unsatisfied with our attempts to explain
phenomena disclosed by the demonstrations.

I have to smile at the idea of your having to "undergo a good deal
of re-education," and I don't think you have "missed" anything. The
difficulty, I believe, is one of communication and my inept use of terms.
We could get ahead much more effectively if we could sit down together and talk it over, and from my point of view I consider it sufficiently important to drop down to see you if from your point of view
you think it would be worth while.

---

* It seemed necessary to make a verb out of the noun "illusion."

But in any event I will try by writing to explain why I used the terms that you properly question.

The paragraph you had difficulty with was the following—

The particular lode star that is pulling me at present is the disclosure of our various demonstrations that the simplest perceptions (in a transaction of living) are an inseparable integration of specifically unique aspects involving specific unique purposes and value-qualities and transactions (in "time and space") and specific unique undetermined emergence *with* universal common aspects involving universal purposes and value-qualities out of "time and space," so to speak.

—and I don't wonder. In the first place, "emergence" in the fifth line was through a typographical error written as "convergence" in my letter to you. Moreover, I failed to state that the "universal common aspects involving universal purposes and value qualities out of time and space, so to speak," referred to the phenomena disclosed by our demonstrations that we have called *assumptions* and the *assumptive world* or *Form World*.

But to go back a little.

We started by trying to get a better understanding of why we see what we see, or the nature and origin of perceptions. Our demonstrations empirically disclosed more and more *inter*-related phenomena except for which ("but for"), perceptions themselves would not exist, e.g., prior experience, purposes, expectancies, action, etc. It became apparent that perceptions aren't entities on their own account but only exist as an aspect of the transaction of living, and that our understanding of perceptions can only be increased to the extent that we can increase our understanding of transactions of living, and further, thanks to you, that neither the "subphenomena" that constitute the "phenomenon" of the "transaction of living" or the phenomenon of the transaction of living itself can be understood if they are thought of as entities existing on their own account, *inter*acting on similar entities but only as aspects of transactions. To quote you:

Einstein's treatment, arising from new observations and new problems, brought space and time into the investigation as among the events investigated. It did more than that: it prepared the scene for the particle itself to go the way of space and time. These steps were all definitely in the line of the transactional approach: the seeing together, when research requires it, of what before had been seen in separations and held severally apart. They provide what is necessary at times and places to break down the old rigidities: what is necessary when the time has come for new systems. ("Interaction and Transaction," *J. Phil.*, 1946)

Further to quote you:

What is called *environment* is that in which the conditions called physical are enmeshed in cultural conditions and thereby are more than "physical" in its technical sense. "Environment" is not something around and about human activities in an external sense; it is their *medium*, the *milieu*, in the sense in which a *medium* is *inter*mediate in the execution or carrying *out* and *on* of every human action; it is the channel through which they move, and the vehicle *by* which they go on. Narrowing of the medium is the direct source of all unnecessary impoverishment of human living; the only sense in which "social" is an honorific term is that of the cases where there is an enriching and refining of the medium in which human living goes on. ("Common Sense and Science," *J. Phil.*, 1948)

Among other things that these demonstrations apparently disclosed was that in essence every individual's perception was different from every other individual's perception, i.e., perception is specifically individually unique, due to the person's unique point of view both in space and from his position in his unique history with his unique purposes, etc. This holds equally true of "transactions of living."

In the earlier stages of our work it was not apparent to us that the demonstrations provided any evidence of a "common" non-specific world or a "milieu" in which a common world could exist. But a more considered analysis of what we experienced with the demonstrations apparently made it evident that they also disclosed phenomena that might be the basis for a common (non-"specific") world. This phenomenon is what we have called "assumptions." But for these assumptions apparently perceptions themselves would not exist.*

I know you will remember that about a year ago I sent you some of my notes dealing with assumptions and the assumptive world. They were very preliminary and not well thought out, but they referred to different examples of assumptions which we thought the demonstrations disclosed and presented some of our thinking about them. To save you the bother of hunting up this correspondence I am sending a collection in one folder of all our preliminary notes on assumptions, including your correspondence with me, with the parts which may have a bearing on our matter of discussion marked with a red pencil.

The reason for making this collection is that Professors Cantril and Lawrence and Mr. Ittleson of the Psychology Department of Prince-

---

* It may be pertinent that in our inquiry into the nature and origin of illusions it is becoming apparent that every illusion is transrelated to assumptions. For example, we would not have the illusion of motion in the balloon demonstration if we did not assume the balloon itself remained constant in size. I am not sure that we would even experience "hitches" but for "assumptions."

ton and Professor Hastorf of the Psychology Department at Dartmouth are all going to be here during the summer, and one of our main undertakings will be to try to clear up our thinking about assumptions and the assumptive world. I got what material we had on the subject together and sent it to them so that they would have a chance to do some thinking about it before they came up.

To recall for you some of the examples of assumptions. We would not perceive distance but for the assumptions that similar things are identical and that things are wholes, etc. We would not perceive motion but for our assumption of size constancy. Now apparently everybody makes these same assumptions, i.e., they are common, universal, for all people and everybody makes them irrespective to the specific "thing" to which they apply them. They remain the same, so to speak, no matter where in space or in time people are. Everybody makes assumptions of the same nature in their perception of "inter-action," "causality," and in their social perceptions.

On the chart I sent you I represented assumptions in the left hand column of the rectangle marked *Form World*. As shown, they have their origin in prior "transactions of living" and are trans-related with the purposeful, valueful and conceptual aspects of our Form World as shown. They are non-conceptual, sub-sensorial and not subject to voluntary recall. They only come into operation in trans-relationships with impingements from "otherness."

What specifically intrigued me and led me to write the paragraph in question was that when one was in the midst of a transaction of living, as I am now, one aspect of the transaction is not only unique to me but has to do with unique specificities in time and space (my purposes are specific and unique, my perception is specific and unique, the "immediate otherness" is specific and unique, my actions are specific and unique); *but*, another aspect of the transaction, what we call assumptions and our assumptive world, are not unique to me and do not have to do with specificities. They are the same as they were when they were operative not only in my prior transactions of living but are the same as they will be when they are operative in my future transactions of living. Moreover, they are the same as (common with) those that are operative in many other persons in their transactions of living. It would seem (and I don't know how to express this) that they are not detailed and specific in nature but generalized or universal.

In using the term "universal common aspects involving universal purposes and value qualities," I didn't have in mind anything in the nature of absolutes existing in their own right, but was trying to emphasize and bring out the common general nature of the assumptive aspects of our perceptions as contrasted with the personally unique and specific nature of the "prognostic directive for purposeful action" aspects of our perceptions.

As to my use of the phrase "out of time and space." As you so clearly put it:

*Trans-action* regards extension in time to be as indispensable as is extension in space (if observation is to be properly made), so that "thing" is in action, and "action" is observable as thing, while all the distinctions between things and actions are taken as marking provisional stages of subject-matter to be established through further inquiry. ("Transactions as Known and Named," *J. Phil.*, 1946)

I didn't mean that we could have assumptions if there wasn't time and space. But what bothered me and still bothers me (maybe I am confused) is that the "milieu" limited to time and space seems to me to be too "restricted a medium" for assumptions to transact in, as it also seems to me that time and space is too limited a medium for the transaction "valuing-values" and many other types of "transactions." Somewhere in your writings, I couldn't find it again, you object to the use of the word "field" to describe the "milieu" of transactions, I presume because of its connotation of space. As I see it, any word connoting "time" would be equally objectionable. And a time-space field wouldn't be any better.

In one way it almost seems as if our assumptive worlds themselves could be thought of as an indispensable part of the milieu for transactions between different people.

I hope this will clarify things. It may at least explain why I expressed myself as I did.

Kindest regards,
Adelbert Ames, Jr.

June 18, 1949

Dear Ames:

I still have to explain why I am so dilatory in response to yours. My infliction hung on for 4 or 5 weeks, and one doctor advised a sea cruise to relieve a congested throat. We just got back yesterday. Some improvement, no great change.

I meant to write you at once to thank you for yours of the third, which threw some light on the questions. If I get your point it would mean in my language that certain "ideas," especially scientific formulations, *deliberately abstract* from any given or specified date or place in order to be available for any (at least a very wide range of) events in a great variety of dates and places. In that sense, I can understand "out of time and space"—i.e., out of any specified date or place, position, etc.

But I'll have to write at greater length later.

Sincerely yours,
John Dewey


[Postcard]

June 20, 1949

Dear Ames:

We shall be going to New Alexandria, Penn., for I hope the summer, soon—about 2000 feet elevation—and when we get settled there I hope to have time to write to you something in response to the material of yours I have on hand.

Yours,
John Dewey


New Alexandria, Pa.

July 20, 1949

Dear Ames:

I haven't had the pleasure of direct communication with you lately. The fact is that my rather limited working time has been completely occupied with writing an Introduction to my *Experience and Nature*, published about 25 years ago, and out of print for some years. Beacon Press is going to republish it when I manage to get a new Introduction to them, and I've written and re-written—largely because I think of so many things to say. It's the devil to get the thing organized. Well, today I had got far enough along to write what I am now sending you a copy of, as after it was written it seemed to be an example, on rather a large scale, of the kind of assumption which in every field today stands in the way of a scientific report consonant with facts—with the exception of a small number in physics—and even Einstein writes at times as if "relativity" were to a knower who is outside—instead of inside—the temporal-spatial world.

I had been speaking of some of the defects of the philosophical movement that is "modern" in the sense that it flourished from the 17th century well into the end of the 19th or beginning of the 20th, and which in its account of "experience" as the thing to be relied upon (instead of on tradition) held "experience" to be the true voice of "nature"; defects because it (the movement) put its dependence upon the Newtonian science in which space-time were external, fixed and independent entities outside what went on within them as their envelope and immutable atoms, merely changing position but not undergoing change themselves within this envelope. Then I went on to say in effect that the deficiencies are not chargeable against the *men* who carried forward the scientific movement till the scientific change re space-time and atoms came about, saying,

The most ancient and most deeply penetrating of all the emotive-motor attitudes that affect human beliefs about the world in which they are involved is dread and dislike of any change which seriously disturbs the habits that have become so embedded in a cultural community to which men are accustomed, and upon which they have to draw to obtain either the way or the material of knowing-understanding anything; that there is more cause for surprise that adherence to unchangeability as the necessary and indispensable property of objects of scientific knowing was questioned by only a few in the vanguard of science after four hundred years of the "new" science than that it took so long a time. To observe—in the sense in which observing is heeding as well as seeing—that the kind of immutability in question constituted a hindrance rather than an aid to scientific inquiry, demanded getting rid of an assumption which was virtually worldwide in extent and as enduring as the ages man had been on earth.

Nevertheless it is a kind of unconscious tribute to the fact that genuine knowing is inquiry that is freed from limits set in advance that the *objectives* of inquiry were converted by reification into entities taken to exist as ready-made antecedents to inquiry—preferably eternally so; the kind of tribute that hypocrisy is supposed to pay to virtue. A humorous, but regrettable feature of the present situation is that some philosophers who have been forced by present science to see that existences which are the subject-matters of science are *events*—hence spatial-temporal—nevertheless attempt to preserve the old canonic assumption of immutability by making such events so minute that they do not occupy any time, being mere mathematical instants, and no space because they are only mathematical points.

I add what I didn't say in my mss that Bertrand Russell is an outstanding sinner in this respect. C. S. Peirce said a long time ago that the vice of philosophy is "aping mathematics."

Well, it was only after I had written as above that it struck me, as

I've said, that here is an example on a large scale of treating assumptions not as postulates-positings for use, but as inherently fixed and in control.

Sincerely yours,

John Dewey

July 27, 1949

Dear Dewey:

I was most delighted and excited to get your letter of July 20 on the "large scale treating of assumptions not as postulate-positings for use, but as inherently fixed and in control."

We all have been working for a long time on a paper on Scientific Methodology drawing heavily on your and Bentley's "transactional point of view" and on "inquiry" and "hitches" and "knowings-knowns," and were entangled in trying to tell people "of the kind of assumptions which in every field today stand in the way of a scientific report consonant with facts." And we were finding, as you say, that "it's the devil to get the thing organized."

So we were most helped in our immediate task by your letter.

But it did more for me. Your statement "The most ancient and most deeply penetrating of all the emotive-motor attitudes that affect human beliefs about the world in which they are involved is dread and dislike of any change which seriously disturbs the habits that have become so embedded in a cultural community to which men are accustomed, and upon which they have to draw to obtain either the way or the material of knowing-understanding anything; that there is more cause for surprise that adherence to unchangeability as the necessary and indispensable property of objects of scientific knowing was questioned only by a few in the vanguard of science after four hundred years of the 'new' science than that it took so long a time. To observe—in the sense in which observing is heeding as well as seeing—that the kind of immutability in question constituted a hindrance rather than an aid to scientific inquiry, demanded getting rid of an assumption which was virtually worldwide in extent and as enduring as the ages man has been on earth," raises again in most definite form on a larger scale the problem we have been sweating with ever since our demonstrations showed that we could not have a perception including "heeding as well as seeing" but for *assumptions*. To be sure they are only tentative and their form changes at least to some extent with every active experience, but they are nevertheless assumptions, and we couldn't have perceptions, including heeding, without them.

As I see it, habits are assumptions of a still less tentative nature and reflexes are assumptions that are fixed, i.e., not tentative at all. Experience has proved to us that the prognostic reliability of reflexes for effective action is so good that even if they lead us into a hitch we can't even enter into an inquiry that will enable us to change them.

What I am getting at is that it seems that in a "transaction of living" assumptions and "form" are indispensable "but for's."

Isn't the necessity of the being, existence, of assumptions and Form explainable if we recognize that the essence of a "transaction of living" is its *emergent* aspect (specifically the emergence of value quality)? For without Form there could be neither emergence, change, nor a direction for emergence. The emergence in itself means change of flow of assumptions and Form.

Apparently our work shows that such changes take place in the Form World on which our Perception is based following every action carrying out the purpose determined by the perception. It seems to be a matter of repeated Form and Flow, Form and Flow.

We have to believe, have faith, in our assumptions, Forms. We must keep them unchanged until, because of a hitch in our transaction of living, we *have* to change them.

But do we abandon them? Don't we rather preserve them as special cases of more inclusive assumptions or Forms? For example, Newtonian assumptions are of as much practical use as ever. In a way we haven't changed them; we retain them as a part of the more inclusive assumption of Relativity. And can we abandon *inter-actional* assumptions? Aren't they still indispensable in the larger framework of trans-action? And haven't we similarly got to retain certain aspects of *self-action*, at least in regard to higher organisms like man, due to the unique, personally responsible emergence aspects of his transactions of living?

In this general connection there is a further interesting consideration brought up by our demonstrations. That is, the more inclusive the "milieu" in which an assumption provides the basis for a prognosis for effective action (i.e., the greater the number of other functional activities the assumption includes), the more tentative it is. For example, the assumption of "size constancy" or of "wholeness" which provides the basis for prognosis for effective action is apparently more fixed or less tentative in the perception of static aspects than the same assumptions are in the perception of motion. And we presume they would be still more tentative in the perception of "interaction." And they apparently are still more tentative in Social Perception.

If we turn back to reflexes, which are assumptive habits for the prognosis of effective action, it is apparent that, although the reliability of the prognosis is much higher, the extent of the "milieu" they have to do with is very limited compared with the "milieu" that is the basis of visual perception and social perception, for example.

At the other limit of the scale from reflexes we have "value-judgments." The "milieu" in which they provide a prognosis for effective action is very extended, but their reliability is relatively low compared with that of reflexes and they are relatively very tentative. However, in exercising "value-judgments" and especially if the reliability of the judgment is confirmed by action and we sense that "All's well with the world," we experience value qualities that are their own reward. Perhaps the concept of the experiencing of emergent value quality by functional activities in the transactions of living (being) is as far as we can go in our conceptualizing in grasping something which in its own right has an excuse for being.

We are looking forward to reading the whole of your new introduction to *Experience and Nature*.

As soon as we finish our paper on Scientific Methodology we will send you a copy. I believe you will find it worth your while to read. We have used so many of your ideas it would be a great favor to us if you would let us know if we have done violence to them.

Kindest regards,
Adelbert Ames, Jr.

July 31, 1949

Dear Ames:

Thanks for yours of the 27th; I am glad you found something helpful in the sketch I sent you, and I hope it would not seem an ungrateful response to your kind comment if I raise a question on one point. That question concerns the apparatus, organic physiology or psychology, that carries the assumptions without which, I fully agree, we couldn't have perceptions and which enter into every observation we make. They are sine qua non's, or as you say, "but for's."

I enclose a brief statement containing something I wrote quite a number of years ago indicating to me that the "apparatus" in question is of the order of habit, *habit* being in this view the behavioral equivalent of Form. (I think it is involved in what is said in the quote about "contains within itself a certain ordering or systematization of minor elements of *action*" which accordingly is the projective aspect of a habit, carried over into further activity formatively, coordinatingly.)

The part of my statement that doubtless seems most speculative is that which refers to what amounts to the unceasing operating of habits. As I stated the matter in one place, we wouldn't hear *a* sound unless we (our auditory apparatus) were already, while engaged in overt activities of quite a different kind, engaged in hearing—and in that hearing the native auditory apparatus—sensory-central—participates as modified or formed through prior activities. We can hear—perceive—*sounds* when someone speaks a strange language; that the tendency of one who doesn't under-stand, i.e., perceive, *words* is to call the sounds "gibberish" would seem to indicate that it is difficult even to perceive *articulation* in such cases. I don't pretend to be able to prove such is the case, but it seems to me that your demonstrations prove it in the case of perception of sights, things seen. The technical difficulties in demonstrating the principle re perception of sounds would be I suppose greatly more difficult, but not insuperable in theory.

Now all this apparently is in disagreement with what you say about the fixity of habits and the low degree of responsibility among them. If habit is not the apparatus—that may not be a good word—of assumptions I can't see what can be.

I appreciate of course that there *are* habits which are of the kind you say. But I think they are *bad* habits—not in a moral sense but biologically-psychologically as having been formed under bad conditions. (I found a few days ago a quotation from Confucius—no identifying reference given—in which he is reported to have said "Every one's errors are due to his environment. By studying the type of errors, one learns the extent of the influence of the environment.") For instance, a good deal of edu-cational practice (not as much now as there used to be) is based upon forming habits by "drill"—so far as the method succeeds—which for-tunately it is too contrary to human nature to do very well—the habits are of the kind that are mechanically fixed. A better example is habits formed on the basis of adaptation to the operations of machines in a factory; as far as that goes on without any opportunity for judgment of conditions entering into the formation of habits, the habits formed are worse in their consequences than reflexes can be, for they have a certain physiological or natural relation back of them. In short, it seems to me that the reputation habits seem to have as resisting re-adaptation to changed conditions is because social conditions demand from a large part of the population a kind of unthinking activity that results in an abnormal type of habits. As society improves its own order, habits *gen-erally* will become as tentative as they are now in the case, say, of a scientist operating experimentally by keeping tab on the consequences of what he does and varying the operation of his habitual lines of activ-ity correspondingly.

However, all this is secondary to finding out what in your view is the biological or psychological seat of assumptions and what is the mechanism of apparatus by which their working is improved. Is there anything in the nature of habit which stands in the way of its providing a basis for prognosis in the degree in which its milieu is inclusive? Is there something in habit *as such* which tends to limit the milieu? Are the successful men in any line those whose habitual lines of action are tentative? Isn't that the lesson taught by the replacement in scientific inquiry of dogmatic theories to which observations must conform to be accepted as dependable by hypotheses tested by observations experimentally conducted?

Perhaps of course the difference there seems to exist between us is just one of different uses of a word, but if so my interest is in learning what the factual counterpart of assumptions are or may be.

Perhaps there is something in the subject matter and process of value-judgments that precludes habits the office I would assign them. In that case, ignore all I've said and reply in terms of value-judgments exclusively. But it always seemed to me that the title "The place of values in a world of fact" was stupid in wording a genuine question as to the place of value *facts* in relation to other facts in a way that made it a puzzle not a question.

Of course I'm looking forward eagerly to your paper on scientific methodology and if the question I've raised is answered in that paper don't bother to reply to this letter.

Sincerely yours,
John Dewey

[Enclosure]

From *Human Nature and Conduct*, pages 40-41:

The word habit may seem twisted somewhat from its customary use when employed as I have been using it. But we need a word to express that kind of human activity which is influenced by prior activity and is in that sense acquired; which contains within itself a certain ordering or systematization of minor elements of action; which is projective, dynamic in quality, ready for overt manifestation; and which is operative in some subdued subordinate form even when not obviously dominating activity.

Need for a word that expresses the place and use of (1) *acquired* activity in influencing subsequent activity; (2) what is *acquired* consisting of an organization or ordering of a number of minor activities; which

(3) projects itself *whenever possible* into subsequent activities, in a way which when it does not (a) overtly control them, none the less (b) enters into them in some covert way.

To which I would be inclined today to add the statement that whatever name be given this mode or way of behaving—as pro*duced* out of a continuum of activities and pro*jected* into a future continuum, as intermediate, is a never ceasing activity as long as we are awake—and may go on more or less when we sleep, if as seems probable dreaming is a manifestation of it—and may even be what the psychiatrists make a mystery of under the name of *the* subconsciousness as if it were an entity.

[Postcard]

August 2, 1949

Since writing yesterday it has occurred to me that the extent and complexity of the milieu is in ratio to the number or variety of habits. The more varied the habit equipment, the less fixed any given one and the wider the milieu.

Sincerely,<br>John Dewey

August 15, 1949

Dear Dewey:

In your letter of July 31 and your postcard of August 2 you raise most important questions. I haven't had time to properly consider them because we are in the midst of finishing our paper on Scientific Inquiry, nor will I be able to give them due attention until the Princeton group leaves about September 1st.

However, I do want to say at this time that I don't think there is any basic disagreement between us, and that all the questions you raise can be answered at least to the extent of giving rise to more important questions.

Would there be any possibility of our getting together and talking the matter out? We could thereby accomplish so much more than by writing. If you expect to return to New York I could run down to see you.

Kindest regards,<br>Adelbert Ames, Jr.

August 21, 1949

Dear Ames:

I am not likely to be in New York City for a few weeks yet. But of course there is no hurry about the point I raised and I realize that I use the word "habit" in an unusual way. I wish there were another word to express the modification that takes place in activity because *of* activity—the *immediateness* of the *readiness* and its constancy.

Sincerely yours,
John Dewey

August 30, 1949

Dear Dewey:

I am enclosing our paper on Scientific Inquiry about which I wrote you.

You will see we have leaned very heavily on you.

Your criticisms will be of great help to us.

I was most happy to get your note about your use of the word "habit." I had surmised that you had used it in your desire to get a word that had a trans-actional connotation which the words "Assumption," "re-flexes," "action," "Perception," and "conceptions" all lack. Maybe the word "habit" has a trans-actional connotation because we only know of habits because of our mistakes—mis-action, action at the wrong time or place, so we relate to the word "activity—the immediateness of the readiness and its constancy" (to use your words). What bothers me about using the word "habit" as you suggest is this. If we do, what naming will we use to refer to the "named" which is referred to by the word "habit"?

Kindest regards,
Adelbert Ames, Jr.

September 9, 1949

Dear Ames:

You said in your letter that you would like criticism; so far I haven't got any, but I do have a query on one rather minor point. In connection with the action of "external impingements" you speak of them as cryptogrammatic. (I am not sure you employ the word "external"—maybe I am reading that in, but I won't stop now to look it up.)

My query doesn't concern the fact that a lot of "translating" has to go on, but as to whether the living organism is not so constructed from the start that there is a certain congeniality between it and the medium in which it lives, which seems to be denied by the use of the word "cryptogram"? There isn't a Leibnitzian pre-established harmony, but the organism and its medium (environment) have developed together within the same natural world, and "hitches" occur, do they not, *within* life-transactions that proceed or go *on?*

It is quite likely that I introduced the word "external" above as expressive of the feeling I get from the words "impingement" and "cryptogrammatic," which seem to me to be too extended or, so to speak, wholesale transferring to the relation of organism-environment as such considerations that hold in occasions to be *specified*.

But maybe I'm tending to make a mountain out of a molehill.

Sincerely yours,

John Dewey

September 13, 1949

Dear Dewey:

I have just gotten your letter of September 9, raising questions as to our use of the words "externality," "impingements" and "cryptograms." As always you put your finger on the essence of "things."

In general I agree that the use of those words implies an inter-actional rather than a trans-actional relationship. And I agree with you "that from the 'start' there is a certain 'congeniality' between it (the organism) and the medium in which it lives."

But before going on (to explain our ideas as to the nature of the "congeniality") I would like to bring up this point. That is, when we go into inquiry we make use of conceptual abstractions. One essential characteristic of conceptual abstractions is that they are meanings referring to partial togethernesses apart from other partial togethernesses and apart from the whole, i.e., to relatively determined separable aspects of togethernesses apart from other relatively determined aspects of togetherness.

That is, they are nouns and "specifications" constructed on nouns. How, therefore, when we go into inquiry and use conceptual abstractions, can we avoid operating on an inter-actional basis, at least to some degree? In an actual "occasion of living" we exist trans-actionally, i.e., everything is operative. But isn't it just impossible in our conceptually abstractional processes to bring into awareness at once everything that is operative in a trans-action of living? We in our thinking are caught in the bedevilment of an interactional point of view in our use of the words "environment," "converging phenomena," "differentiated physiological patterns," "higher physiological processes," etc., and especially so when we use the words "externality," "impingements," and "cryptogram."

I might first explain why we used these words "impingements" and "cryptogrammatic." First as to the word "impingements": we used it in the meaning as defined by Webster—(1) "To strike or dash (on, upon, against) especially with a clash or with sharp collision; of radiant or aerial waves, to come sharply (on or upon a body)"; (2) "to encroach or impinge (on or upon)"; (3) "to come into close contact"—as a general term to express that external aspect of the "field" or "milieu" relation between the organism and the medium in which it lives, at a particular conceptually isolated "now in space and time," in which the direction of the effect is from the environment towards the organism. (Purposeful action by the organism is the external aspect of the "milieu" in which the direction of the effect is from the organism towards the environment—both aspects are necessary for a "milieu" for a "transaction of living.") On our chart we called "impingements" "converging phenomena."

We used the word "externality" as synonymous with "environment" and I think it is probably a poor word to use.

We used the word "cryptogrammatic" as descriptive of the character of the "stimulus pattern" produced on our terminal physiology (the retina, for example) by "impingements" from the environment. It seemed to us that such a designation was necessary to make clear that the physiological stimulus patterns, in themselves alone, are without meaning. There can be no more meaning inherent in stimulus patterns than there is meaning in the electrical chemical disturbances that continue to take place (are physically registered) in the wall of a house where shadows of the leaves of a branch fall upon it. We go on to speak of the "stimulus cryptograms" being translated by higher physiological processes in terms of our "Form World." Perhaps the use of the word "translated" is unfortunate as it suggests a process for which we have no explanation. Maybe it would be better to say that the characterized "stimulus cryptograms" activate specific characteristics of our "Form World."

Your questions make clear that more elaborations are necessary to bring out more clearly the "congeniality" between the organism and its environment. As we see it a toe hold is given for an understanding to "congeniality" in physical terms from our conceptual recognition that at any one time (within the rate of speed of radiations) every point of the whole of nature is represented at every other point. For instance, in this room in which I am sitting light rays from every "atomic disturbance" in every part of the room converge at every other point in the room. Everything is represented everywhere. (Similarly all the radio waves from everywhere on the earth and rays from the solar system are converging at every point in this room.) This representation of the whole at every point is completely undifferentiated in any terms that are significant to us as organisms or that we can conceptually understand.

Consider the converging light rays from all parts of this room that are coming together just before they enter my pupil. Every direction is undifferentially represented at every minute point. As far as I am concerned it is an undifferentiated mass. It is only because of the dioptrics of my eye that rays coming from one direction are differentiated from rays coming from another direction relative to my particular point of view. But the dioptrics of the eye are the organism's own special creation for its own special "purposes." (It is interesting that whenever organisms make use of light rays they differentiate them in terms of their relative direction to the organism's position.)

Now this differentiation of the immediate impingements into relative directions, as useful to the organism as it may be, gives the organism only a part of the trans-relationships inherent, so to speak, in the "milieu" of the impingements themselves. Relative direction to a point of view does not disclose that everything is represented everywhere.

As we see it, these relative directions of impinging radiations are registered as "stimulus patterns." But relative directions in themselves alone have no significance to the organism whatsoever. They must be translated into terms of absolute (egocentric) direction from the organism. Moreover, the characteristic patterns created by the differentiated radiations, in themselves, don't disclose the significances of the sources from which the radiations emanate. They too must be translated into terms of significances to the organism. It is for these reasons that we called the physiological stimulus patterns "cryptograms" requiring "interpretation" or "translation."

I said in the paragraph before the last that the immediate impingements do not disclose that everything exists everywhere. However, isn't that disclosure made evident to the organism when through translating his "stimulus pattern cryptograms" in terms of his Form World he integrates his biological and life's history, spatial as well as temporal, with his immediate environment? And don't hitches arise from the integration of the togetherness of the past with the emerging togetherness of the future?

To go back to your question—"But as to whether the living organism is not so constructed from the start that there is a certain congeniality between it and the medium in which it lives, which seems to be denied by the word 'cryptograms'?" With what I have expressed above in mind —isn't the use of the word "cryptogrammatic" as applied to our stimulus patterns helpful rather than otherwise in getting a trans-actional grasp of the picture?

I don't like the word "impingement" so well, as it implies something *from* something else. Maybe "we ought to give that word up and use 'converging phenomena' in its place."

As to that part of your question: "whether the organism is not so constructed from the *start* that . . ."—for the "start" it would seem that we have to look back into early biological history. Organisms didn't develop their eyes without which they could have no awareness of relative egocentric direction or thereness or thatness and make use of light ray impingements until late in their history. It would seem that sensitiveness to light, and later eyes, would only have evolved if much earlier in their history organisms had developed processes to record the significances of trans-actional experiences and also processes to take account of the significances of such recordings as related to their purposes in carrying out their "transactions of living" in their immediate "nows."

I hope I haven't "sidestepped" your questions.

I expect to be in New York the weekend of September 24 and 25. Will you be there at that time? I could drop in to see you either before or during or after this weekend.

Kindest regards,
Adelbert Ames, Jr.


September 13, 1949

Dear Ames:

This communication is to be some remarks about habit. First I'll say I used the word to name something which I felt to be of importance (whether the word is good or not) before I used "transaction"; the *action, activity* part of transaction undoubtedly weighed heavily with me. In relation to assumptions, there is the question of what *activates* it? What is its active vehicle? Its carrier, or its apparatus? The sort of thing I used "habit" to name or stand for would illustrate my meaning.

I have no dictionary here, but I take it for granted that the word habit is from Latin *habeo;* the word *have* seems to be important; habits have us and we have habits. It doesn't seem accidental to me that be-have names what it does name; a habit is a *way* of be-*having;* the "be" is important too. Be-lief. The following is just playing with words but there may be something more than puns in it.

The word habit (like the word experience) is double-barrelled. In its passive, receptive aspect, it is habit*uated to,* accustomed to, used to, this and that. In its active outgoing aspect it is ability, *habile,* a specific form of skill. Put the two together and the amalgam covers habit as a mastery of something over us: "Poor man—he can't break his habit of drink—his fondness for liquor"; and our mastery over things: "He is very skillful at this or that." A habit is a *facility*—it ensures ease in doing—man has as many readinesses as he has habits. To be ready is preparedness plus: "Make ready, *Go.*" Habits are inclinations, *bents* in a certain direction—the bent *may* be a distortion as when a man is mastered by a habit, but it isn't necessarily one.

I haven't anything of Whitehead's with me; but as I recall it "route" is a favored word of his. Actively a habit is a route in which to move, to travel—route is often used as a transitive verb—as in giving instructions: "Route the goods by such and such a line." (Route, I would say, is definitely a trans-actional term.) *Routine* may be either active or passive according to context; ruts of course are cases of being overpowered by a habit.

In what I wrote earlier about the tendency to use habit to designate a *mechanistic* mode of action I was objecting to the common tendency (or "habit") of overlooking the sense in which a habit is a liability.

Accustomed to, habituated, used to—these are where only the context decides whether they refer to something desirable or undesirable, and this statement probably holds of *habit* itself.

Perhaps the nearest approach in ordinary speech to what in lack of a better word I have used *habit* to designate is found when habits are spoken of as "second nature." The second refers of course to their having been acquired, built up, constructed, by means of prior activities. I think I said before that it seemed to me very poor psychology to hold they are constructed of habit rather than its source. To indulge in one more play on words: Habits are habitations we build; they may be of a kind we are ashamed to live in and with, or the opposite.

I hope that at least the foregoing will make it fairly evident why the word in my case has a certain kinship with "assumption." If "position" only carried with it also the sense of *positing,* it might be the word to express what I'm after. To *take* AND to *hold* a position in the active sense of both taking and holding—maintaining, *up*holding.

Sincerely yours,

John Dewey

September 17, 1949

Dear Ames:

Thank you very much for your full and very satisfactory answer to my "query." It filled the bill. Somewhere in our writings, Bentley, who did the writing on the "transactional in physics," pointed out that it was perfectly legitimate to take segments within the transaction and subject them to independent treatment which according to the conditions of the case *might* be interactional, provided it was noted that in the end the treatment was recognized to be within the larger context of a transaction. I have been meaning to ask you to send him a copy of your *Psychology and Scientific Research,** and also, if you have them to spare, a copy of the *Characteristics* † paper. I have sent him a copy of the Lawrence talk which Cantril was good enough to send me. Bentley isn't as old as I am but he is just over 80 and I am sorry to say he recently had a stroke—a "minimum" one, he writes me, but I fear it will interfere with his work.

I think the *Characteristics* paper is very important; in fact it is so valuable to me that I am asking you to send him a copy instead of sending mine on to him. The point about *values sensed* is very clearly stated; there can be no doubt whatever, judging from my experience, that they are basic to value *judgments* and are practically constant in *every* experience we have while evaluative *judgments* occur only periodically under specific conditions. I was struck of course with the statement that we have to accept the sensing of value-qualities even though we have as yet no adequate explanation of them. Judging from my own experience with them in relation to refletctive thinking in respect to the *psychology* of what, if and when formulated, would be, I believe, *logical,* they are connected somehow with a sense of direction—the *way* things are *going*. Years ago after Galton's writings on the visualist type (which I am zero if not minus in), I was interested in the topic, and realized that I am of the so-called "motor" type; and it was in that connection that I found how completely I depended on immediately sensed or felt directions occurring before and much more frequently than any deliberate logical analysis in following any exposition involving a train of thought or course of reasoning. I noticed more than once that when I was reading along I had a certain feeling of check or "hitch" at a certain position on a page and that when I went back afterwards and examined the passage at that place on the page I found what seemed to me to be a logical

---

* Published in *Science*, Vol. 110 (1949), Nov. 4, 11, and 18, pp. 461-464, 491-497, and 517-522.

† Published as *The "Why" of Man's Experience* by Hadley Cantril (New York: Macmillan, 1950).

flaw in the subject matter presented. The reason I indulge in this bio-graphical item is that reading the Institute's paper made me realize how stupid I had been in not generalizing the experience as one of value, since I've long been interested in value from the standpoint of philosophy and had decided that it is not confined to some special field—which is the way it is now usually treated—but is pervasive. One philosopher has actually written a book "The Place of Value in a World of Facts" as if value wasn't itself one of the commonest of facts.

In writing on Logical Theory I employed the word "situation" to indicate that knowing as inquiry takes place within a "problematic situation" which being *sensed* is wider than the problem that is explicitly *stated*, as an "intellectualization" of the situation for the purpose of straightening out the whole situation—that is, the *end* is not just solving the problem as stated because the latter is a means to the resolution of the directly experienced *"situation"*—for lack of a better name.

This is recurrence of what I have experienced before—that I find my courage strengthened when I read your findings—and all the more so because the approach is from a different angle.

Sincerely yours,
John Dewey


September 20, 1949


Dear Dewey:

Your communication of "some remarks about habit" of September 13th is most illuminating and helpful.

As I see it, before you began to use the naming "transaction of living" you used the naming "habit" to refer to much the same "named."

I think you agree that the "named" you have in mind when you use the words "transactions of living" includes much more than the "named" you had in mind when you used the word "habits." And what we have in mind when we use your term "transaction of living" may be still more inclusive. As we said:

For an occasion of existence to be a whole or for a "trans-action of living" to be complete, "growth" or "emergence" and enhancement of value-quality must take place. For growth and emergence to take place the following phenomena must have occurred:

(1) Purposeful action, the results of which have failed to fulfil the purpose of the action. That is, the person must have experienced frustration of purpose (encountered a "hitch").

(2) Process of "inquiry" to determine the "why" of the "hitch," leading to
(3) further purposeful action, modified by the disclosures of the inquiry, the results of which action fulfil the purpose of the action.
(4) Alteration of the Form World as the result of the experience of this action.

The word "habit" is especially useful because, as you point out, it connotes so many different "activities," "processes," as listed below:

$$
\text{habit}
\begin{cases}
\text{have} \begin{cases} \text{They have us} \\ \text{and we have them} \end{cases} \\
\text{behave} \\
\text{mastery} \\
\text{ability (specific form of skill)} \\
\text{facility} \\
\left. \begin{array}{l} \text{inclinations} \\ \text{bents} \end{array} \right\} \text{purposes} \\
\text{"routings"} \\
\text{second nature}
\end{cases}
$$

But as inclusive as all these connotations are, they cover only a small section of the "activities," "processes," that play roles in a "complete transaction of living."

Because of their nature, isn't it impossible for any *single naming* to refer to more than a very small section of all the "activities" that constitute a "complete transaction of living"? Of necessity mustn't we use a whole series of "namings" (which moreover have to be related in an intrinsically reasonable pattern, of the nature of what I think you mean by "specifications")?

And among other namings, isn't "assumptions" a most useful one to refer to a limited section of a "complete transaction of living"? In adopting it I think we had in mind, among other things, the need of some word to emphasize the prognostic nature (i.e., not a disclosure until after action of our relationship to our environment). We also wanted a word to refer more specifically to the relatively determined aspects that play a role in a "transaction of living," of the same nature you mention that the word "habit" connotes when you said, in regard to habits, that "they have us and we have them" and that they are "second nature."

We have been using the word "form" to refer to those relatively determined aspects.

The *"action, activity"* aspects of transactions of living are essential aspects, but apparently what can be thought of as temporarily inactive "form" also plays an essential role.

Does this in part answer your following question in regard to the word "assumptions"? "There is the question of what activates it? What is its active vehicle? Its carrier or its apparatus? The sort of thing I used habit to name or stand for would illustrate my meaning."

There follows below a number of connotations of the word assume, taken from Webster:

|  |  |
|---|---|
| | 1. Take up or into, adopt. |
| | 2. To take to or upon oneself; to invest one-self with (a form, attribute or aspect). |
| Assume: | 3. To pretend to possess. |
| ad + sumere | 4. To take as one's own, to appropriate, esp. by usurpation. |
| (to)  (to take) | 5. To take for granted, or without proof; to suppose as a fact; to suppose arbitrarily or tentatively. |

As we see it, this taking was done in past transactions of living, and what is taken constitutes what we called our Form World.

In themselves "assumptions" haven't any "ability" or "facility." We may or may not act on our assumptive perceptions. They may be only tentative. Aren't "habits" assumptions that we have found so reliable that we act on them without awareness? And isn't some word necessary to refer to that part or aspect of habits and also reflexes?

As you say, there is a close kinship between assumptions and habits. Habits are assumptions and more. And it seems to me that "positing" is a good word to refer to relatively fixed aspects of assumptions but not to their tentative aspects, and it doesn't seem to me as good a word as habits because it doesn't connote "ability" or "facility."

Best wishes,
Adelbert Ames, Jr.

October 5, 1949

Dr. John Dewey
1158 Fifth Avenue
New York 29, N. Y.

Dear Dewey:
I haven't been able to stop thinking on that most important question we briefly touched upon in our visit with you—namely, what degree of

"self action" have we in our transactions of living? It involves the question of "free will" and "determinism."

My thinkings on the matter seemed to take pretty definite directions, and I am writing them to you in the hope that you will check if I am going too far astray.

You and Bentley, in the presentation of your transactional concept of the universe, clearly point out the inadequacy of the formerly held "self active" and "interactional" hypotheses.

However, in the development of our ideas in formulating an intrinsically reasonable explanation of the characteristics of living man in a transactional universe it seems to be indicated that in the emergence of value-quality man apparently does play a causal role. In that role there are apparently two aspects of his causal activity; first, his activity in making a choice in formulating a value-judgment (directive for action); and second, his actions in carrying out his prognostic value-judgment. It would seem that in such activities there is at least an aspect of what is commonly thought of as "self action."

We are in complete agreement with you that no such thing as "self action" can exist in a non-transactional universe, and we are faced with the question as to whether or not we are correct in our conclusions that man does play a causal role in the emergence of value-quality in a transactional universe.

Perhaps the first step in the inquiry is to try to become more clear as to what the "named" is that is referred to by the "naming"—"self action"—and the "naming"—"the causal role man plays in the emergence of value-quality in a transactional universe."

As I understand it, the "named" referred to by you when you use the "naming"—"self action"—are: firstly, that the "thing" that acts in "self action" exists in its own right apart from other "things" in the universe which also exist in their own right; secondly, that the nature of the action is determined solely by the "thing" acting free from any influence of any other "thing" in the universe; thirdly, that the effect of the action alters other specific "things" in a definite determined manner, resulting in a "fait accompli." *

The "named" we refer to in using the "naming"—"the causal role man plays in the emergence of value-quality in a transactional universe"—are differentiable from the "named" referred to above by "self action,"

---

* It is apparent that no such "named" could exist in a "trans-actional" universe: firstly, because no "thing" exists in its own right apart from other "things"; secondly, no "thing" determines its actions free from the influence of other "things"; thirdly, the effect of action is never limited to specific other "things," is not definite and determined, is never a "fait accompli" or a "fact."

in that: firstly, the action is by an actively living man existing only because of the existence of innumerable other functional activities; secondly, the nature of his action is influenced by the activity of innumerable other functional activities; thirdly, the effect of his activities is not on "things" or altering them, can never result in definite or determined alteration of "things," is never a "fait accompli" or a "fact." (For as you so clearly show, there is no universe of "things" or "facts" or "faits accomplis.") Isn't it that the effect of man's action is primarily on the nature of existing value-quality and that that effect results, firstly, from the effect of his value judgments and actions on himself, i.e., on his "assumptive value Form World," and secondly, from the effect of his actions in making value-judgments and in carrying them out in so far as they alter other persons' capacities to make value-judgments and their capacity to carry them out?

According to our hypothesis, man's basic interest in increasing his capacity to experience higher and higher value-quality, i.e., in the emergence of value-quality, is because the prognostic reliability of his value-judgments increases with the quality of the experienced value on which the judgments are based. This in turn is because the higher the quality of the experienced value, the greater the spread of the transactional relationships that are taken into account. These questions arise. When a man selects a higher instead of a lower value in forming a judgment and acts thereon, to what extent is he a free agent—i.e., self acting? As you said, in view of his action being transactional, he is a party to the transaction. That is, he is a contributor. It would seem that he is also responsible with a unique responsibility, different from whatever existed before or will exist again.

If he makes the right value choice he will be freer from hitches that he would otherwise run into in the future. And by the effect of his choice and action other people will be free from hitches that they would have run into in the future.

Man's range of choice is very limited. He doesn't have free will to the extent that he can choose any value-quality. His freedom of choice is determined by his "assumptive Form World" that he brings to the occasion.

But within the range of his choice what he decides and does is stupendously important. One aspect of its importance is because so much more than the man himself in his immediate "now" is involved. The making of a value-judgment and acting on it can't exist by itself alone. It must involve other human beings and their value-judgments and actions. The transaction is communion in the most profound sense of the word. The phenomena involved in the transaction are not "things" or "objective phenomena" but values and their emergence.

My own inquiry, it seems to me, has been blocked because when I think the word "transaction" I think of the example of a transaction that you and Bentley have used—a transaction in a market place involving not only a seller but also a buyer, the object, "thing" dealt with, the market place, and many other transrelated "objective" phenomena. So the conceptualized abstractions that are associated with the word transactions, that lie in the penumbra of my intellectual processes, all refer to "things," "objects," physical phenomena existing in time and space in their own right, which you so clearly show can't exist. So I am thereby prevented from getting the very point of view that you and Bentley are trying to communicate.

It seems to me that I can avoid that block in so far as I can substitute valueful purposes and emergent value-quality in place of "things" and "objects" and physical phenomena as the processes that constitute a transaction in a "milieu" more inclusive than time and space. And while I agree with you and can't see any possibility of self action existing in a universe of "things" and "objects" and "physical phenomena," it does seem to me to be intrinsically reasonable that an aspect of self action involving personal responsibility can exist in a universe of valueful purpose and emerging value-quality.

But before this question can be satisfactorily answered, further inquiry is necessary as to the nature of valueful purposes and value emergence.

In your letter of September 17, you say you "had decided that it (value) is not confined to some special field—which is the way it is now usually treated—but is *pervasive*."

If value permeates the "milieu" in which transactions of living take place, can't it be thought of as an aspect of the "milieu"? This would seem to be true for those relatively determined value aspects which together constitute what we called our "assumed value Form World" which are common and universal to us all: for example, the sensed value of good will of other men, or more specifically the tentative value assumption that the personality we are transacting with is honest.

Still more relatively determined are the sensed values we call emotions, as of hunger and as of sex, which we think of as being reflexly related to specific physiological conditions.

In transactional activities where there are no "hitches" * these universally commonly assumed value aspects are automatically effective, i.e., the individual exercises no choice, his value-judgments are automatically made for him. So under these conditions there would appear to be no aspect of personal "self action" or "contribution."

* This is an idealized situation, as in every actual transaction there apparently are at least vestiges of hitches.

It is this relatively determined value form "milieu" in which and from which we operate in our transactions of living. It is the up-to-the-now heart and soul of the universe, a form providing a take-off from which we emerge into the continually new and undetermined aspects of the "now future."

This emergence is in terms of new emergent value which becomes part of the relatively determined value form "milieu" and adds to or detracts from its *quality*. It would seem that it is in this emerging aspect of value that the individual is a responsible contributor and might exercise an aspect of "self action."

For in this undetermined emergence due to the presence of new factors that never existed before the value aspects of the relatively determined "value Form World" of necessity will have a low prognostic reliability because they do not take account of the new factors.

It is under these conditions of personally unique specificity that the individual can recognize and take account of new emergences and can formulate a personally unique value-judgment as a prognostic directive for action that will have a higher reliability of success in furthering his purposes.

I am not confident as to how much sense this will make to you, but it at least may provide some toe holds for an inquiry into the subject, which seems to me to be of the greatest significance.

We enjoyed so much seeing you.

Very kindest regards,
Adelbert Ames, Jr.


October 9, 1949

Dear Ames:

My failure to reply to your last two letters is not due to lack of interest but to the fact that I've been rather below par physically.

With respect, first, to the matter of assumptions and habits. I finally realized that we were talking about two distinct and yet intrinsically connected things; at all events, that is the conclusion I've arrived at. What I was talking about was the process, the active conditions, under which assumptions as *net outcomes* are instituted, established—i.e., become, as the word *establish* suggests, etymologically, become *stabilized*. I wasn't attempting to substitute *habits* for assumptions, although I now see the way I wrote would leave that impression. So that I was gratuitously writing as if the word "assumption" were used to name the process or operation by which assumptions are instituted and established, brought into being. It seemed to me too *intellectual* a word to cover the active mechanism or apparatus. And in the account that appeared in the *Times*, written by Laurence, the words "conceive," "unconscious weighing," etc., were used as equivalents of assumptions. On the other hand, Lawrence of the Princeton Psychology Department in *his* statement pointed out the importance of recognizing on the basis of your experimental demonstrations that "sensation" is the name for a state or process in which the total sensory apparatus of the entire organism is involved, not of anything which can be isolated through reference to some specific sensory organ located at a particular place and occurring at a particular date in time. What I was using the word "habit" to name was this *same* fact when viewed from the "motor" aspect of the so-called *sensori-motor* circuit—that is, the need for seeing that we have the *habit* of perceiving, seeing, observing, heeding, rooms in which we spend our time when indoors *as rectangular*. But, on the other hand, the *assumption* that they are rectangular is in fact a net *intellectual* outcome of the habit, and I should have recognized that fact earlier if it had not been that my *own* habits had led me to a rather one-sided intellectual interest and assumption—one in the means and processes by which outcomes—as ends or results—are brought into existence.

Now, having said this, I must add that I am not trying, by implication or inference, to commit you to the particular interpretation or understanding about *assumption* that I have set forth in the foregoing.

The question raised in your other letter I find more difficult to state a considered conclusion about, one which I would be willing to stand by.

I can make a beginning, however, by saying that, given my own philosophical background and its assumptive outcome or "form world," I do not find it helpful to put the question of the degree or kind of self-action involved, in a context of "free will and determinism"—and by saying this I don't mean to attribute to you an undue or exaggerated interest in that context. If I had been inclined to attribute to you any such interest, the fact that you immediately go on to discuss the matter in terms of the "emergence" of value-qualities, would have completely deterred me. For *that*, I think, is the *factual* context in which the question becomes an issue to be taken into account. When put in that context, I find myself somewhat halted or "stumped" by what seems to me a current serious ambiguity re "emergence." It—the word—is used by some writers—including, unless I am wrong, those who first systematically employed the term—to name the appearance *in perception* of something which had been *there all the time*, in line with the earlier view entertained by some who regarded themselves as "evolutionists," that whatever *e*-volves, must have been previously *in*-volved.

I do not mean to suggest that you are putting any such significance into the word *emergence;* on the contrary I take it that you have reference to the occurrence of something authentically *new.* But if so, it seems to me that the question becomes one of *fact* rather than of general theory. That is to say, the transactional point of view assumes, rather than denies, the active participation of the organism, self, person, or whatever, as a necessary participator engaged in a given transaction; the question of the degree and kind of participation is, on that basis, a question of fact to be settled on the ground of the evidence available in a given case. It is doubtless true that the *word* transaction is over-loaded with commercial associations; I have read more than one letter objecting to its use on that account. But the convenience of *commercial* transaction as illustrating certain aspects of *any* transaction —especially its reference to a long and wide range of spatial-temporal considerations, should not be permitted to override the fact that the transactional point of view in its generalized application demands that attention be systematically paid to the actual content and bearing of a given transaction—in this case, by way of example, the *kind* of transactions that are the *occasions* of value-qualities.

This is what I mean by the issue being one of specific fact rather than of abstract theory, and I think that in *this* factual context the issue is well worth following up, and that while the question of *freedom* is undoubtedly involved, any suggestion that it has to do with the question debated under the designation freedom of *will* is jumping into a briar patch in order to recover vision. The question of indeterminacy *is* involved without doubt. But one of the stock objections against my general theory of logic as concerned with inquiry as *fact* is that it points out that every genuinely problematic (or *hitch*) situation involves in its occurrence an aspect or quality of factual (so-called "objective") indeterminateness. If it didn't, all that would be necessary would be simply to bring by some immediate *psychical* action our own mental views into line with existence—the whole operation of experimentation to change existent fact so as to change what is observed would then be entirely needless.

I hope that at least what has been said indicates why, and at what point, your reference to the occurrence of value-qualities (with the implicated recognition of the necessity for methods of scientifically determining *how far occurrent qualities* can be treated as *properties*) is so important.

Sincerely and gratefully yours,
John Dewey

October 13, 1949

Dear Dewey:

I was especially happy to get your last letter because what you say assures me that the results of our inquiries were in conformity with your philosophy and point of view.

First as to assumptions and habits. As you say, the "named" referred to by "assumptions" and "habits" are two distinct yet intrinsically connected things. Isn't it that assumptions are "conceived" in the action of actual transactions of living? Likewise habits are "conceived" in the action of actual transactions of living. Assumptions are operative, not in the abstract, but only in later actual transactions of living intrinsically connected with the "habits" that were "conceived" when the assumptions were "conceived"?

As to the degree or kind of self action involved in transactions of living. I agree with you that it is confusing to put the questions into the context of "free will and determinism." What you say about the ambiguity of the word "emergence" is most helpful to us. In using it, I had, as you gathered, in mind reference to the occurrence of something authentically new. I had not thought of its use to refer to "something which had been *there all the time*"—"that whatever *e*-volves, must have been previously *in*-volved."

It makes it all clear sailing for me when you state, "That is to say the transactional point of view *assumes*, rather than denies, the active participation of the organism, self, person, or whatever, as a necessary participator engaged in a given transaction." And your statement bringing in "indeterminateness" is splendid. . . .

Very kindest regards,
Adelbert Ames, Jr.


October 13, 1949

Dear Ames:

. . .

I omitted in my previous letter to call attention to the wide scope of the words *thing* and *things* when used idiomatically; I find virtually always that the idiomatic use of a word is more genuinely philosophical than a conventionalized "philosophical" usage. The original signification was a *meeting* for deliberative purposes; then like the French *chose* (Latin *causa*) the *subject under discussion*, as in the legal sense (even now) of a *cause*. And when used for *articles*, it was in its earlier history usually when the articles involved were regarded as *valuable;* reference to *physical* things is definitely secondary. Like the Latin *res*, a thing was a *matter of concern*, like res publica—a matter of *public* concern. As I think I said in my other letter—the commercial reference is suggested simply because it brings out so clearly the *indefinitely* extensive spatial and temporal referent of the word. An event isolated in time or narrowly located spatially simply cannot be a transaction; even a commercial transaction involves a long legal history in which an indefinitely large number of persons have participated and can only arbitrarily or conventionally be held to exclude moral reference—*mores*, when account is taken of the central place held and exercised by communication in Mores. That there are cases of communication when the *subject matter* involved approaches closer to "communion" than in other cases is, I suppose, what is to be expected; and it is likely that in such cases the *sense* of expansion, of freedom from external restriction, would be liveliest. But the freedom seems to me to belong to the *transaction*, not to one of its component factors: such is the ground of my dissatisfaction with introduction of freedom of *will*.

There is one other point on which I should perhaps comment briefly —the question of a "universe of *facts* or fait accomplis." There is a sense of course in which I deny the existence of a *fixed* universe of facts. There is another sense in which I hold that the world of things *known* is the world of facts—that what we *know*, in the specifically distinctive sense of "knowing," as over against being and having, is that which *has* happened; we think with reference to the future *facienda* but know with respect to what is over with—things done, *facta*. I don't know that this point is of any special significance with respect to the subject under discussion. But I believe that intellectually *fact* is much more significant than *truth*—which to me is a *moral* name, not a cognitive one, since in the case of propositions and conclusions of a cognitive nature, it's a question of *validity* rather than of truth.

I hope I haven't over-emphasized the point I have in mind, and that I haven't written, for the sake of brevity, too didactically.

With regards,
John Dewey

[Postcard]

October 14, 1949

This is just to say that if I had read yours of the 13th before writing and mailing the piece I sent this a.m.—I wouldn't have written or sent it —I had compunctions as it was.

Yours,
John Dewey

November 3, 1949

Dear Dewey:

.   .   .

I am in the midst of an inquiry of the trans-relationships of "illusion-ism," "surprise," and "frustrations" in transactions of living, and have gotten far enough to be sure the inquiry will be most fruitful. It is very exciting and has already given a toe hold on the named referred to by the namings "humility" and "charity."

I want to add a word about the occasion of your ninetieth birthday dinner. Mrs. Ames and I and our daughter and son-in-law were there with the Princeton group. We were all profoundly affected. It was my first experience of *communion* on a large scale, using that word as re-ferring not simply to the communicating of ideas but in its older sense as referring to mutual sharing and playing a role in "becomingness" and "growth." You should have been very happy.

Kindest regards,
Adelbert Ames, Jr.

November 5, 1949

Dear Ames:

Thanks for note; sorry we didn't have a chance to meet personally —including the other members of the family. "Communion" is just the word; I told my wife I could *sense* the friendliness of the gathering— I was searching for some expression for the *immediate* quality of what was communicated.

.   .   .

Yours,
John Dewey

April 7, 1950

Dr. John Dewey
504 South Street
Key West, Florida

Dear Dewey:

I got your manuscript "Importance, Significance and Meaning" a few days ago. I am very much impressed by its *importance*, although I have not yet thoroughly digested it in spite of having read it a number of times. I always have difficulty in translating philosophical terminology into my own remembered experiences of "transactional living."

What you say raises for me so *many* important questions and hitches, some of which I would like to write to you about later. I will now only attempt to give you a couple of examples.

What is the named you refer to by the phrase "the ongoing course of behavior that has been proceeding smoothly" which is *"deflected"* by a "hitch" and is *"resumed"* after the "hitch" has been resolved? I take it that by that statement you are referring to an immediate aspect of a particular person's "transactional existence" ("continuance in life" —Webster). The word "course" implies direction. The word "smoothly" implies a direction satisfactory (value aspect and importance) to the particular person. The word "interference" implies negation of satisfaction. The word "deflection" implies a cessation of the totality that is being taken account of in straight-away behavior and a diversion of what is being taken account of into the particular "channel" of deliberative reflective conceptual activity *—a "going over"—a conscious recalling of the conditions (conceptual aspects) of direct straight-away behavior.

Am I wrong in thinking that the significance to others of your most important paper will be directly related to their understanding of the nature of what you are referring to by "the ongoing course of life's activity" since only then can we be aware of "importance," i.e., why "we want to go to a particular town or cure a patient." This as I see it raises the question "what for?" We may make use of immediate "signs" and meanings to know "what to do" or "how to act" in the immediate situation of time and space to resolve the hitch. But no immediate "signs"

---

* Cf. the following statement by Freud which I just this morning received from Cantril: "When making a decision of minor importance, I have always found it advantageous to consider all the pros and cons. In vital matters, however, such as the choice of a mate or a profession, the decision should come from the unconscious, from somewhere within ourselves. In the important decisions of our personal life, we should be governed, I think, by the deep inner needs of our nature."

or "meanings" will tell us "what for." As I see it the "what for" involves the totality of our existence from the beginning of biological time and extending into the future in a "milieu" more inclusive than time and space, and is related in some way at least to what we have been reaching for and what Cantril tried to express in the whole of his paper, namely, a personal participation—through action in the immediacy—in the emergence of "value-quality" which is inseparably related to increased probability of success in accomplishing our purposes and the successful continuance "of the ongoing course of life's activity."

Secondly, I am not clear as to the named referred to by "hitch." Your examples of the motorist and doctor are of hitches that arise from "environing condition" but don't other and more important kinds of "hitches" arise from the organism; e.g., from wrong reflexes, habits, assumptions, of which we are aware through paradoxes, frustration, surprise, illusions, lack of surety? In these cases it would seem that the inquiry would involve entirely different kinds of signs and meanings.

Your distinction between "use" and "operate" hits the nail right on the head.

There are many other questions I would like to ask, but before doing so I want to study your paper more thoroughly. In that task it would greatly help me if I could get page 9 that is missing in the manuscript (see page 12 of the typewritten copy) and the word that is missing before "means," third line from the bottom, page 11, typewritten copy; the word that is missing before "been," third line from the top, page 13, typewritten copy; and the word that is missing before "reorganization," sixth line, second paragraph, page 18, typewritten copy.

Thank you so much for sending the manuscript.

Best wishes,
Adelbert Ames, Jr.

[Postcard]

Key West, Fla.

April 20, 1950

Dear Dr. Ames:

This is to say that my failure to write is due to the fact that I've been having a second and more violent attack of the virus infection that is rife here and I guess quite widely. I'm not up to much yet.

Sincerely,
John Dewey

1158 Fifth Avenue
New York 29, N.Y.

May 11, 1950

Dear Ames:

I am still having to inflict my handwriting on you, but I hope with some improvement.

I felt when I asked you with *what world* the "assumptive world" contrasts, that it was not likely the sense of the question would be evident. I don't suppose it will become much if any clearer if I say that it seems to me that a *thorough-going* acceptance of the *transactional* point of view necessitates that the assumptive world is either all-inclusive or else is limited to detected *delusions* or those in process of being so detected. What I want to add now is a reference to Berenda's article, April, 1950 *Philosophy of Science*, in which he designates my theory of knowing-knowns as "*logical* empiricism,"—a name I had not thought of myself but which I'm inclined to believe is technically the accurate one. The gist of the article for me is summed up on page 132. It makes a better statement of both the positive and the negative (sceptical) aspects of the generalized (inclusive-exclusive) commitment of the transactional point of view to the *assumptive* world as coinciding with the *world* as *known* than I could have made.

Very sincerely,
John Dewey


November 8, 1950

Dear Dewey:

You may remember that last spring you sent me a copy of your manuscript "Importance, Significance and Meaning." We were much impressed by it and it led us into a field of inquiry as to types of "hitches" one runs up against other than what we are calling the "how-to-do" hitches which you primarily deal with. Most important of these, apparently, are what we are calling "what for" hitches, or the "why" of our actions.

Cantril and I are just finishing up a paper entitled "What For Hitches" and we want to refer to your paper "Importance, Significance and Meaning." Has it been published yet, and if so, where?

My activities were interrupted in the middle of the summer by my having my gall bladder removed—most successfully—and I am now back to work again.

I hope you continue in good health.

Kindest regards,
Adelbert Ames, Jr.

November 9, 1950

Dear Adelbert Ames:

I am happy to infer from your letter that you are well over the operation in its conditions and consequences.

Nothing has been done about the Importance article. For some unknown reason one page was missing from the sheets I sent to have properly retyped; by the time I got around to attending to the gap, I was down with a rather severe virus attack, and the after effects, in connection with other deficiencies proper at my age, prevented my doing any intellectual work at all for about six months—which among other things accounts for your not having heard from me for such a long time. About a month ago I got a new physician who made a different diagnosis from that of other doctors and adopted a different line of treatment—in consequence of either that or the passage of time I have had an upsurge of vigor; I got out the old type-copy the other day, and decided it was overloaded with material—and now have the idea of breaking it into parts, one of which will include what may be called the logical pattern involved, hitch, discovery, development and formulation of problem converting a trouble or disturbance of behavior into an intellectual statement which can be handled reflectively so as to indicate a way of treatment which in resolving the problem will also make possible a reinstatement of the course of behavior that has been interrupted—though of course on a plane of greater significance of content. The other article would be psychological, stating the bearing of the analysis of knowing as intermediate and mediate behaving in ongoing life behavior upon such topics as "sensations," "ideas," understanding and misunderstanding, emotional difficulties, etc.

I am so far behind in things to which I was committed I don't know how soon I can get at them.

An article on valuing should later emerge from the two just-mentioned. I have a lot of mss on the subject written two or three years ago but laid aside as unsatisfactory—I think the proper line of development should be indicated as to origin or source, content and office from the two articles just mentioned. The earlier material was written with the intention of providing a basis for scientific treatment of "social" subjects—humanics. Instead of scientific treatment of them requiring elimination of value-reference, the latter is in my judgment the *only* ground on which a treatment which is scientific can be based.

I feel sort of obliged, now that I am in communication with you, to say that my objection to the use of the *word* "Assumption" has grown stronger instead of weakening—though it is hardly sound to say so without giving any reason why.

With best regards.

Sincerely yours,
John Dewey

November 10, 1950

Dear Dewey:

In answer to your letter of November 9th: I am most happy to hear of your "upsurge of vigor." May it continue.

As a line of thought Cantril and I are presenting in our paper "What For Hitches" was given rise to by your ms "Importance, Significance and Meaning," we of course wish to refer to it. Could we refer to it as a ms. which you are now re-writing? I may be mistaken, but from what you say I think that both your and our inquiries are along very similar lines. We are just finishing up our paper and will send you a copy in a few days, and will be most interested to get your reaction to it.

I am most interested to learn that your "objection to the use of the word 'assumption' has grown stronger instead of weakening," because during the last year our group has been conducting a long series of experiments which apparently conclusively show that the phenomenal processes which could be referred to by some such name as "assumptions" play an indispensable role in transactions of living.

Most cordially,
Adelbert Ames, Jr.

November 17, 1950

Dear Ames:

I hasten to say that my comment was at the farthest remove from any doubt about or difficulty with the "phenomenal process" which your experimental work has demonstrated. On the contrary, I think your work is by far the most important work done in the psychological-philosophical field during this century—I am tempted to say the *only* really important work.

My difficulty is with the word "assumptions" as applied to the interpretation of the word: not to the word just as a word which would be a purely verbal matter but to the *implications for theory* that assumptions as *name* for the demonstrated processes seems to me to carry with it. I hope my later notes made this point clearer.

You certainly make any use of my mss you may care to do; I shall be honored by the reference.

Sincerely yours,
John Dewey

# Bibliography

PSYCHOLOGICAL MATERIAL PUBLISHED BY ADELBERT AMES, JR.

"Binocular vision as affected by relations between uniocular stimulus patterns in commonplace environments." *American Journal of Psychology,* 59 (1946): 333-357.

"Architectural form and visual sensations." *Building for modern man,* ed. Thomas Creighton. Princeton: Princeton University Press, 1949, 82-91.

"Sensations, their nature and origin." *Transformation,* 1 (1950): 11-12.

"Visual Perception and the Rotating Trapezoidal Window." *Psychological Monograph,* 65 (7) (Sept., 1951): Whole No. 324.

*With* Hadley Cantril, A. H. Hastorf, and W. H. Ittelson. "Psychology and scientific research." *Science,* 110 (1949): 461-464, 491-497, 517-522.

*With* W. H. Ittelson. "Accommodation, convergence and their relation to apparent distance." *The Journal of Psychology,* 30 (1950): 43-62.

"Reconsideration of the Origin and Nature of Perception." *Vision and Action,* ed. S. Ratner. New Brunswick, N. J.: Rutgers University Press, 1953.

"An Interpretative Manual. The nature of our perceptions, prehensions and behavior." Princeton, N. J., 1955. 130 pp.

# Index